FINDING THE MONEY

Finding the Money

*The Complete Guide to
Financial Aid for Students,
Actors, Musicians and Artists*

PREETHI BURKHOLDER

McFarland & Company, Inc., Publishers

Jefferson, North Carolina, and London

LIBRARY OF CONGRESS CATALOGUING-IN-PUBLICATION DATA

Burkholder, Preethi.
  Finding the money: the complete guide to financial aid for
students, actors, musicians and artists / Preethi Burkholder.
        p.   cm.
  Includes bibliographical references and index.

    ISBN 978-0-7864-3692-7
    softcover : 50# alkaline paper ∞

    1. Student aid—United States.   2. Humanities—Scholarships,
fellowships, etc.—United States.   3. Arts—Scholarships,
fellowships, etc.—United States.   I. Title.
LB2337.4.B86   2009
378.3—dc22   2009000740

British Library cataloguing data are available

Cover image ©2009 Photo Objects

Manufactured in the United States of America

McFarland & Company, Inc., Publishers
  Box 611, Jefferson, North Carolina 28640
    www.mcfarlandpub.com

I dedicate this book to my parents, who taught me what is important in life, and who made selfless sacrifices to send me to a land far away, so that I would have a better life. I thank my father, who taught me to believe in myself and advised me to avoid the pitfalls that lay on my path to success; and my mother for setting an example of what it means to be a woman and for shining a spiritual light. Thank you, Amma and Thatha.

Acknowledgments

Thank you to my husband, Trent, for being a supportive spouse and for standing by me during good and bad times. Thank you to my sister and Dileepa, for offering me a roof to live under and for guiding me when I was rather lost. Thank you to my brother, for chauffeuring me around for piano lessons, as a little girl growing up in Sri Lanka. Thank you, dear Fremont, for being a great friend. Finally, thank you to my baby daughter, for re-igniting my passion for life.

Table of Contents

Acknowledgments   vi

Preface   1

1—An Introduction to Financial Aid   5

2—Federal Student Aid Programs   11

3—Getting Money for College   21

4—The College Essay   35

5—The Art of Winning Scholarships   50

6—The Hunt for Loans   58

7—The World of Grants   79

8—Congratulations! You Have Been Awarded
Financial Aid   120

9—The Alternate Aid Route   127

10—Around the Globe   136

11—Working Along the Way   141

12—The Acting Connection   143

13—Investing Strategies   156

14—Resume Writing   178

15—Cyber Aid   201

16—Listing of Grant Directories   213

17—Useful Websites Every Financial Aid
    Seeker Should Know   217

18—Financial Aid Myths   238

19—Marketing Tips   242

Glossary   249
Bibliography   257
Index   259

Preface

Performing artists are unique individuals. They have a secret side to them—a side that gets unfolded mostly through their art. At least, this has been one of my discoveries as a pianist. My journey as a performing artist spans the gamut of emotions and experiences—success, joy, failure, despair, loneliness, and betrayal; and my journey is far from over.

I woke up to the sounds of Beethoven and Mozart every morning. It was a habit instilled by my father, a lover of classical music. Although my father had the inspiration to study piano, his parents could never afford to give him a music education. Due to the lack of finances, his musical talents were never cultivated at an early age. My father worked hard to give his three children a luxury that his parents could not afford.

If the inspiration to study music came from my father, then the aspiration came from my mother. My father handled the cassette player while my mother handled the money. I mention the part about money right at the start of the book because, without it, I may not have become a musician, nor would I be writing a book about financial aid. The bottom line is, you have to get some kind of financial support to make it in the performing arts world. Without money, many a talent has gone unheard, unused, and uncultivated. Lack of money has turned many dreams into dust.

My piano teacher in Sri Lanka, Shanthi, sparked my musical talents at the young age of five. After completing high school I was offered several scholarships by American universities. It was a life-changing step that would never have been possible had I not received any financial aid.

I came to the United States at age nineteen, brimming with hope and ambition. It was a frightening and exciting journey for a young girl who had never stepped on a plane before. All that accompanied me were two suitcases. They held the basic items that I needed to get my life started in a new territory: willingness to work, resilience to rejection, and a desire to stand on my own feet. My dreams, however, far exceeded the space of those two bags.

My love for piano ignited into a flame during college. Catherine, my teacher, introduced me to the masterworks of Schumann, Mozart, and Beethoven. I practiced constantly, working like a dog, spending hours on a single note, and staying awake till two in the morning, while everyone else had gone to sleep. I attended world-class music festivals and delivered my piano skills to the elderly at nursing homes. I discovered that performing music was a great way to connect with people and to bring healing to those in pain.

I also found that practice and performing were not enough. After a while I had to say, "Enough with the applause. Now show me the money." I say this because there were many nights when I came back to my apartment after a piano recital, and did not have enough money to buy groceries to enjoy a decent meal. Just a few hours earlier, I had received a standing ovation for performing Beethoven's sonatas.

Here is what I discovered: no matter how talented you are and how hardworking you are, sometimes you need financial support to make it in the performing arts industry. A few us may be lucky enough to have a parent, close friend, or a relative able to secure that path, and to advise us on the many pitfalls that lie on that journey. I was not one of those lucky few. I had to seek it on my own, in a new country. Of course, a few generous individuals opened doors for me along the way. For them, I will always be grateful.

After completing a master's degree in music I had difficulty securing a job in piano performance. No one seemed to be willing to give me the break that I needed. When the bills keep pouring in and the paychecks do not, you have to temporarily adjust your priorities. I was forced to let my musical ambitions rest—for ten years. Music was always in the back of my mind, though.

My interests went in different directions during that decade. I ended up working as a carpet hauler, cashier, waitress, prep-cook, and receptionist. In retrospect, these seemed to have been some of the darkest and most discouraging years of my life, but they were also the most growing. The person that came out of that dark phase was driven to succeed. Nothing stopped her from moving forward.

After years of aimless wandering I got up one morning and told myself, "I want my life to change." The rest is history.

Here is the key point: the desire for change to enter your life must come from within. I forced a change in my mental thinking process. Yes, I had the power to turn my life around. If no one else was going to give me a break, then I would have to seek it myself. I learned the art of transforming the word "no" to yes, and that has made all the difference.

From then on, it was a series of life-changing steps that steered my life and career as a performing artist. Firstly, I changed my geographical location. Secondly, I cultivated friendships with those who had aim and direction in life. Thirdly, I sought spiritual direction. Today, I am a professor of piano performance, a writer, a wife, a piano performer, and a mother. I am rewardingly exhausted almost every day, consumed by happiness rather than regret.

I have found that it is not so much the destination, but the journey that brings out the best (and sometimes worst) in us.

Financial aid changed my life—and it will change yours too.

May every reader of this book accomplish his or her dreams and goals in life. You deserve it.

I shall be telling this with a sigh
Somewhere ages and ages hence:
Two roads diverged in a wood, and I—
I took the one less traveled by,
And that has made all the difference.

—*Robert Frost, "The Road Not Taken."*

1

An Introduction to Financial Aid

An Overview of Financial Aid

Winning financial aid is not about being smart. It is about being persistent. You may have all the inspiration in the world, but if you don't have the perspiration to accomplish your dreams, most likely you will end up as an individual with unfulfilled dreams. Sure, there are many smart and talented performing artists out there, but if they are not willing to work hard and channel their talents in a productive path, that is a lot of potential being wasted.

Financial aid is any grant, scholarship, loan, or work study program offered to help a student meet his or her educational and career needs. Few students can afford to pay for education without some form of financing. If someone is able to fund your educational and career goals throughout your journey in the performing arts, there is little need for you to seek financial aid. If that were the case, you would never have picked up this book. Chances are you need outside support to pursue your dreams and ambitions.

Financial aid encompasses a variety of programs funded by colleges, private organizations, individuals, and state and federal governments. Approximately two-thirds of all student financial aid comes from federal programs administered by the U.S. Department of Education.

Many people shrug off the idea of financial aid because they don't think they will qualify. If the idea of financial aid has crossed your mind, you probably qualify. The worst that can happen is you apply and get turned down. It's free to apply, so why not?

Perhaps the most common myth is that a family must be financially very poor in order to receive federal aid. This simply is not true. Student financial assistance programs in general are designed to help as many people as possible.

Any person, regardless of age, sex, academic background, and economic criteria, qualifies for financial aid in the United States. Performing artists in virtually all fields qualify for aid. Some of these fields include:

- Dance
- Music
- Theater
- Puppetry
- Street performance
- Acting

Financial aid may come in many forms. However, all forms can be grouped into two major categories: gift aid and self help aid. Gift aid is free money, money that you don't have to pay back or work for. Naturally, this is the kind of aid most people want. Self help aid is money that requires a contribution from you. That can mean paying back the money or working for the money.

There are restrictions and stipulations on most aid programs. Some places may award financial aid to five-year-old children, while others may award financial aid to 90-year-olds. Typically, however, applicants in the 15-to-45 age range have a higher probability of receiving aid as there are more options available to them. Determining which places give aid to address a specific need is half the battle.

Performing artists can apply for financial aid addressing various needs. Some of these needs include:

- College tuition
- Music and acting lessons
- Research purposes
- Postgraduate funding
- Emergency living aid such as mortgage, medical bills, and food expenses
- Travel purposes
- Starting a performing arts school
- Loans

And more.

> **Smart tip:** The most widely sought-after financial aid is for college. Whether you are a senior in high school about to attend college for the first time, or a 50-year-old single mom wanting to get a degree, there are options for financial aid available.

Nuts & Bolts of Financial Aid

Performing artists applying for traditional aid, such as loans, grants, and scholarships, need to meet some basic requirements in order to qualify for aid. The guidelines for federal financial aid, i.e. those provided by the government, are fairly standard, whereas the guidelines from private funders are more flexible.

A performing artist applying for federal financial aid at the college level must typically be:

- A U.S. citizen or eligible non citizen (see below)
- Attending half- or full-time or planning to enroll at an accredited trade school, college, or university
- Registered with the Selective Service office, if applicable (males 18 and older)
- Registered with the Social Security office (exceptions for non-citizens)
- In good standing on any previously received federal financial aid (no defaults)

> **Smart Tip:** For questions concerning basic eligibility requirements for federal financial aid, check with a financial aid counselor or the Federal Student Aid Information Center on the web at www.studentaid.ed.gov or by phone at (800) 4FED-AID.1

Eligible Noncitizens

All federally funded aid programs, such as loans and grants, are available only to U.S. citizens, their spouses, and permanent residents of the United States. Although the majority of federal aid is given to U.S. citizens, there are certain categories of non–U.S. citizens who are eligible as well. The federal government requires documentation from all noncitizens who request federal aid for schooling. These documents include:

- A passport stamped "Processed for I-551 or I-151"
- An Alien Registration Receipt Card, typically referred to as a "green card"

In addition to the above, individuals in the United States with one of the following stamps on their passports will be considered eligible noncitizens:

- Cuban-Haitian entrant, status pending
- Refugee
- Asylum granted
- Conditional entrant (if issued before April 1, 1980)

> **Smart tip**: While U.S. federal government aid programs may be less for non U.S. students who don't meet certain requirements, there are hundreds of private scholarships open to all students based on criteria other than United States citizenship.

- Indefinite parolee and/or humanitarian parolee

Residents of the Federated States of Micronesia, the Marshall Islands, American Samoa, Swain's Island, and Palau are also eligible for U.S. government financial aid.

Dependent Students

One common factor involved in all federal and state aid applications is determining your status as dependent or independent from your parents. Students who are claimed on their parents' yearly income tax forms and who receive financial support from their parents are classified as dependents. When filing for financial aid, dependent students must report their parents' yearly income and assets on their aid applications Students applying for aid may have dependents of their own. Those who qualify for dependent status under a student's care for dependent status can include natural children, adopted children, foster children, or any other person who receives over half of his or her support from the student during the award year. For example, an elderly parent or grandparent under your care can be declared a legal dependent.

Independent Students

Independent students are financially self-supporting and are not claimed by their parents for tax purposes. If your parents don't claim you as a dependent on their tax forms and you are 24 years of age or older, then only your income will be used to determine your ability to pay for college, thus increasing your eligibility for financial aid.

In the case of students under 24 years of age and whose parents don't clam them as dependents, the U.S. government believes parents are still chiefly responsible for their children's education whether or not they are classified as independent. Because of past abuses, more proof of independence is now required (see below). Under new laws, the parents of so-called under-age independent students may still have to provide income and asset information on financial aid applications even if they don't officially claim the student on their tax return forms. While it is difficult for students under the age of 24 to establish independent status, the possibility is worth pursuing if you are having extreme difficulty getting your parents to contribute to your college expenses or even signing your application forms.

As a student, you qualify as independent if you meet one or more of the following criteria:

- Are at least 24 years old by December 31 of the award year
- Are married
- Are a U.S. Armed Forces veteran
- Are enrolled in a graduate or professional program
- Are an orphan or ward of the court. Former wards of the court over the age of eighteen can declare themselves independent if they were wards up to the age of eighteen
- Have legal dependents other than a spouse

Veterans

You may declare yourself a veteran if you were honorably discharged (or will be as of June 30 of the award year) from any branch of the U.S. Armed Forces (including the Coast Guard). Students who attended a military academy in the United States and left in good standing can also be considered veterans. Veterans have many opportunities awaiting them to return to school or to engage in other educational pursuits.

Drug-Related Offenses

A new law suspends aid eligibility for students convicted under federal or state law of sale or possession of drugs. If you have been convicted of drug possession, you will be ineligible for one year from the date of a first conviction, two years after a second conviction, and indefinitely after a third conviction. If you have been convicted for selling drugs, you will be ineligible for two years from the date of a first conviction and indefinitely after a second conviction. If you lose eligibility, you can regain eligibility early by successfully completing an acceptable drug rehabilitation program.

Financial Aid Night

At senior high schools around the country, financial aid night has become a common fall event. With financial aid becoming more complex, many high school counseling offices are wisely choosing to invite the experts in to discuss the details of applying for and accepting financial aid. One thing to remember is that if your high school does not offer such an event, you can most likely invite yourself to another local high school's financial aid night. The information should be as relevant to you as if it were given to you by your own high school. Topics that may be covered include:

- What is financial aid?
- Cost of attendance (COA)
- Estimated family contribution (EFC)
- What is financial need?
- Categories, types, and sources of financial aid
- Special circumstances

2

Federal Student Aid Programs

Your financial aid package is likely to include funds from the federal student aid programs. These programs are administered by the U.S. Department of Education. Not all schools participate in every federal student aid program offered by the U.S. government. Check with your school's financial aid office to make sure your school participates in the federal program(s) you are interested in.

> **Smart tip:** Here is a good website to visit, to learn about federal aid: http://www.ed.gov/programs/fpg/index.html

Here are some of the common types of federal aid:

- Federal Pell Grants
- Academic Competitiveness Grants
- National Science and Mathematics Access to Retain Talent Grants
- Federal Stafford Loans (formerly Guaranteed Student Loan)
- Federal PLUS Loans (Parents)
- Campus-Based Programs
- Federal Supplemental Educational Opportunity Grants
- Federal-Work Study
- Perkins Loans

Here are some figures of how federal aid is awarded.

S for Subsidized and Unsubsidized, Direct, and FFEL Loans Academic Year 2006–2007:

	Dependent undergraduate student	Independent undergraduate student	Graduate and professional student
First year	$2625	$6625—No more than $2625 of this amount may be in subsidized loans	$18,500 for each year of study—No more than $8500 of the annual amount may be in subsidized loans
Second year	$3500	$7500—No more than $3500 of this amount may be in subsidized loans	$18500 for each year of study—No more than $8500 of the annual amount may be in subsidized loans
Third and fourth years (each)	$5500	$10,500—No more than $5500 of this amount may be in subsidized loans	$18,500 for each year of study—No more than $8500 of the annual amount may be in subsidized loans
Maximum total debt from Stafford loans when you graduate	$23,000	$46,000—No more than $23,000 of this amount may be in subsidized loans	$138,500—No more than $65,500 of this amount may be in subsidized loans. The graduate debt limit includes Stafford loans received for undergraduate study

The source for this chart is *The Student Aid Guide 2005–2006*, page 21, U.S. Department of Education.

Eligibility for Federal Student Aid

Not everyone qualifies for federal student aid. You can receive federal student aid if:

- You are a U.S. citizen or national; a U.S. permanent resident; or an eligible non citizen
- You are enrolled in an "eligible" program at an "eligible" school
- You have been certified that you are not in default on any federal student loans (unless you have made satisfactory repayment arrangements), nor have you borrowed in excess of the allowable limits
- You are registered with Selective Service (males age 18 through 25)
- You promise that all money received will be used for educational expenses at XYZ College

- You have a high school diploma or its equivalent, or have met other basic standards as established by your state. Home-schooled students without the equivalent of a high school diploma are eligible for federal student aid if they have completed a secondary school education in a state-recognized home school setting
- You are making satisfactory progress in your course of study
- You have a valid Social Security Number
- You show you have a need to qualify for any need-based program

Government Merit Aid

In addition to federal aid, government merit aid is also awarded to deserving students. Check online to see the current requirements for each of the following awards.

- *Byrd Scholarships:* Grants of $1500 a year to outstanding high school graduates, renewable annually for four years. Each state's scholarship agency selects winners in its state. To obtain a listing of state scholarship agencies contact the State department of Education in your state.
- *Paul Douglas Teacher Scholarships:* Grants of up to $5000 a year (but not higher than the student's cost of attendance) to outstanding high school graduates who plan to teach in elementary or secondary schools. They are renewable annually for four years. A student must agree to teach two years for each year he gets the money. Winners are selected by state scholarship agencies.
- *National Science Scholars:* Grants to encourage outstanding high school seniors to study science, math, or engineering. The maximum grant is $5000 (check amount online), renewable for four years.

Free Application for Federal Student Aid (FAFSA)

All schools use the Free Application for Federal Student Aid (FAFSA). In order to qualify for financial aid at almost every public and private college in the United States, you need to fill out the FAFSA, the federal financial aid form, which can be found at www.fafsa.ed.gov. Most high school guidance offices also have copies of it. The FAFSA is processed by the U.S. Department of Education.

Often at public colleges and universities, the FAFSA is the only form that needs to be submitted. When the form is submitted to the Department of Education it computes the estimated family contribution (EFC). According to the Department of Education the EFC is the amount that is expected to be paid by the student and his or her family for college costs.

The FAFSA is used mainly by students applying for federal, as opposed to state aid. However, some colleges or universities will allow you to use this form to apply for state aid as well. Contact the financial aid

Smart tip: FAFSA has a very good website that holds your hand through the whole process. It is found at http://www.fafsa.ed.gov/

office at your school for its policy. The FAFSA needs to be sent in as soon after January 1 as possible, and no later than May 1.

The FAFSA covers the following kinds of financial aid: Federal Pell Grant, Federal Supplemental Educational Opportunity Grant, Federal Work Study, Federal Perkins Loan, and Federal Stafford Loan (subsidized and unsubsidized) programs. With the exception of unsubsidized Stafford Loans, these programs are need-based. That is, when determining eligibility for funds from these programs, your estimated family contribution as calculated through the FAFSA process is considered.

On the FAFSA you can list six colleges to whom you want your financial information sent. You can have it sent to even more after your data have been processed. There is no cost for this service. If you are applying to more than six, here are some suggested strategies.

- List the six schools with the earliest deadlines. If you start the process early, you have plenty of time to get your data to others.
- List your top six schools. If you are running short on time, make sure your preferred colleges get your information first.
- List the six most expensive colleges. If you will need financial aid to afford the school make sure the price school gets your data before it runs out of institutional aid.
- List public colleges first, then private institutions—a reverse of the advice above. Most private colleges use PROFILE and/or their own financial questionnaire to get the same information and they can use this information to begin estimating your eligibility for financial aid.

Within four weeks after you mail your FAFSA you will get a response from the U.S. Department of Education. It will contain either a request for more information or your estimated family contribution.

Information Required on the FAFSA

Here are some of the documents that you will need to prepare the FAFSA:

- Taxable income for both parents and students, including wages, pensions, capital gains, rents, interest, dividends, annuities, unemployment compensation, alimony received and business income
- Non-taxable income, including worker's compensation, welfare

benefits, housing and food allowances, child support payments received, untaxed social security benefits, veteran's noneducation benefits, tax-exempt interest income, and earned income credit
- The value of cash, savings, and checking accounts (as of the day you plan to sign the application) for both parents and the student
- The net worth of other investments: stocks, bonds, commodities, precious metals, and trusts
- The market value of real estate other than your home
- Net worth of investments. Investments include: real estate (but not the home you live in), trust funds, money market funds, mutual funds, CDs, stocks, stock options, bonds, other securities, Coverdell ESAs, 529 savings plans, installment and land sale contracts (including mortgages held). Investments don't include the home in which you live, the present value of life insurance and retirement plans, or the value of prepaid tuition plans
- Net worth of owned businesses and/or investment farms (does not include a farm that you live on and operate)
- Current balance of cash, savings, or checking accounts
- A copy of your latest tax return and all bank and investment account statements.
- Adjusted gross income from the tax return
- Earned income from wages, salaries, tips, etc.
- Nontaxable benefits including earned income credit, child tax credit, welfare benefits, and nontaxed social security benefits
- Nontaxable income including payments to tax-deferred pension and savings plans, IRA deductions, payments to SEP, SIMPLE and Keogh plans, child support received, tax-exempt interest, foreign income exclusion, untaxed pensions, or IRA distributions, and housing, food, or other living allowances paid to the military or clergy
- Deductions from income for FAFSA purposes including Hope and Lifetime Learning tax credits, child support paid because of divorce or separation, taxable earnings from Federal Work Study or other need-based work programs, or any scholarship, fellowship, or Ameri-Corps award that was taxable

Personal Identification Number (PIN)

The Department will mail a personal identification number (PIN) to

> **Smart tip:** Your goal is to lower the estimated family contribution (EFC), which is calculated from the FAFSA. The lower the EFC, the greater the possibility of student aid, which may include grants, federal student loans and employment.

most students who apply for aid. If you do not receive a PIN number from the Department you can apply for one at the Department of Education website at www.pin.ed.gov.

Visit the Department of Education's websites to familiarize yourself with the web based FAFSA application. Once there, you can navigate to the PIN website, www.pin.ed.gov, and request a PIN for both yourself and your parent. To be clear, your parent must request his or her own, and you must request yours. Within a few working days, or even shorter in some instances, you will receive your Department of Education PIN number in your email account. It is wise to check your junk mail filter at this time to be sure you will receive your communications from the department and from FAFSA. Once received, you will be closer than ever to filling out your FAFSA. If you are not given a FAFSA worksheet, either ask your high school counselor for one, or print one off from www.fafsa.ed.gov . This worksheet is not an actual application, but it is a good place to gather the information you'll need once you sit down at your computer to begin the web-based FAFSA application.

You can use this PIN number to:

- Access your SFA program records online
- Make corrections to your application information through the Internet
- Access your Renewal FAFSA in subsequent years
- Take the place of your signature if you apply using FAFSA on the web in subsequent years.

The Student Aid Report (SAR)

After filing a FAFSA, the student receives a Student Aid Report (SAR), or the institution receives an Institutional Student Information Record (ISIR), which notifies the student if he or she is eligible for a Federal Pell Grant and provides the student's EFC. The SAR, sent in the mail by the Department of Education, is a multi-page document that reports your EFC in the upper right corner of page one. The EFC is the most important information it contains but the SAR serves other useful purposes.

The SAR tells you if your EFC is low enough to be eligible for a Pell Grant. If it is, you probably are in line for a generous package of financial aid built upon the Pell. You will learn the size of your Pell Grant in your award letter from the college. If you are eligible for a Pell Grant, the SAR will include a Pell payment voucher that must be sent to your college. Be sure to make a copy for your records.

CSS PROFILE

Some colleges ask their financial aid applicants to fill out a PRO-FILE form. The PROFILE is administered by the College Board, a not-for-profit association of schools and colleges. This mainly asks for information about your family's income, expenses, and assets. The online form is customized to your situation, so you won't be presented with too many questions that don't apply to you.

The Financial Aid Profile Form grew out of changes made by Congress in 1993 to the federal student aid formula used to figure a family's ability to pay for college. Rather than adopt the new federal guidelines, some private colleges decided to create their own aid application forms. For families applying to several colleges, this often meant filling out the federal FAFSA plus a separate aid application for each college under consideration, often five or six lengthy, complicated applications.

The Financial Aid Profile Form eliminates the need to fill out separate applications by creating a standard form with one customized section. This section contains the additional, non-standard questions from all the schools selected by you on your registration form. Remember, however, that not all schools will require this form but all will require the FAFSA when applying for federal financial aid. Be sure to confirm with each school you are considering whether or not it is necessary for you to complete a Financial Aid Profile form.

The core of PROFILE is similar to the FAFSA, but the College Board customizes each form with additional questions as requested by the colleges to which the student is applying for aid.

Colleges that use PROFILE generally follow the Institutional Methodology (IM) for calculating a student's need, an approach that differs in several ways from the Federal Methodology (FM) followed by FAFSA. Since the IM is meant to give a more complete picture of your finances, it is not surprising that the PROFILE is longer than the FAFSA. It is the same general concept but you will need to gather more records to answer all the questions, and it will take more time to fill out.

The PROFILE doesn't replace the FAFSA. You still need to complete that, too, because that is the form required for federal student aid, which any college will expect you to seek before they give away their own institutional funds. The schools that require the PROFILE do so because they believe it gives a more complete account of your financial situation to guide them in awarding their own funds. The College Board provides the colleges with your PROFILE information, and the colleges use it to calculate your estimated family contribution and your need.

The College Board analyzes your data and reports them to the colleges to which you are applying. The schools then apply their own need analysis formulas, usually based on the Institutional Methodology, to figure out your estimated family contribution (EFC). From this analysis, they determine how great your need is and how much institutional financial aid to give you.

It is best to submit the PROFILE at least one week before your earliest financial aid priority date. Registrations are accepted beginning October 1 of the year before you intend to start college. If you file late, you will have to make do with whatever funds, if any, are left over.

You may need to submit the PROFILE ahead of the FAFSA, depending on the deadlines your colleges set. In fact, some of the colleges that require the PROFILE will ask you to submit it before you submit your FAFSA. This is especially likely if you are applying for an early decision or early action for admission to the college. If a college requires the PROFILE before January 1, you can submit a PROFILE with estimated income figures for this year based on your year-to-date pay stubs and your previous year's tax return, then send corrections to the college later if necessary.

Filling Out the CSS PROFILE Online

The PROFILE is available online only; you can't file it on paper. The upside of this is that PROFILE is available 24 hours a day, seven days a week. Furthermore, its online system edits and alerts you to missing or incorrect information before you submit the application, thus eliminating a potential source of delays.

To start the process, obtain a copy of the PROFILE booklet from your high school guidance office or college financial aid office. Complete the worksheet included in the booklet *before* actually registering with the College Board, the organization that processes the forms. When you feel you are ready, go to www.collegeboard.com to register for the CSS/ Financial Aid Profile. Registration involves answering sixteen preliminary questions and paying a fee. Have your credit card ready as well.

You can get ready to complete the PROFILE with the Preapplication Worksheet, available from the PROFILE site at www.collegeboard. com. You can also download and print out the PROFILE Registration Guide and Application Instructions from the same site. You will need to create a collegeboard.com account with a username and password before you can file. Setting up the account is free. If you previously registered online for the SAT you already have this account.

Registration will involve providing some preliminary information such as your date of birth; mailing address: the year in school for which you are seeking aid: whether you are a U.S. citizen, a veteran, or an orphan; whether you have dependents or have separated or divorced parents; and whether your parents own a home, or all or part of a business or farm.

During registration you will also be asked a few very basic questions about your family's finances. These determine whether you will be asked certain questions that usually don't apply to low-income families.

It takes approximately one week for your information to arrive to your schools or scholarship programs after you submit your profile. Any revisions you wish to make will have to be sent directly to your school or program at this time.

> **Smart tip:** Register for the Financial Aid Profile application only if the schools from which you are seeking aid request that you complete this form. But remember, you have to register first in order to receive the customized PROFILE application packet.

Most families will have to pay a fee of $23 to register for the PRO-FILE and to have their information sent to one college, plus $18 for each additional college. You will need to give their CSS codes. You can add more colleges to this list after you register, or even after filing your application. Just go to the PROFILE website and click on "Add Colleges to Submitted Application." The fee can be paid with most major credit cards, some bank debit cards, or by an electronic withdrawal from your checking account. Low-income families applying for the first time may qualify for a fee waiver.

After you complete your PROFILE you will receive an online PROFILE acknowledgment that confirms the colleges to which you are sending the information and gives you the opportunity to correct any data you submitted. You should print the acknowledgment, which includes the list of colleges and the data you entered on the form. Once you submit your PRO-FILE you can't revise your information online. Use the printed acknowledgment to make changes, if necessary, to the PRO-FILE information, and send those corrections directly to your colleges.

> **Stat fact:** According to a study done by the College Board in 2004 titled "Trends in Student Aid," about 25 percent of full-time undergraduate students enrolled in public colleges and universities and 60 percent at private institutions received institutional grant aid totaling $46 billion. In addition to the in grants, 10 million taxpayers benefited from federal education tax credits or tuition and fees deductions. Also, there are numerous federal, institutional, and private student loans available to students with very low interest rates.

Information Required on the CSS PROFILE

It is a good idea to gather the necessary records before you start and have them handy as you work on the PROFILE. The CSS PROFILE requires all the information contained in the FAFSA and more. Here are some of the documents you need:

- Records for both yourself and your parents
- U.S. income tax return for the year before you start college, if completed; pay stubs and other income-related records for estimates
- U.S. income tax return for the year before that
- W-2 forms and other records of money earned the year before you start college
- Records of untaxed income for those two years
- Current bank statements and mortgage information
- Records of stocks, bonds, trusts, and other investments
- The value of the parents' home and amount owed on the home
- Funds paid for private elementary, junior high, and high school tuition for dependent children
- Savings and investments held in the name of the student's siblings who are under 19 and not in college
- The name and address of the non-custodial parent and whether there is a court order requiring support. In addition, the form asks if there is a formal agreement that the noncustodial parent will be paying for education.
- The year in which your home was purchased and its original purchase cost
- The year and model of any vehicles owned
- The current value of your IRA, 401(k), or other pension plans
- A supplemental form asking for income and assets of the noncustodial parent

3

Getting Money for College

Getting Your Feet Wet in the College Aid Process

For many college-bound students, the amount of aid they will be eligible to receive determines the school they choose to attend. It is very important to estimate the general costs of each institution that a student is considering. Remember, though, financial aid is designed to supplement, not replace, a family's contribution to college costs. Therefore, all institutions expect a family to pay their fair share.

You should always give yourself as many options as possible when considering a college or university. Instead of just applying to one or two schools, apply to six or more and see which school offers the best deal. Don't limit yourself to schools you feel are "in your range." A private university with a $25,000 price tag that offers you a $22,000 aid package is a better deal than a $7,000 state college that only gives you $2,500 in aid. Aim high for some of your choices, but also pick a few lower-priced schools just in case.

The outlets available for getting college aid are many. To get an idea of how much money is out there, consider the following statistics for 2007 taken by the College Board:

Total Aid for 2007 in Billions (120.9 billion)

Federal loans 51%	$61.4
Federal grants and work study 17%	$20.7
State grants 5%	$6.3
College-offered scholarships 20%	$24.1
Outside scholarships 7%	$8.4

> **Smart tip:** Financial aid experts recommend that you apply for financial aid before deciding which college or university you are going to attend. High school seniors are not usually notified of acceptance at an institution until long after the deadline to apply for aid has come and gone.

The first rule of college financial aid is simple: the colleges are the places to find it. College-administered financial aid comes in two basic varieties: awards based on academic merit or special talents, and awards based on need. Your first major decision in the financial aid search is whether or not to apply for need-based aid. In most cases the answer should be yes.

The factors that determine how much financial aid a family qualifies for include the parents' and student's income and assets, the size of the family, and the number of children attending college. The more income and assets a family has, the more college costs it is expected to pay. Even if your family income is several hundred thousand dollars a year, there is still a chance you may qualify for something, and some non-needs awards require an aid application.

College Fairs

Attend college fairs where representatives distribute information and talk to prospective students and their parents. Attending these fairs will also help you get a feel for a college or university by talking to students or faculty. The fairs are held in most major cities across the nation during the course of a year and they usually begin in September.

If you live in a small town, college fairs may not be that readily available. In such cases it may be worthwhile to organize a trip to the nearest big city where college fairs are being held. For example, if you happen to live in the small town of Basalt, Colorado, most likely there will be no college fairs frequently organized in that area. Denver may be the closest city where one can be found.

Questions you should ask at college fairs include:

- What percentage of students attending your college receives scholarships and financial aid?
- What percentage of the scholarship is based on financial need?
- What percentage of the scholarship is based on merit?
- What is the name of the financial aid director?
- What is the deadline for the application for admission?
- What is the deadline for the application for financial aid and scholarships?

Financial Aid Office

Once you have applied for financial aid, the student financial aid office takes over. All colleges have a student financial aid office. One of the primary functions of this office is to assist students, parents, and school counselors in understanding the financial aid application process and the various student aid programs, as well as how to finance college costs.

For college students the financial aid administrator (FAA) can be the most important person on campus. The financial aid administrator at each school in which you are interested in can tell you what aid programs are available and how much the total cost of attendance will be. The FAA can draw from the money under the college's direct control or certify the student's eligibility for money not under the college's control. The FAA can also decide on the contents of the student's aid package. Once your financial need has been calculated, the Student Financial Aid Office will develop a comprehensive student aid package that may include need-based federal and state grants, merit scholarships, loans, and work-study employment.

Make sure you update your financial aid status every year, or whenever your family situation changes. This is a vital part of making certain you receive all the aid you are entitled to. Remember, just because you receive a certain amount in your financial aid package your freshman year doesn't mean you will get the same deal in your sophomore or junior years. Keep the FAA informed of any and all changing circumstances.

After you have received aid from the financial aid office don't assume that you will not have to deal with the FAA again. You may have to renew certain scholarships, inform the office about new forms of aid that you have received, or notify the office that your family circumstances have changed. Many types of aid don't renew themselves automatically. You must submit the FAFSA and supplemental forms (CSS PROFILE or Institutional Aid Application) every year by the published deadline. At many colleges the renewal of merit scholarships is tied to grades and/or some other conditions. You need to determine the minimum grade point average to renew the scholarship. In some cases, if the student does well, additional scholarship money may be available. It is the financial aid office that determines all these answers. Therefore, being in close touch with the financial aid office throughout your college years is to your advantage.

Some of the functions of the financial aid office include:

- Advising students and parents on student aid programs
- Determining final eligibility for federal and institutional need-based aid
- Providing a student-aid package

- Sending a financial aid award letter that details the types, amounts, and conditions of aid
- Setting disbursement procedures for institutional, federal, and state student aid.
- Providing alternatives, if needed, for helping to meet college expenses

College Entrance Tests

Tests are often a requirement of admission at many colleges. Students seeking aid can take achievement tests to qualify for them. These must be prepared in advance.

Recent high school graduates are typically required to submit the College Board's Scholastic Assessment Tests (SAT), or the American College Testing Program's examination (ACT Assessment) results.

Many colleges that enroll large numbers of adults either do not require a formal test or offer adult tests that are specifically designed for them. About one-half of all adult students in the U.S. are enrolled in two-year community colleges. Virtually none of these institutions require the SAT or ACT of adult applicants. Four-year colleges will very often have an application process for adults that also does not require the SAT or ACT.

The tests for graduate-level funding differ according to the field. Some schools may require the Graduate Records Examination (GRE), while others may not. Contact your specific graduate school to find out about tests that you have to take in order to qualify for aid.

Information and registration forms for the SAT can be obtained from local high school guidance counselors or from:

The College Board
SAT Program
Box 6200
Princeton, NJ 08541-6200

The ACT Assessment consists of four tests of 35 to 50 minutes each. The multiple choice questions focus on analytical and problem-solving skills and also require some general subject knowledge. ACT information and registration forms are available from high school counselors or from:

College Aid Process
ACT Registration
Box 414
Iowa City, IA 52234

Estimating Your College Budget

College costs differ greatly from one campus to another and depend on several factors. Whether or not you live on campus, attend an in-state or out-of-state school, or work during the year are factors that influence the amount of money you will need to cover expenses. When estimating your school budget, include the basic costs of tuition, room and board, and books and supplies. Don't forget money for yourself. One of the most common mistakes students make in budgeting is not to consider money for personal expenses such as clothing, transportation, and medical bills.

> **Smart tip:** Also remember, you are going to college to get an education, not to party all year long and spend your parents' hard-earned money. There is no need to look too fashionable and spend money on the latest clothing every semester, nor is there a need to rent a BMW to drive around campus to show off to your buddies.

How to Cut College Costs

When estimating costs, also think about ways to cut costs. Help your parents out a bit. Don't become a leech and try to have it easy simply because you parents are paying your college expenses. Consider the following if you are on a tight budget or just want some extra spending money:

- Leave your car at home, if possible. On most campuses, a car is simply not needed, and parking, maintenance, and insurance costs add up quickly.
- You don't have to go out to clubs, bars, and concerts every weekend. Nothing wrong in enjoying the environs of your own room or campus every once in a while too.
- Save on clothing. Don't buy new clothing every semester. Wait for sales, wear hand-me-downs, or buy clothes from thrift stores.
- For entertainment, try your school's free offerings, such as movies or plays. Also try cheap activities like basketball, rock climbing, or lifting weights at the school gym.
- Use online bookstores to find better book bargains such as Amazon.com or www.varsitybooks.com.
- Check to see if free tutoring is available.
- Try to make the bulk of your cell phone calls during your free-minutes hours or look into using an Internet connection for free phone calls.
- Try not to eat out. Grocery shopping and cooking your own meals are a lot cheaper.

- Look for used textbooks, which are often half as expensive as new books.
- Stay away from credit card purchases. Use credit cards only for emergencies.

The Financial Aid Paper Chase

Application forms of one kind or another are required for all college financial assistance programs. Unfortunately, students are unable to receive financial aid through a phone call alone. At first glance, these forms may appear confusing and difficult, causing many students to avoid filing for financial aid altogether. Don't be intimidated by a few directions specified on sheets of paper. Taking the time to read through them and filling them out can change the direction your life may take. If you carefully follow the directions, you should be able to avoid most trouble spots.

> **Smart tip:** When you contact a college regarding financial aid, ask these two very important questions:
>
> - What is their financial aid deadline for college aid?
> - What is their financial aid deadline for state aid?

If you are filling out paper forms, ask for two copies of any requested form. Students often make mistakes during their first attempt to complete the form or, worse yet, they misplace the form. Photocopy all parts of each form and use these copies as rough drafts. Be sure, however, to send only the original form back to the appropriate address.

Students with divorced parents often have special concerns when filling out financial aid forms: namely, trying to figure out which parent or step-parent has responsibility for supplying the parental information. Typically, if you are determined to be dependent, and your parents are divorced, only the income of the parent with whom you have lived for the greater period of time prior to filing the form should be used. That custodial parent, unless remarried, should complete the FAFSA as a single head of household, listing only his or her income and an appropriate portion of any joint assets and debts. However, some schools will request information from the non-custodial parent, which may be used in the determination of eligibility for state and/or institutional aid. Remember, your financial aid office can guide you step-by-step through this process and answer any specific questions you may have about your particular home situation.

Before you begin the task of filling out your forms, gather all financial data that may be needed, including:

- Previous year's U.S. income tax return forms
- If your return isn't completed before you apply for aid, an estimate of your income and expected earnings
- If applicable, your parents' return, and your spouse's return information
- W-2 forms and other records of earned income during the previous year
- Records of untaxed income
- Bank statements
- Records of benefits received through the Department of Veterans' Affairs, Social Security, and any other federal or state agency
- Records of investments (such as stocks, bonds, property, savings)
- Mortgage information
- Medical and dental expenses for the previous year
- Farm or business records
- Driver's license and Social Security numbers

Completing the Financial Aid Forms

The single most important thing you can do when completing financial aid forms is to submit them as early as possible. The reason is that colleges and universities have a limited amount of funds to disperse to students. If you send in your aid request too late, you will simply be out of luck.

Keep in mind that these forms are evaluated using computers. Forms must be neat, clean, and free of stray markings in order to register properly. When completing your financial aid applications, fill in every appropriate blank. If an answer is zero or not applicable, indicate that, rather than leaving the space empty. This will help get your forms processed faster. Don't forget to sign the forms, either. In addition, financial aid advisors also recommend that you:

- Use a black ballpoint pen on the FAFSA. Do not use felt-tip pens, markers, or colored pencils. For other forms, read instructions carefully.
- If you make a mistake, start over with a new form or clearly mark over your mistake. Do not use "white-out" or any other correction fluid.
- Use exact figures whenever possible. Do not enter a range of figures, such as "$500 to $1,000."
- Never put two separate amounts in one answer blank.
- Do not write in the margins of the forms; stray markings can cause the computer to register incorrect information.

- Be sure that everyone who provided information to you for the completion of the form places his or her signature in the appropriate section.

The final submission of the forms are also important. After investing all the time and effort to filling out the form, don't be sloppy about how you mail it out. Here are some mailing tips:

- Do not return completed forms that have been torn, crumpled, or stained; the computer will be unable to scan them properly.
- Do not send any extra materials, such as tax forms or letters, along with the required forms. Send only the form. If you would like to make comments, do so only in the appropriate sections.
- Send the original application, but make a copy of the completed form for your own records.
- Do not send any form via certified or registered mail (unless specified). Students (or parents) who do this slow up the process.

Timeline

In order to maximize your financial aid planning strategies, you should implement them a few years before enrolling in college. The following is not a strict timeline for applying for financial aid. Nor should you despair, thinking it is too late, if you are already a senior in high school. However, here is a basic outline of when you should embark on the financial aid process if you are applying for college-based aid:

8th Grade

Find out what courses you should take in high school to best prepare you for college. Think about subject areas that interest you.

Create a filing system. Be sure to set up a file where you can keep track of all the information from each school. Include the names of the administrators that you meet, especially in the financial aid office. Better still, file all your information in a computer, cell phone, or electronic notebook that you can easily access.

9th Grade

Talk to a school counselor about your future, what colleges might best serve you and what they might cost. Work with your parents to establish a plan to finance college.

Spend time in your library, researching four-year colleges, performing arts schools, community colleges, and alternative schools.

10th Grade

Write to colleges for catalogs and brochures to get an idea of their offerings, admission requirements, and financial aid policies.

Take the PSAT to prepare for college admission tests.

Create your own personal databank of all the information that you may need to complete applications for colleges: scholarship applications, FAFSA, and any other form required pertaining to college.

11th Grade (Fall):

Attend college fairs, meet with college representatives who visit your school to talk about specific institutions.

Make a list of colleges that interest you. Write for the admission and financial aid information.

Talk to your counselor about your PSAT scores and their implications for your college career.

Visit a library at school, in your community or at a nearby school to research lists of private scholarships for which you might qualify.

11th Grade (Spring)

Develop a resume of high school activities and awards that you can update as necessary.

If you haven't taken any achievement tests like the SAT or ACT, and your college asks for achievement tests, then take them.

Narrow your list of colleges and make plans to visit them. Write for an appointment at the admissions office. Allow time to talk to students and professors.

Research scholarships online. Begin your offline and online search for possible scholarships that match your interests, skills, academics, and talents.

Create a list of scholarship possibilities from your online and offline searches. Be sure to watch for deadlines for each. Retain the contact information for future use, including name of organization, eligibility, prizes, requirements, and deadlines.

Write to private scholarships requesting information.

Write several basic essays and be prepared to revise one at the last minute to meet a deadline for a scholarship application.

11th Grade (Summer)

Request admission and financial aid forms from the colleges to which you intend to apply.

Review your career plans and decide which type of college is right for you—large or small, public or private, two-year or four-year. Contact the admissions office of each college in which you are interested to obtain information on admissions, scholarships and financial aid.

Apply for private scholarships, government grants, and student loans.

12th Grade (Fall)

Make sure you are taking courses to meet the requirements of colleges for which you are applying.

Think about your application essay. Talk to your counselor and English teacher about it.

Attend college fairs and meet with college representatives.

Watch the mail for college acceptance letters and financial aid award letters to determine the college and package that best that meets your needs.

Request letters of recommendation from counselors, teachers, volunteer contacts, pastor, etc. Provide each person a copy of your resume to inform them of your high school work, employment, and activities. Send each a note of thanks for the letter.

Sign up to retake the SAT/ACT to better your score. Order scores to be sent to possible colleges you plan to attend. Make sure your scores are sent to the colleges to which you may submit applications in the future.

Compare the financial aid award letters received and watch for response deadlines. You must sign and return a copy of your financial aid award letter to receive financial aid. Also, once you have selected a college, notify the colleges you decide not to attend.

12th Grade (Winter)

Respond immediately to any request for more information or additional documents in your financial aid application.

After you get letters of acceptance and financial aid awards, decide which college you will attend. Accept its offer by its deadline or the spot may go to someone else. Decline other offers in writing.

Be sure your high school sends a transcript to colleges where you have applied.

Work with your parents to collect financial information. Submit financial aid application as soon as possible after January 1. As soon as possible after January 1, complete the FAFSA and submit electronically or by mail.

Review the financial aid package with your parents. Be sure you understand each kind of aid offered to you. Schedule an appointment with the school's financial aid director if you have questions.

Graduate School Aid

The type of graduate school aid available differs according to the institution. The biggest source of financial aid for graduate school comes from the university that you are applying to and the faculty who work there. The more they want you, the more of their resources they will offer you.

The amount of funding available will depend on the school, how large the department is, how forward-thinking the faculty is, how motivated the faculty is to get grants and share them with the students, and many other subtle factors that run through every graduate school department. Many of these factors are hidden behind the scenes.

Merit alone is often not the only or the decisive factor determining graduate school aid. Especially once you have been accepted to a department, there are other factors that can play a role in whether or not you continue to get aid during your graduate school years. Unlike undergraduate level, at the graduate school level, you may be at a specific institution for five or even ten years, depending on the program, research assistantships that you get and how long you take to complete a PhD. In the case of international students, remaining a perpetual student may help to ease the visa issue and remaining legal in the United States.

Here are some tips to consider when you are seeking financial aid in graduate school:

> **Smart tip:** remember, people who get "A"s in college don't necessarily get "A"s in life. Don't assume that excellent academic grades alone will assure you a great future. People skills, team work, a strong work ethic and a spiritual foundation are important factors as well.

- Don't step on any toes. Performing arts faculty consists of somewhat erratic and even unpredictable personalities. As a fresh student, avoid stamping on everyone's toes to indicate your importance.
- Get along with the faculty.
- Be willing to step out of the "academic" boundaries and perform favors. For example, if you are asked to do an accompaniment for chamber ensemble outside your usual sphere of activities, step up to the plate.
- Don't complain.
- Have a positive attitude.

• Always try to do more than what you are asked to do. Don't try to get away, doing the least amount of work. Professors know when idleness is involved.

Funding for Graduate Students

In many graduate school programs the available funding is published in a leaflet or on the web, or can be obtained through a discussion with the faculty chair. The following are some of the common forms of funding for graduate students.

Tuition scholarships and waivers. For professional degrees this may be all you can expect, and you may receive only partial tuition support. The rest of your education will have to be paid for by campus employment, savings, spousal income, and/or loans.

You do not have to pay back scholarship money, and most of the time, you don't have to work for it either. If the scholarship has no service requirement, it is not considered taxable income. Therefore it should not appear on W-2 or 1099 forms, and you do not have to report it on your annual 1040. You do not have to report it when applying for loans or state aid. However, you can't claim the tuition bill covered by the scholarship as an educational expense, either. If work is required for your tuition scholarship or waiver, the money may be considered taxable income. Be sure that you have in writing what work, if any, you need to do for scholarship money.

Sometimes, state schools find it easier not to bill someone than to find scholarship money because state legislatures are very tight with tax dollars; hence the invention of tuition waivers. You are simply not billed for the courses taken, or the additional out-of-state tuition charge be waived. Sometimes partial tuition scholarships are called fellowships. You receive a cash award that is promptly subtracted from your tuition bill.

Stipends. A stipend is supposed to allow students the time to devote their full attention to their studies instead of having to flip burgers to pay rent. In return for nine months of career-related work, you will be paid a stipend to cover your living and otherwise uncovered educational expenses. A stipend may be associated with a title: full-time graduate assistant, half-time teaching assistant etc. The important things to know are how many hours you are supposed to work and for how many dollars per semester.

You also need to know how many academic years you are guaranteed a stipend, assuming satisfactory academic progress. Of course, your next question should be-what is the average time it takes students in your discipline to earn a degree? There may be a gap in funding between the two, and you need to ask the director of graduate studies how students support themselves after the assistantship runs out.

The career-related work associated with the stipend should add luster to your curriculum vitae. Less experienced teaching assistants will supervise course laboratories, grade examinations, give guest lectures in class, run tutorials, or lead discussion sections. More senior graduate assistants may actually design their own courses and give all of the lectures.

If you are planning an academic career, get as much experience as you can, assisting with a variety of courses in your discipline. Not only does it look good to a faculty search committee, but it also gives you ready-made courses or laboratories for when you start your career.

The amount of the stipend money that you receive will vary among schools, among departments within a school, and even among students within the department. The amount of stipend may also be independent of the amount of time you put in. On average, graduate students work about 16 hours a week towards teaching assistant (TA) duties, but this varies.

The stipend is taxable income (federal, state, county, and city), and if you are classified as an employee, you may also lose part of your paycheck to FICA. It is important to know how much of your earnings will disappear before you get your paycheck.

You may be expected to pay school fees, supplies, and books out of your stipend, as well as tuition. Don't forget medical insurance and health center fees, along with parking. There are normal living expenses such as room, board, and transportation as well.

Research assistants (RA). Research assistants get a stipend for doing research for a faculty member. The amount of the funding will vary depending upon the discipline. The source of your stipend as a research assistant may be a government grant or the university coffers. Grants require frequent renewal to keep the money flowing, so this route may appear risky. But university RA money is not guaranteed either.

In general the faculty members who get the research grants hand out research assistantships. Therefore, if the faculty member happens to be your graduate advisor, and you have a good relationship with him or her, you may be the first in line. Even if your advisor doesn't have any research dollars, another faculty member may.

In general, research assistantships pay more than teaching assistantships. Both have their advantages. The TA gives you teaching experience, the RA gives you research experience.

Fellowships from the university. Receiving a fellowship is an honor. Every academic department, however, will have a different definition of what a fellowship is. The best fellowships will last three to five years and include a 12-month stipend. How do you get in line for free university fellowship money? Unlike fellowships awarded by foundations or the government, there usually is no separate application. The department will nominate you based on your application to graduate studies.

Extramural fellowships—that is, awards that don't come from faculty research grants or university coffers—are funding sources for which you apply directly, independent of the school. Some of the largest extramural fellowships come from the government, while some of the most prestigious come from private foundations. Some fellowships support you for several years, others just for one year while you are getting started, doing field research, or writing your dissertation. A few fellowships even support a year of travel between college and graduate school. There are, however, few fellowships offered by foundations or the government that apply to students in professional schools or in master's degree programs.

Extramural fellowships usually supply a healthy stipend and a partial or full tuition scholarship. Sometimes you will also get an educational allowance. Because you are supported by an institution or organization outside of the university, you shouldn't have to teach or do research for a faculty member. Some fellowships will, however, have an academic requirement to teach courses sometime during your graduate career.

4

The College Essay

Writing College Essays

Often, the essay may be the entry point of saying hello to a college. Writing essays is one of the most essential components of your scholarship search when applying for college and financial aid. Essay composition is required for most college and private scholarship applications and is probably the most important part. This is the spot where admission reviewers get to see what you are like as a person and what you want out of life. In addition, they simply get to see how you develop an argument and where your writing skills are in comparison to those of other applicants. Either way, the essay is extremely important and a good one can make your application stand out.

Learning to write a good essay is important to your success. In many cases, this letter may be an applicant's first and only chance to make a good impression. In fact, there are many scholarship competitions that are based solely on the quality of your essay.

The essay is your opportunity to take charge of the impression you make on a college or a scholarship committee and to provide information that does not appear in grades, test scores, or other materials. The main purpose of the essay is to give an in-depth view of you as a unique individual. Most essay questions are designed to help evaluators discover the values, ideals, achievements, and traits that make up your personality. Therefore, a well-written essay may give evaluators a glimpse of your inner self through your ability to compose a cohesive, well-thought-out writing sample.

The essay allows you to reveal your talent, intelligence, sense of humor, enthusiasm, maturity, creativity, sincerity, and writing ability. These factors all count in an admission evaluation and financial aid.

When admissions officers read essays, they search for evidence of curiosity, strong moral character and the capacity to commit to meaningful endeavors. They want to get a sense of your unique voice and distinctive qualities. Write in a way that holds the reader's interest. The admissions reviewers and scholarship judges read plenty of really boring essays about "how wonderful I am" and "my plan to end world hunger."

You will likely be asked to provide an essay related to a specific topic. Different schools might ask for different essay topics. The idea of writing dozens of essays for the possibility of a scholarship award may seem like a waste of your vital time and effort. But if you gather your potential scholarship applications together and review the specifics of what the essays are supposed to address, then you may find that one or two well-crafted essays can be used for multiple applications.

Basic Steps in the Essay-Writing Process

Writing an admissions essay involves much more than simply putting pen to paper. There are no hard and fast rules on what steps you should follow. Adhering to some of the steps described below may help. Here is how to get through the process, from the first inkling to the final revision.

Brainstorm

You will need to brainstorm to come up with some ideas for topics. Even though you may be given a prompt on the application, you will still most likely need to come up with a unique and creative topic that allows you to write an interesting and compelling essay. Brainstorming involves more than coming up with a topic, however. It also involves seeing whether or not you can expand upon a topic. Basically, you have to determine whether or not a topic is worth writing about.

Outline

With your subject securely implanted in your mind, it is time to do some preliminary writing work. You need to flesh out the topic into an outline for your essay. You can do this by thinking of the various approaches you can take on a topic. If the essay is to be argumentative, you will need to develop an outline that emphasizes the main argument and the supporting points you will make. If you are writing about your life, you may want to steer clear of the five-paragraph essay and go for something a little more linear or narrative in form, as though you were telling a story. The outline of the essay will mirror the structure the essay will take, and the structure the essay will take is based heavily on the content your essay will contain.

Talk with People

Before you dive into actually drafting your essay, take some time to talk to someone who is familiar with the process of essay writing. Your high school counselors are there to help you with precisely this sort of thing, so be sure to take advantage of their services. If you don't have a counselor, why not ask for help from an instructor? More often than not, they are delighted to help students who want to go to college.

You need to talk to someone before you set your draft down onto paper so that you get an idea of what is at stake and what your competition is like. You will probably be able to get your hands on sample essays, and your counselor can give you some hints and tips on what admissions reviewers are looking for. Don't go into the essay-writing process without having this knowledge.

Write It Out

With all of this fresh knowledge in your head and your outline in hand, you can finally begin drafting your admissions essay. Don't worry too much about structure at first. After all, you want to get your most creative ideas out on paper first, before you start complicating it with structure. You probably have the ideas in your head, so just let them flow out as naturally as possible. Once you have them all down on the page, try to set the whole thing aside for at least a week—preferably, two. This is the "marinade" stage. This way, you can come back to the table with a fresh perspective.

Revise

Revision is probably the most important step of the entire essay-writing process. When you revise your essay, you will be looking first at the content you have created. Do you support your points logically? Is your thesis clear? Is the focus of your essay concise? Do you provide enough examples for each point you make? Is any one point "heavier" in content than another? If you find issues in these areas, fix them first. You will also want to double-check your facts, if any, at this time.

Next, you will need to revise for structure. Does your essay have a solid introduction, supportive body paragraphs and a strong conclusion? Do you make smooth transitions from one paragraph to the next? Does anything seem out of place? If so, rework these parts until they are clear and consistent. You want one sentence to flow logically to the next.

Edit, Edit, Edit

Once you have completed the big revisions on your essay, it is time to get down to the nitty-gritty stuff like fixing grammar issues and spelling

> **Smart tip:** Remember how much better vegetables taste when you allow them to marinade in soy sauce for a couple of hours before grilling them? The same principle applies to essay writing. Allow your draft to marinade for a couple of days. Then, revisit it and edit it.

errors. Edit your essay several times. Cross out unnecessary words, fix punctuation errors, and watch your word usage. These may seem like nit-picky things to be concerned with, but you have to show the admissions reviewers that you take your writing very seriously. The more you edit it, the stronger it becomes. Avoid doing the writing, editing, and submission of the application in one sitting. Come up with a fairly finished draft and let it sit for a few days. You will notice things you may have overlooked had you done it all in one sitting.

Peer Edit

Once you have gotten your essay as good as it can be, let someone else have a glance at it. There is always room for improvement in writing and another set of eyes can help catch those small mistakes you might have skipped over. Peer editors usually don't catch big mistakes, but they do catch grammatical errors. Make sure you select someone you trust for this duty, like a counselor, teacher or parent.

Adhere to Deadlines

Keep track of your deadlines. As you start researching colleges, you will find that there are many places where you can apply. Being aware of their deadlines is important. Develop your own method of keeping track of deadlines. Technologically savvy writers can use Outlook. Old-fashioned writers can jot down the deadlines on a calendar or post them on the refrigerator door.

Don't put off writing your essays until the last minute. Plan them during the summer before your senior year, if you can, or early in your senior year, and write an individual essay for each college. Spend quality time with your essay. Give each application individual attention. Don't rush your writing because you have to meet an overnight deadline. Simmer your writing, research your topic, and spend time with your application. Seasoned reviewers can detect whether or not an application has been crafted at the last moment.

Attune Yourself with the College

Attuning, or finding your voice, refers to the way you decide to approach the essay. During the process of attunement, you are likely to find your unique voice. There are several ways of seeking attunement. Visiting the college website is an excellent start. Although every college website is different, most of them follow similar formats and include the academic calendar, student activities, financial aid, faculty, course curriculum, and more. Know your prospective college: research, research, and research some more.

Obtain as much information as possible about a prospective college. Understand the mission of the college, and study its programs and focus. Be sure to make a note of any academic preferences and/or limitations. See if your ideas fit within the guidelines of the college. Read through them and get a feel for the school.

When possible, talk with someone in the financial aid college who has a decision-making role or capacity. This gives you a sense of their preferred style of communication. Note whether their style is formal, scientific/technical, or community oriented.

Write Right—College Essay Writing Techniques

Learning to write a cohesive and persuasive college essay is crucial to the financial aid process. Write right. Writing is the medium through which you communicate with the admissions officer, the financial aid officer, and the awards committee. It can determine how much aid you might receive.

Avoid unnecessary words and redundancy. They waste your space, waste the reviewer's precious time, and may confuse the reader. Never send your reader to the dictionary by using uncommon and unfamiliar vocabulary. Whatever you plan to write, say it once and say it right.

Here are some tips to improve your writing skills.

Avoid Jargon

Using language that is used by a particular group, profession, or culture, especially when the words and phrases are highly technical for someone outside the discipline to understand, can be a disadvantage. Jargon can also convey a sense of pretentiousness and meaninglessness. If you must use a technical term, define it when you first use it.

Here is an example of a sentence using jargon:

The Fresnel lens that was invented in 1822 revolutionized the study of pharology.

If the reviewer does not know what a Fresnel lens is or what pharology means, your point and its significance are lost. You are making the reviewer's job more difficult by using jargon.

Instead of being too specific about the Fresnel lens, which is a type of illumination introduced to lighthouses by France in the 19th century, and using the word "pharology," which is the study of lighthouses (the word comes from the first recorded lighthouse in history, the Pharos Lighthouse of Alexandria around 290 B.C.), this sentence can be restructured so as to avoid jargon:

> The invention of the Fresnel Lens, which was a type of illumination used in lighthouses in the 18th century, revolutionized the study of lighthouses.

Explain Acronyms and Terms

Make yourself clear. You cannot assume that readers who will judge your proposal will know the same acronyms or buzzwords that are common to your organization or field of interest. While they may understand that HUD refers to the U.S. Department of Housing and Urban Development, a self-coined acronym like CARA, for the Connecticut Arts Response Action, can confuse the reader. Give readers the full name or title on first reference, followed by the acronym in parentheses.

Write Short Sentences

A sentence gains clarity when it is brief. Avoid long sentences. When sentences get too long, wordiness creeps in and it is easy for the reader to get lost in the phrases and lose your train of thought. By the end of the sentence the reader may have forgotten what was written at the beginning. Eliminate wordiness as it is likely to lead to grammatical errors. Take a look at the following sentence:

> "Give Peace a Chance" was a dance recital that our high school presented, in which I played a leading role in depicting movements of conflict from around the world.

Here is how you can make life easier:

> "Give Peace a Chance" was a dance recital presented by our high school in summer 2008. I played the leading role of performing scenes of conflict and despair faced by people living in war-torn countries.

You want to get your point across, not bury it in words. Your prose should be clear and direct. If an admissions officer has to struggle to figure out what you are trying to say, you are in trouble. Make your presentation as strong as possible and keep it to the point.

Write Cohesively

Organize your thoughts clearly. Arrange the elements of your thoughts in a way that creates a particular structure within the proposal. Cohesion is key. Organizing your thoughts forces you to eliminate unnecessary details that make the essay disconnected. Make your sentences short and powerful. Repeating the same things over and over

> **Beware:** Typically a sentence in a college essay needs to be less than twenty words. If a sentence has fifty words then it most likely needs revision.

again will lead the reviewer to believe that your academic and extracurricular background lack substance, just like your writing does.

The following is an example where the thoughts are disjointed. The request is made by an individual applicant to seek funding for a photographic project:

> I will be visiting Varanasi, India, to conduct a photographic documentary on Varanasi, India. It is one of the oldest living cities in the world. It captures the essence of India. I want to show how old ideas exist with modern trends.

Here is how you can organize your thoughts better:

> "Varanasi, India, is one of the oldest living cities in the world. In many ways, Varanasi captures the essence of India, filled with contrasts between the old order and the new, ancient civilizations versus contemporary globalization, and the sacred and the secular. My goal is to conduct a photojournalism project titled Tradition vs. Modernism in Varanasi, India. "The theme of the photo project will be to study how traditional rituals are being assailed and benefited by modernism and globalization.

Avoid Expressions of Uncertainty

> **Smart tip:** Trim the fat from your writing. Avoid unnecessary words.

The language in a college essay needs to be authoritative. Uncertain words and sentences like "may," "basically," "it appears to me," and "I might be able to," show uncertainty on the part of the applicant. Such phrases leave the reader to wonder whether or not the applicant offers promise. The following is an example of a sentence expressing uncertainty:

> It appears to me that there is a shortage of classical chamber music performances in the university curriculum, I think.

The college essay equivalent of the above statement is as follows:

> Less than 30 percent of all classical music recitals in the university curriculum feature chamber music.

Avoid Using Former and Latter

Using the words former and latter slows the reader down. Some reviewers may have to reread the previous text to determine what was "former" and what was "latter." Here is an example:

Trans fat foods in public schools have led to unhealthy eating while green salads, although less popular, add nutritional value to meals. There is a national effort to eliminate the former and increase the latter food type.

Here is a clearer sentence:

Although many schools around the country continue to use trans fats there is a push for green salads to replace them. Salads are considered healthier and add more nutritional value to meals.

Get Rid of Puny Language

A little amount of emotion may be helpful in college essays, but too much of it is likely to ruin your chances of winning aid. If you think that the reviewer is going to be touched by your emotional statements and not facts, then you may be in for a surprise. Although most people are sensitive and can be swayed by emotions, too much emotional writing can be a disqualification.

Emotional sentences are referred to as puny. They try to communicate your project through feelings, and not through facts. Lamenting about your mortgages, unpaid utilities, and ill health within a proposal may not be the best strategy to crafting a proposal that requests funds to buy a guitar to advance your musical career. Grant proposals require a straightforward and matter-of-fact style of writing. Get rid of puny language and convey your ideas pungently and precisely.

The following is an example of a sentence that is puny:

Our Board feels that the establishment of gallery space is a wonderful idea. It will give local people the opportunity to display their fascinating works of art. Unfortunately, though, the recent loss of our executive director, who died of a terminal illness, the fire that destroyed our office space, and an increase in rent have crushed our organization financially. We are trapped in a sad situation and truly need your help.

Here is a better way of writing it:

The establishment of a gallery space will enable local artists to display their work free of charge. It will also bring our arts council a monthly income through juried art shows, entry fees, and the sale of artwork, thereby enabling our organization to advance financially.

Avoid Tag Questions

A tag is a short question that is added to the end of a sentence or command. We are used to adding tags in conversations. The following is an example of a tag question used in conversation:

You mailed the greeting cards to the client, right?

When it comes to grant proposals, however, there is only one thing to do with tag questions: lose them. Here is an example of a tag question:

Public art is one of the most ubiquitous forms of art, don't you agree?

In writing college essays the above sentence needs to be rephrased as follows:

Public art is one of the most ubiquitous forms of art.

Spell Check, Stylistic and Grammar Checkers

Spell checkers are now generally integrated into word processing programs. Some of these programs automatically alert you to the presence of misspelled words as you type. Word processing programs can generally check for the following types of incorrect or poor usage:

- Sentences that are too long
- Paragraphs that are too long
- Passive versus active verb constructions
- Adjacent identical duplicate words
- Vague phrases
- Incorrect punctuation
- Missing spaces
- Too many spaces between words or sentences
- Overused words

You want to get your point across, not bury it in words. Your prose should be clear and direct. If an admissions officer has to struggle to figure out what you are trying to say, you are in trouble. Make your presentation as strong as possible and keep it to the point.

If your essay is filled with misspellings and grammatical errors, admissions representatives will conclude not only that you do not know how to write but also that you are not smart enough to get help. Use a spell check. Be especially careful about punctuation. Check (and double-check) for typographical errors. Above all, submit a clear and readable essay.

Don't Disappoint the Reader

Be aware that a heading, a subheading, or a topic sentence is essentially a "promise" to the reader about what he/she will find in the text that follows. Remember to include them. For example, if you write, "The chart below gives an indication of how many elderly residents in nursing homes have experienced falling injuries at Sunny Hill Nursing Home in 2007" but there is no chart, you are betraying the reader.

Don't Blow Your Own Horn

Remember the adage, "Tis the empty can that makes more noise?" Don't brag about your project to the funder as being the best. It might go against you. Show substance in your achievements and allow them to speak for you. Avoid an undue amount of self-praise. Let your data speak for you. Avoid statements like the following:

> Our outstanding and exceptional method of...
> Our organization is the best in the continent for...

Be Politically Correct

Be politically correct, particularly when you are writing your college essay. Say "people with reduced mobility," not "disabled people." Use "minority individuals," or terms such as African-American or Native American when you have to be specific about ethnicity. "People of color" or "minority individuals" is safer than "colored people"; "developing countries" sounds better than "third world." Use inclusive, nonsexist language by substituting she/he and his/her.

Avoid Using Modifiers

Examples of modifiers include "very," "really," and "certainly." Use these sparingly in your essay. Using them frequently is an indication that you are trying to get the attention that is slipping by you because you have limited vocabulary to write what you want.

Using excessive modifiers also indicates one's insecurity in relying on simplicity. The following is an example using a modifier:

The Center for Organic Foods, which is an extremely credible organization in the industry, promotes a very important message about eating very healthy foods.

A more effective way of writing it is as follows:

> *The Center for Organic Foods* plays a strategic role in raising awareness about eating healthy foods.

Use Metaphors to Strengthen Your Argument

A metaphor is a figure of speech that enhances the meaning of a sentence with colorful imagery. A metaphor helps to create a written painting with words and adorns your style of writing. Notice how the quality of the following sample is enhanced by a metaphor:

> Despite the ongoing peace treaty several signs have indicated that the country is treading unsteady territory. War can erupt at any moment.

The grant writing equivalent, using a metaphor, is:

The peace treaty is hanging by a thread.

Create a Visual Painting with Your Words

Make your paragraphs create images appealing to the visual, aural, and gustatory senses when possible. This will entice the reviewer to read your proposal further. Make your writing style a work of art. The longer a funder lingers on your essay, the more likely it is that you will get funding. Adopt an arresting writing style that will grab the reader's attention and make him not want to stop reading.

The following is an example of creating a visual painting with your words:

> Aromatherapy massage is relaxing to give as it is to receive. Concentrated essences extracted from plants have been valued throughout history for their therapeutic properties. The ancient Egyptians and Greeks greatly appreciated fragrance. Cleopatra is said to have indulged in herbal essences as part of her beauty regimen and healthy lifestyle. The goal of my project is to promote aromatherapy massage as a healer. Lotus Spa will produce herbal essences that are healthy for the skin.
>
> Lotus Spa will incorporate a wide variety of essential oils into massage treatments. Basic massage strokes such as fan stroking, kneading, and circular pressures work effectively in aromatherapy massage. Massage with aromatic oils softens the skin and aids healing. Some of the herbs used to create essential oils are juniper, lavender, geranium, marjoram, and rosemary. Lotus Spa will offer clients an array of choices on aromatherapy massage, fragrance products, and healing methods.

Stick to One Tense

Avoid changing tenses within the proposal. Using present tense in one section and past tense in another can confuse the reader. Here is an example:

> A CD recording of the music helped to increase awareness of the different types of singing found in Native American reservations. It was released in record stores last week. The recording is helpful to schoolchildren. It was also helpful to musicians, healers, and scholars. Schoolchildren are listening to the CD in the classrooms.

Here is the college essay writing equivalent:

> A CD recording of the music helped to increase awareness of the different types of singing in Native American reservations. It has been widely received by schoolchildren, musicians, healers, and scholars.

Give your College Essay the Human Touch

Don't get too technical and dense your essay writing style. It can be a turn-off for the reviewer. Most people have feelings. It is up to the writer to reach out to those feelings through writing. Use anecdotes, provide real-life examples, supply actual quotes from those who have benefited or will benefit from your services, emphasize the needs of those you serve, not your own, and describe the situation in terms that are not only factual but also of human interest.

Don't Be Romantic in Your College Essay

Remember—this is not a romantic letter. Timing your cover letter to get there on Valentine's Day and pasting pictures of Cupid or provocative photos of yourself on the application pages is not going to increase your chance of getting into college.

Don't pester the essay reviewer with such childish behavior.

Don't Put Down Other Applicants

Avoid assuming that you are the only applicant worthy of being accepted to a specific college. By putting down other applicants and giving the impression that you are the only individual worthy of acceptance, you are likely to hurt your chances of winning any aid. Acting in isolation does not sit too well with today's thinking. The strategy is to show how your acceptance can blend well with the rest of the student body. When you put down another applicant, it looks bad on you.

Don't Put All Your Eggs in One Basket

Create a healthy mix of college applications. Apply for private as well as state colleges. Spending six months on only one application is not recommended. Work on several simultaneously. Diversifying is key.

Avoid a Tone of Arrogance

Remember, it is up to the college to decide whether or not to accept you. They are on the higher end as far as admission is concerned. Demanding admission arrogantly from a college is never a good idea. Humility creates more positive overtones than arrogance.

Do Not Use a Cookie-cutter Approach

A cookie-cutter approach is when you submit the same college essay to ten different colleges without tailoring each one separately. It is also known as the shotgun approach. Using the cookie-cutter approach is disadvantageous because the guidelines of each college are different. You may have to reduce the word count, rewrite some of the paragraphs, and do some editing of text. It is critical to tailor your proposal for each college and to format it specifically to the individual funding source.

Writing a single "boilerplate" college essay that can be sent out to many colleges is not recommended. A single college essay is right only for the funder for which it is written. Sending it to dozens at once is usually a waste of resources. Sending a boilerplate proposal skips over the important steps of matching the potential college with your program and presenting the match in a way that the particular reviewer will find pertinent and compelling.

How to Select a Topic for Your Student Admissions Essay

Even though you will most often be given a prompt of some sort for your admissions essay, you will still need to come up with a topic that is individual and unique to you. There are plenty of things you can write about; you just need to look long and hard to find them. Here are a few tips for evaluating potential topics you come up with.

Eliminate What Can't Be Expanded

Some topics may look good as the focus of your essay, but once you try to expand it at all, you soon realize it will only make for an essay that is very thin and low on content. Look through the list you've compiled. Do you see any topics that you can't expand upon? If so, scratch them off the list right away.

Choose a Topic That Gives Hope

At some level, everyone is looking for hope. Let's face it: the world is a pretty depressing place. There are so many sad things going on that our eyes cannot see. Despite the harsh realities affecting the majority of the people, hope makes them keep on living. When you are selecting a topic, choose one that leaves room for hope. Hopelessness creates negative overtones.

Eliminate Clichéd Topics

Choose a topic with a unique angle. Are any of the topics on your list things that have been talked about over and over again? If this is the case, it's time to move on to other topics. You want to write an essay the reviewers will remember, not one that they feel as though they have read before.

Choose a Topic That Makes a Good Impression

If a topic does nothing to impress the judges or to portray you in a positive light, then you should not use it. Quite simply, you need to select a topic that will leave a lasting impression on the reviewers. They read many essays a day, which makes it hard to distinguish one from another after awhile. You have to work your hardest to make your essay stand out from the whole host of other essays the reviewers receive. To do this, you need to eliminate the topics and subject matter that you could take or leave. Maybe you could write about how you ran for class president and what you learned along the way, but maybe that is not the most exciting or unique thing you have done. It may take a while, but try to figure out which topics need to be eliminated.

Don't Look for Pity

When you write an admissions essay, a lot of the time the prompt will call for you to write about something that has happened in your life. The things we usually remember are the events that were either tragic or negative in some way. It is okay to write about such things, but be careful. Even though it was heartbreaking to lose your pet fish, this may not be a good topic for your college essay.

Avoid Sensitive and Offensive Topics

There are many issues that you should avoid on a college application essay. For instance, issues that may be offensive to others should be avoided at all costs. Anything that causes problems in the world between groups such as religion or politics should not be discussed, unless you are going to be discussing it in such way that it only pertains to you. Rather than writing about why everyone should be a Christian, focus on how the religion has affected you and helped you to become a responsible individual. Race is also a sensitive issue. This is not the time to be stepping on toes.

Smart tip: You don't want to make the topic of your essay how you overcame a drinking habit or how you stopped partying on the weekends. While such recovery from drinking and partying may be personal triumphs, remember, you are competing with students who never got addicted to them in the first place. So, don't reveal your weaknesses too generously in your college essay.

Eliminate the Negative

The admissions essay is your chance to shine and to impress college admissions reviewers. You don't want to depress them and you certainly don't want to show off your every little flaw. For example, you don't want to make the topic of your essay how you overcame a drinking habit or how you stopped partying on the weekends. Even though you may have really overcome these things, the admissions reviewers are going to be caught up in the fact that you ever partook of alcohol or drugs or had certain things as a weakness at all. If you can, it's better to avoid the things that make you look bad.

5

The Art of Winning Scholarships

Basic Guidelines for Winning Scholarship Aid

Each fall represents the unofficial beginning of the scholarship hunting season. Let's assume you are planning to attend college in fall of a particular year. If this is the case, from October of the previous year through the end of spring of the target year, you should be in hunting mode.

The key to winning scholarship money is to find awards that match your talents, skills, academics, and interests. No matter how good a student you are, if you fail to match the eligibility requirements for a particular scholarship, you are in a tight spot.

Since there are countless scholarship opportunities out there, the idea of searching through the masses of scholarship search sites and matching services can seem daunting. If you go into the process blindly with no game plan you may give up on the whole idea before you really even start.

To begin with, fill out a personal data form, a very thorough compilation of all of your cultural, ethnic, family, religious, academic and extracurricular activities. The more specific and inclusive you are the better your chances are of finding more scholarships for which you qualify. The object of the game is to win money. The more scholarships that are appropriate for you to apply for, the greater your odds of getting that money. The trick is to uncover all the sources you are eligible to receive. Failing to match

> **Smart tip:** Having an Internet connection can be really useful and a timesaver in your scholarship hunt. If you don't have Internet access, don't despair. Most public libraries have free Internet. Of course, if you are in school or in college, you can get Internet access that way.

yourself to sources even in one category could mean missing out on free money.

Find a few scholarship search engines that you are comfortable with. Make sure they are legitimate. They should not be requiring any payment, banking information or commitment to any type of deception. Once you have found your favorite sites, bookmark them for easy reference.

It will help your scholarship search efforts if you make a list of all your achievements, interests, and other qualifications before you start. Enter your data as requested, making sure to include every activity, organizational membership, or community service you have been involved with. Ask your parents and friends if your list looks complete. It is very easy to overlook some participation or commitment you made years ago. Creating this personal profile can help. The profile will also be useful as you begin filling out applications and writing essays.

Many college admissions applications contain applications for financial aid as well. Therefore, whether you are applying for admission or a scholarship, pay close attention to all the sections of an application because you have to be admitted to a college before you can win a scholarship sponsored by it.

Read the instructions carefully. Scholarship programs receive hundreds and even thousands of applications. Don't lose out because of failure to submit a typewritten essay, if required versus a handwritten one or to provide appropriate recommendations. If you have a question about your eligibility for a particular scholarship or how to complete an application, contact the scholarship sponsors.

> **Smart tip:** An important strategy for your successful scholarship search is to begin at the end of the alphabet. That is, when searching for scholarships in each listing or directory of foundations, begin at the back of the book and work forward. Most students will begin their search from A to Z but will quit before identifying the foundations that start with letters from the end of the alphabet. This strategy improves your chances dramatically.

Most of the time when you locate a scholarship that you are interested in, you will have to request the application packet. To do this you will write a letter. The letter should be short and to the point. You will want to include such things as:

- Your name
- Your grade or the year you will graduate
- Your GPA if the scholarship is academic
- Test scores, if they are a requirement for eligibility
- The reason you are eligible for the scholarship

> **Smart tip:** Remember, not all scholarships are based on grades or test scores. For example, you can get a scholarship because you were born in Texas or just because your dad works for the railroad.

- If the scholarship requires a financial need, include a brief explanation of your circumstances

Reading a Scholarship Listing

Scholarship listings usually include four sections: the award, eligibility, application requirements and contact information.

The award section details how much the award is for, whether it is renewable and based on financial need, etc. The eligibility section is very important. Reading the eligibility requirements is a must. Don't waste your time on a scholarship that you are not eligible for. Application requirements detail a list of materials you will be expected to submit in order to apply for a particular scholarship. Please note that in many cases you will have to contact the sponsoring organization requesting application procedures prior to submitting an application. Contact information will include the web and e-mail addresses, fax, phone and physical address.

Sometimes, the wording of the information may be a little different. Some directories or websites may have information in greater detail with additional information such as geographical limitations, age limitations, and the history of the scholarship award.

Here is an example of a scholarship listing:

Susan Glover Hitchcock Scholarship *(Four-Year College, Two-Year College, University, Vocational/Occupational/Scholarship)*
Purpose: Award for women who are majoring in music. Must be a Massachusetts resident. Application deadline is April 15.
Focus: Music.
Qualifications: Applicant must be: female, full-time student. High school students not considered. Award available to U.S. citizens.
Funds Available: Minimum award amount: $500. Maximum award amount: $800.
No. and Amount Awarded Last Calendar Year: $15,000 total.
To Apply: Required: application form; transcript; essay.
Deadline: 4/15.
Contact: Sandra Brown-McMullen, Vice President, 617-722-3891.

Merit Scholarships

Merit scholarships are money given to students on the basis of demonstrated ability—academic, performance, service, athletic, etc. Most scholarships come from the colleges themselves and vary widely from institution to institution. There are also some scholarships available from businesses, alumni organizations, and programs like the National Merit Scholarship.

The more heavily a college invests in merit scholarships the less money it has for packages based on need. Since the students who win merit awards (particularly those based on standardized test scores) tend to come from well-heeled families, merit scholarships represent a significant money transfer away from high-need applicants towards lower-need ones.

Private Scholarships

Private scholarships are non-federal scholarships that originate outside of the college, and generally require the student to file a separate application. Although academic standing or financial need may be conditions for some private scholarships, these funds may also be awarded based on such qualifications such as field of study, religious affiliation, ethnic background, leadership skills, place of residence, or other criteria.

High schools, Dollars for Scholars, churches, local businesses, and civic service organizations frequently have scholarship programs. So may the company where a student's parent works. Information about private awards, including how to apply for these funds, is usually available at the high school or local library.

Private scholarships are sponsored, administered and awarded by a wide variety of private agencies, organizations or individual donors. Much of the private scholarship money is restricted. It could be for students of a certain religious faith or ethnic heritage, for children of military or union members, journalism majors, theater majors, students from certain towns, etc.

Be aware, however, that private scholarships can change the amount of financial aid that you can get from a college. Some schools automatically reduce the financial package by the amount of outside scholarships. Others ignore any outside money. Still others consider it on a case-by-case basis.

National Merit Scholarships

The National Merit Scholarship Program is an academic scholarship competition for recognition and college scholarships administered by the National Merit Scholarship Corporation (NMSC), a privately funded, not-for-profit organization. The program began in 1955. NMSC conducts two annual competitions for recognition and scholarships: the National Merit Scholarship Program, which is open to all students who meet entry requirements, and the National Achievement Scholarship Program, in which only African-American students participate (see below). Each year a total of approximately 10,500 scholarships are awarded through NMSC programs. The website for the National Merit Scholarships is www. nationalmerit.org/nmsp.php.

To enter the competition, a student must:

- Be enrolled full-time as a high school student progressing normally toward completion of high school and planning to enroll full-time in college in the fall following the completion of high school;
- Be a citizen of the United States or be a U.S. lawful permanent resident who intends to become a U.S. citizen at the earliest opportunity allowed by law; and
- Take the Preliminary SAT/National Merit Scholarship Qualifying Test (PSAT/NMSQT) in the specified year of the high school program, usually the junior year (11th grade) and usually at one's own school. Students completing high school in three (3) years or less must be in the last or next-to-last year of high school when they take the test. Students unable to take the exam because of an extenuating circumstance, such as severe illness or natural disaster, may be permitted to substitute subsequent SAT results by making arrangements with NMSC no later than March 1 following the exam that was missed.

National Achievement Scholarship Program

African-American students who meet entry requirements and request consideration when they take PSAT/NMSQT can enter the National Achievement Scholarship Program as well as the National Merit Program. The two programs are conducted concurrently; however, a student's standing in each program is determined independently. African-American students can qualify for recognition, become candidates for awards, and be honored as scholars in both competitions, but they can receive only one monetary award from NMSC. Students who are chosen as both National Achievement and National Merit Scholars receive the monetary award that is most advantageous to them and are recognized as Honorary Scholars in the other program.

Steps in the Achievement Scholarship competition are parallel to those in the National Merit Scholarship Program. Of 130,000 entrants, some 3,000 students are referred to colleges for their academic potential and an additional 1,600 students are designated semifinalists on a regional representation basis. Semifinalists are the highest scorers in the states that make up each region and have an opportunity to continue in the competition for scholarships.

Before receiving an award, a finalist must (a) notify NMSC of plans to enroll in a college or university in the United States that holds accredited status with a regional accrediting commission on higher education, and (b) plan to enroll full-time in an undergraduate course of study leading to a traditional baccalaureate degree. NMSC scholarship stipends are not payable for attendance at service academies, virtual universities, and certain institutions that are limited in their purposes or training. A very small number of National Merit Scholars do not receive a monetary award because their educational plans or other awards preclude receipt of a monetary scholarship; however, these students may be honored as Honorary Merit Scholars, a designation that acknowledges achievement without providing any financial assistance. The website for the National Achievement Scholarship Program is www.nationalmerit.org/nasp.php.

Tips for Filling Out College Scholarship Applications

The first item that college and scholarship administrators will see is your application. If your application is sloppy, it will make a weak impression before administrators get a chance to formulate positive assessments and think about what aid to offer. This impression may cause them to scrap your entire application. There are no strict rules as to how you should fill out scholarship applications. Individual requirements may vary.

The following are some of the main steps for filling out your college scholarship applications.

Type It Out

All applications should be typed unless the application requests that you print. Check your work. Proofread your applications for spelling or grammatical errors, fill in all blanks, and make sure your handwriting is legible. Avoid using correction fluid or correction tape. Keep extra copies of the application handy, or first work on a photocopy before transferring the information on to the original copy. If you are working online on a program like Word, reread the information before printing out the final version that you are going to e-mail or mail to the school. Be sure to sign and date each application and include all of the required materials.

Submit Early

Applications should be turned in as far in advance as possible. There are many scholarships issued on a first-come, first-served basis. Once the funds are depleted you cannot apply until the following year. Apply as early as possible for scholarship programs. If you can, do it in the fall of your senior year, even if the deadlines aren't until February or March. Very often, scholarship programs award all their funds for the year before their stated deadline.

Be sure to organize your applications by deadline, with the earliest deadlines first. Make a checklist for each application on a scrap of paper or sticky note for the front of the application. Mark off each item as you complete it. If you have time between applications, proofread your essays, address envelopes, and follow up with potential donors to see if your application has been received. Applications that are missing information, come in after a deadline, have spelling or grammatical errors, or otherwise don't meet the minimum expectations of the donor, will be discarded.

Attend to Your College Test Scores

Arrange to have your scores from the SAT and other standardized tests sent to the colleges shortly after your applications arrive, if you have not already done so during the registration phase for the tests. Make sure to check with the colleges and universities to ensure that they have received the scores. If you feel you could have done better at the SAT or ACT, take them again, and have the new scores sent to the schools.

Be Organized

Set up a file system for all copies of applications so that you can locate them easily as deadlines draw near. It is a good idea to create a separate file for each scholarship and sort them by their due dates. If application materials get lost, having copies on file will make it easier to resend the application quickly.

Maintain Rapport with the Colleges

Before applying for financial aid, you should contact the schools you are interested in attending to find out which form they prefer, CSS or FAFSA. Even though you cannot officially file any of these forms until after January 1 of the year you plan to attend college, obtain one of the forms early and gather all the information you will need to fill out the form completely.

Make Copies

Keep copies of all scholarship material. Before sending out an application always have a copy on file for your records, including the essay and any other enclosures. You may need to review it later at a scholarship foundation awards program. Apart from having it on computer, it is recommended to have a hard copy as well. You may lose your hard drive, disk, or CD-ROM, thus making it difficult for you to access your information if it is saved only on the computer.

Allocate Application Components as Necessary

All sections of the application that you are not directly responsible for should be given to those who are responsible for them as soon as possible. Such outside materials include recommendation forms from counselors, teachers, and friends, or secondary and mid-year school reports. Sometimes it may take days, weeks, or even months to get the material from external sources properly filled out. Repeated reminders and follow-ups may be necessary to secure information from others. Give yourself adequate time to gather the material from outside sources.

Include Supporting Materials

Include attachments when available. With your applications include articles that may have appeared in your local newspaper about you or your activities. Any media publicity can weigh in your favor. Include samples of your work that are extraordinary. Send tape recordings or CDs of your musical performances, comedy roles, dance recitals, and acting skills. Flaunt any special talent or hobby that you have. It makes your application stand out from others.

Include a Resume

Include your personal resume. Most applications have space for you to list your activities and special awards, but it looks more professional to include a resume, unless specified otherwise. Never leave the spaces for this information blank. Instead, type instructions to see additional information on a separate sheet, which will be your resume.

Don't Leave Blank Space

For questions that do not apply to you, write "not applicable" in the answer blank, or abbreviated NA, to show that you have not overlooked the question. Don't leave it blank. It might give the impression that you don't have any information to provide for that particular section.

Beware: There are many sources and free directories that contain scholarship links and information. Be wary of scholarship scams, especially services that require you to pay to see a list of available scholarships.

6

The Hunt for Loans

Applying for Loans

Education loans come in three types: student loans, parent loans, and private loans. A fourth type, consolidation loans, allows the borrower to combine all of his/her loans into one loan for simplified payment.

There are three main sources of loans: the federal or state government; colleges, and commercial enterprises such as banks or firms that specialize in college loans. Many student loan providers offer low-cost government and private loans with high-quality servicing and flexible repayment terms. You may apply online for your loans at various banks.

Federal Student Loans

Federal loans are the largest source of student loans around. These are long-term loans with low interest rates designed exclusively for those needing money to meet the costs associated with education. They have very attractive terms when compared to most other borrowing options— such as lower interest rates, federal subsidized interest possibilities, options to postpone payments, longer repayment terms, easier credit requirements, etc. You will need to complete the Free Application for Federal Student Aid (FAFSA) before you can apply for federal student loans.

Commercial Loans

Several commercial lenders specialize in college lending. These programs allow you to repay the principal on a loan after graduation, though the interest payments need to be made while still in school.

State Loan Programs

In addition to federal aid, most states offer their own loan programs. Usually these programs are designed for state residents. However, in some cases, even out-of-state students can qualify. The terms, interest rates, repayment schedules, and amounts of loans vary widely from state to state. Several states offer special incentive programs to train teachers, doctors, nurses, and other professionals in short supply. Other states offer programs aimed at veterans or those enlisted in the state's National Guard.

Apply to banks that administer the state programs. The individual college's financial aid officer will make the ultimate decision.

College Loan Programs

Individual colleges have their own programs. These vary from school to school and from department to department. The music department may offer no-interest loans of $5000 for piano music majors, while the theater department may offer $3000 loans to freshmen. Inquire from the department chair about the different loan programs that may be available.

Private Loans

You should always plan to look for federal loan options before investigating private loan sources, because these loans are sometimes more difficult to obtain and can often end up being very costly to you in the end. Private loans are designed to supplement federal loan programs and are available from schools, banks and education loan organizations. Private loans are also known as alternative loans and the terms often vary considerably, based on the lender and borrower credit histories.

Alternative Loan Programs

After reviewing the college's financial aid package, you may still need additional money to pay for college expenses. At this time you may want to consider an alternative loan, available from private lenders to supplement a student's financial aid package. Make sure that you have researched all student aid possibilities before you borrow for alternative loan programs, as they are usually more expensive than federal government guaranteed loans.

> **Beware:** Any education loan has to be repaid—even if you don't finish school, are unhappy with the education you received, are unable to find a job, or are making less money than you planned. So, borrow wisely, because the amount of money you borrow will have long-term effects that can influence your lifestyle.

Differences between federal and private loans

Here are some important things to remember about the differences between federal and private student loans

Federal loans:

- Usually have lower interest rates
- Often include federally-subsidized interest
- Provide options to postpone payments
- May have a longer repayment term
- Offer easier credit requirements
- Generally require completion of FAFSA
- Usually require school certification
- May offer borrower benefits in the form of interest rate discounts or rebates

Private loans:

- Don't require completing the FAFSA
- Send the funds directly to you, not your school
- Can help when federal student loans aren't enough to fund your entire education
- Have interest rates and fees that are determined by the lender and often depend on your credit rating
- May require the borrower to have a cosigner, if the student does not qualify alone
- May or may not have deferment and forbearance options depending on the lender in certain circumstances
- May offer borrower benefits in the form of interest rate discounts and rebates
- May offer borrower benefits in the form of interest rate discounts or rebates to encourage students to make timely payments, make automated payments, or agree to enroll in web-based billing and servicing

Points to Consider When Applying for Loans

Taking loans should not be taken lightly. As you begin researching the various loan programs you may want to consider the following questions:

- What is the minimum and maximum I can borrow?
- How long does it take to get the money?
- Does the lender offer pre-approval over the phone or Internet?
- What is the interest rate?

- Will the interest rate stay the same? If not, how often does it change?
- Is there a cap on how much this variable rate can increase?
- What is the length of the repayment period?
- How much will this loan cost me over the repayment period (i.e., principal plus interest plus fees)?
- Can I combine payment of this loan with other loans (e.g., Federal, Stafford)?
- Will I need a co-signer?
- If there is a cosigner, is that person's obligation permanent?
- What criteria are used to determine if a person is creditworthy?
- Is there a penalty for prepayment of principal?
- Does the loan have deferment and forbearance provisions?
- Do I make payments while I am in school?
- What if I go back to school after making payments for a period of time?
- When is my first payment due?
- Does the lender reward borrowers that make consecutive on-time payments?
- Are the interest rates competitive with other alternative loan programs?
- Are there origination fees?
- Are the fees comparable to other alternative loan programs?
- What if I have employment problems?

Tips for Borrowing

Loan borrowing can be a serious business. You need to know what you are getting yourself into. Here are some points to consider when borrowing student loans.

- Always read the documents before you sign anything. If you don't understand any part of the document, ask someone who is likely to give you sound advice and to give you feedback.
- Choose a lender carefully. Lenders will offer incentives or benefits that will affect interest rates and can substantially determine how much you will pay over the life of the loan (principal plus interest total loan cost).
- Borrow what you actually need and only after all other resources have been exhausted. Avoid borrowing for nonessential items.
- Apply for private scholarships and check out all grant programs, e.g., state-funded programs and institutional programs.

- Make sure that you notify the lending institution of any address change. Usually the first payment is late due to the lender's mailing the first bill to your old college address or your parents' home. This can adversely affect your back-end benefits.

> **Smart tip:** Federally backed loans can help create a good credit rating. Almost all lending institutions are willing to make alternative payment plans if you are having trouble meeting your repayment schedule. If you foresee financial difficulty, contact the agency carrying your loan immediately to explain your situation. Do not just skip a payment without explanation.

- Some lenders may be very aggressive. Be careful with those using heavy pressure.
- When choosing a FFELS lender (see next section), be sure to know what repayment incentives are available. Lenders offer a variety of incentives. Be cautious of incentives that are linked to a certain number of on-time payments. Many students miss a payment and do not qualify for the benefit.

Stafford Loans

Stafford loans are probably the largest single form of federal student aid. Federal Stafford Loans are student loans that must be repaid and are available to both undergraduate and graduate students. Stafford Loans are available through many different lending institutions and are fully insured by both state and federal governments.

In addition, the U.S. Department of Education administers the Federal Family Education Loan (FFEL) and the William D. Ford Direct Loan Program. The main difference between the two loan programs is that students receive FFEL funds from private lenders (such as banks, credit unions, and other lenders) who participate in this program, while direct loans funded through the federal government go directly to the school.

Prior to obtaining a Stafford loan you must participate in a loan counseling session that drives home the importance of debt management. A website sponsored

> **Key Characteristics of Stafford Loans**
>
> - Stafford Loans (subsidized and unsubsidized) must be repaid
> - Lenders: banks, credit unions, savings and loans, loan associations, schools, and, through the Direct Loan program, the U.S. Department of Education
> - Insured by lender and reinsured by the state and/or federal government
> - Deadlines: Apply as soon after January 1 as possible.

by various banks allows you to take the session online and will send your "quiz" results directly to participating schools. Once you get the loan, the U.S. Department of Education will make payments to you through your school, usually in two payments a year.

Eligibility Requirements for a Stafford Loan

Students must meet certain requirements in order to qualify for a Stafford loan. Here are some of them:

- You must be enrolled at least half-time in a participating school
- You must be a U.S. citizen or eligible non-citizen
- Unsubsidized Stafford Loans are issued regardless of income
- Students are able to borrow money whether they have financial need or not
- Students studying overseas are also eligible as long as they are earning credit from their state institutions
- You must not have previously defaulted on any other student aid loans
- Junior and senior undergraduates must not have more than $23,000 outstanding from previous Stafford Loans (or GSLs), and graduate students must not have more than $65,000 outstanding from any previous Staffords or GSLs

To receive a Stafford Loan, most applicants need to fill out the Free Application for Federal Student Aid (FAFSA). Apply as you would for financial aid, by filling out a FAFSA form directly with your college. There may also be other forms individual schools require, such as the Financial Aid *Profile* application. Financial aid advisors at the school you are attending or planning to attend can help you determine what forms to fill out. Colleges and universities will use the FAFSA to determine eligibility for the loan.

After your financial aid package is complete and award amounts are determined, you will either receive a Stafford Loan application in the mail from your financial aid office or you will need to request one. Complete the form and make sure that the school you are attending has filled out its section of the form, certifying your registration, the amount of award money you will be receiving, and the total cost of your tuition and expenses. Most schools will automatically check your eligibility for a Pell Grant (see Chapter 7) before announcing the appropriate Stafford Loan amount. If you do receive a Pell Grant, the amount of your Stafford Loan may be less. In some cases, your college or university can certify a loan for less money than you are eligible to receive, or they can refuse to certify your application altogether. If this happens, the school must present you with written documentation for its actions. The school's decision is final and cannot be appealed to the U.S. Department of Education.

Federal Stafford Loans may be subsidized or unsubsidized. A subsidized loan is awarded based on financial need. This means you are not charged interest before repayment occurs or during authorized periods of deferment. The federal government pays the interest for the student. An unsubsidized loan is not awarded on the basis of need. Students are charged interest from the time the loan is disbursed until it is paid in full. The interest rate effective July 1, 2006, for the repayment period is fixed at 6.8 percent. Note that it is possible for a student to have partial eligibility for both subsidized and unsubsidized loans in an award year. These loans have fees up to 4 percent. Also, there are delayed repayment and deferment provisions.

Effective July 1, 2007, through June 30, 2008, the new rates for variable student loans were as follows for loans that were first disbursed between July 1, 1998, and June 30, 2006:

Federal Stafford Loan Rates

Period	Rate
During school, grace and deferment periods	6.62%
During active repayment, including forbearance periods	7.22%

Federal PLUS Rate

Period	Rate
For all periods during repayment, including forbearance and deferment	8.02%

The rates for loans disbursed on or after July 1, 2006 have a fixed rate as follows:

Federal Stafford Loan Rates

Period	Rate
For all periods, including in-school, grace, deferment, and repayment periods	6.80% fixed

Federal PLUS Rate

Period	Rate
For all periods during repayment, including forbearance and deferment	8.50% fixed

Disbursement

Once the application for your Stafford Loan has been approved by the lender, the funds will automatically be transferred back to your school for disbursement. Before receiving your loan money, you must sign a promissory note agreeing to pay back the entire amount you have borrowed. Typically, there is a 4 percent loan fee that is taken out of the loan before you receive the money. The disbursement of loan money is either credited to your account by the school, or paid directly to you, or both. The number of payments you receive is based on your academic calendar. If you attend a school on the quarter system, you will usually be paid three times a year at the start of each quarter (not including the summer quarter). Schools that operate on a semester system pay their students twice a year, at the beginning of fall and spring terms. With the Stafford Loan, disbursements may also be on a weekly or monthly installment plan. Payments may never be more than one-half the amount of your loan. Students who are studying overseas can arrange to receive their funds directly.

Undergraduate students in their first year of study who are also first-time Stafford Loan borrowers must wait thirty days after the start of school to receive their first loan installment. This also applies to borrowers attending an institution with a default rate of over 25 percent. Because of this waiting period, it is very important that you make arrangements to have your tuition and expenses covered until you receive your installment. As noted earlier, many schools will grant emergency loans free of interest to students who have not yet received financial aid. Contact your financial aid office for more information.

Paying Back Stafford Loans

Students who have Stafford Loans based on need are not responsible for making interest payments until after graduation. These types of loans are subsidized, meaning that the federal government supports or pays the interest on these loans while the borrower is in school. Non-need, or unsubsidized, loans will accrue interest while the student is in school and during deferment periods. Borrowers with unsubsidized loans may have the option of letting interest accumulate until they are out of school or until deferment ends.

In addition to the interest you pay and the principal itself, students with subsidized loans will be charged a 5 percent origination fee that is deducted equally from each payment. The origination fee helps the federal government cover the costs of administering the Stafford Loan program. Some lending institutions may also collect an insurance premium of up to 3 percent. This premium is deducted from installments in the same way as the origination fee. Students with unsubsidized loans will be charged a combined origination fee and insurance premium of 6.5 percent, deducted from each payment.

The organization carrying your loan should inform you of the date, when repayment is to begin. However, if this deadline has passed and the company has not contacted you, it is your responsibility to either notify the organization or begin repayment on time. Stafford payments are typically made over a five- to ten-year period, depending on the size of the loan.

If your status changes, you must notify the organization carrying your loan. Often this organization will be different from the original lender, because many lenders sell the loans they carry to other companies who handle the collection process.

If your school does not participate in the Federal Direct Student Loan Program, banks, credit unions and private lenders offer unsubsidized Staffords. Unfortunately, you may not have as many ways to repay. But if you repay your bills on time, the student loan Marketing Association (Sallie Mae, may buy your loan from the private lender. If your loan is bought and first four years of payments are made on time, the interest rate is lowered by 2 percentage points on the remaining loan balance. You can save another 0.25 percent by authorizing automatic deductions from your bank account. If there are two years of on-time payments, Sallie Mae "forgives" the origination fees of more than $250. These steps will allow you to save $386 on a $5,000 loan and up to $7095 on a $60,000 loan.

Your payback plan usually goes into effect six months after you graduate, leave school, or reduce your enrollment to less than half-time. For those demonstrating need, payments don't begin until six months after a student leaves school, and no interest accrues until that time. With an unsubsidized loan, interest accrues immediately after the funds are distributed, usually each semester. If you have a subsidized Stafford Loan, you are not responsible for interest payments during this six-month period. If your loan is unsubsidized, the interest will continue to accumulate.

Deferring a Stafford Loan

Deferring or postponing Stafford Loan payments is possible under specific conditions, as long as the loan is not in default. You must contact the agency carrying your loan to apply for deferment. Be prepared to present documentation to support your request. Your eligibility for deferment depends on the date your loan was first disbursed, the current status of your loan, and the following criteria. For loans first disbursed on or after July 1, 1994, deferment is granted for:

- Graduate or fellowship study
- Half- or full-time enrollment in a post-secondary institution
- Involvement in rehabilitation programs for the physically challenged

The repayment of a Stafford Loan may be canceled or forgiven, but only under the following specific conditions:

- Bankruptcy (in some cases)
- Complete and permanent disability of the borrower
- Death of the borrower
- Going back to school for a teaching certificate
- Teaching full-time in an area serving low-income students
- Teaching full-time in an area with a shortage of teachers
- Volunteering for the Peace Corps, VISTA, or other nonprofit organizations

If you qualify for any one of these requirements and would like to apply for cancellation, contact the organization carrying your loan. Some of these conditions are dependent on the amount of funds available to cover such programs, so check with your loan company for availability.

Up to three years' deferment is granted for:

- Economic difficulties
- Inability to find full-time employment

Forbearance of a Stafford Loan

Any student who is willing to make loan payments but is unable to do so, and who is not eligible for a deferment, may apply for forbearance. Forbearance is a specified amount of time during which you are not required to make any payments on the principal balance or interest of your loan. You must contact the organization that carries your loan and inquire about procedures to apply for forbearance. Most companies require some type of written statement about your present financial situation.

Perkins Loans

Undergraduate and graduate students who have established financial need may be eligible to receive a Perkins Loan. The Perkins Loans program requires a high degree of financial need and is available to graduates and undergraduates. The Perkins Loan program is commonly referred to as a campus-based program because the schools act as lenders and finan-

Key Characteristics of Perkins Loans

- Perkins Loans must be repaid
- Lender: This is a campus-based program with the school acting as the lender
- Insurance: The school insures the loan with the backing of the federal government
- Interest rate: Annual rate of 5 percent (usually subsidized; the school makes the determination)
- Deadlines: Apply as early in the year as your school allows (usually this is shortly after January 1)

cial administrators. While this is a federally funded program, it is the individual schools that determine what constitutes exceptional need, which is the basis for distributing these funds.

Since each college or university determines what the need parameters are for getting a Perkins Loan, don't be surprised if you meet the definition of exceptional need at one school but not at another. So be sure to apply for this loan at each school you plan to attend.

The total amount that your school awards you is dependent on both your financial need and how much money you have received from other aid programs. Once you have qualified for the Perkins Loan, you will need to sign a promissory note to receive your money. A promissory note is a binding agreement between you and the school, stating that you will repay the money you have borrowed.

Eligibility for the Perkins Program

Students must meet certain requirements in order to qualify for the Perkins Loan program. Here are some of them:

- You must be an undergraduate or graduate student
- Your school must have funds allocable to the Perkins Loan program
- You must be attending school at least half-time
- You must be working on your first undergraduate or graduate degree (people working on their second degree are not eligible)
- You must be a U.S. citizen or eligible noncitizen

Remember, this is a campus-based loan program, so applicants need to apply at their school (not with an independent lender). As soon as you know that you will be applying for aid, you should visit your financial aid advisor and obtain the FAFSA or any other necessary forms. Apply early. Schools cannot give out any more money once they run out. Typically, schools ask that you apply as soon after the first of the year as possible. Proving financial need is also important. Talk with your financial advisor and your parents to help you determine the best ways to prove need.

Disbursement

Every school uses a different method for disbursing aid, so check with the financial aid office at your college or university for details on disbursement dates, times, and locations. When disbursements are made, the school will either give you the money or credit your account, depending on the system used by the financial aid office. The number of loan payments you receive each year depends on the amount borrowed and your school's operating system. If your school is on the semester system, you will receive the loan in two payments at the beginning of each fall and spring semester. Schools running on the quarter system disburse loans at the beginning of each quarter, or at least three times a year, excluding summer.

Payment Terms

A Perkins Loan is one of the most advantageous of all loans. Interest rates are only 5 percent. There are no origination fees. Payments don't begin until nine months after graduation or leaving school and usually extend over a 10-year period.

The payback plan for the Perkins Loan includes a long grace period for borrowers. A grace period is the time following graduation, termination of studies, or dropping below half-time status, during which students do not have to make payments on their loan balances. Students have nine months before repayment begins with the Perkins Loan. Grace periods vary from school to school in cases where students drop below half-time. Contact the financial aid office for the exact amount of time given to such students. At the end of the grace period, students begin making monthly payments to their school. The amount of each payment depends on the amount of the loan, the length of the repayment period, and the date the loan was made.

The interest rate is fixed at 5 percent and does not accrue until you start making payments. The outstanding balance can be paid all at once or over a long period. Missed payments, late payments, and payments of less than the full amount are subject to penalty in the form of a late charge or collection fees. Charges on late payments are determined by each institution on an individual basis and will continue until payments are made on time. No interest is charged as long as the student is enrolled in college at least half-time.

Deferment of Perkins Loans

Deferring or postponing loan repayments is only granted under specific conditions. To postpone payments, you must fill out a deferment request form, available from the financial aid office at your school. Make sure you file your request before the deadline set by your school or you will be charged a late fee. Your deferment eligibility depends on the date your loan was first disbursed, and the following criteria.

For loans made after July 1, 1994, deferment is granted if you:

- Are enrolled at least half-time at a post-secondary institution
- Are involved in a rehabilitation program for the physically challenged
- Are participating in a graduate fellowship program
- Are serving in the Armed Forces in areas of immediate danger
- Teach full-time (specific qualifications and areas only)
- Volunteer in VISTA or the Peace Corps
- Work as a law enforcement or corrections officer
- Work full-time as a nurse or medical technician
- Work full-time as a public service employee

Deferment may be granted up to three years for:

- Inability to find full-time employment
- Economic difficulties

If your loan was made before July 1, 1994, contact the agency that carries your loan for deferment qualification.

If you need to apply for deferment and meet any one of the preceding qualifications, contact your financial aid office immediately for application details and deadlines. This will prevent you from missing or making any late payments and help you avoid collection fees and late charges.

Forbearance

Any students with loan debts of 20 percent or more of their gross income can be granted forbearance by their lending institutions. Forbearance is a period in which borrowers do not have to make any interest or principal payments on their loans for up to three years. Students must apply each year through their school to receive this benefit. Forbearance is also granted to students who cannot make payments and are not eligible for loan deferment. Contact the financial aid office at your college or university for application information.

Parental Loans for Undergraduate Students (PLUS)

PLUS is an acronym for Parental Loans for Undergraduate Students. PLUS lenders are financial institutions such as banks or credit unions.

These loans are designed for parents with good credit histories whose dependent children are in school at least half-time. Money for PLUS Loans comes from the same institutions that provide funds for the Stafford Loan Program. However, an important overall distinction must be made between the two loans: a PLUS is paid directly to parents, while the Stafford Loan program considers students the primary borrowers. PLUS lenders loan money to parents who wish to borrow, regardless of need, in order to help them finance a dependent's college education.

The amount of money parents can borrow through the PLUS program is contingent on how much federal financial aid you, as a student, have already received. Parents can receive enough money to cover the entire cost of their child's education, minus any other federal student aid already received. For example, if your college costs are $8,000 total for one year, and you have received a Stafford Loan for $3,000, your parents would qualify for a PLUS in the amount of $5,000 to cover the remaining costs.

Prior to requesting a PLUS application, it is important that you, as the student, make an effort to apply for all other available aid. With the PLUS Loan, interest starts accumulating following disbursement, and your parents will begin repayment on the loan sixty days after it has been issued.

PLUS Loans are not need-based. Parents may apply directly to the school or to an independent lender or state guarantee agency. Parents and graduate and professional students may borrow up to the cost of attendance (COA) minus any financial aid awarded (COA - other aid = maximum PLUS Loan). Colleges will determine the actual PLUS Loan amount.

Contact your own bank or another local lender to determine whether they issue these types of federal loans. Upon finding a lender, it is important to ask about the insurance fee (up to 4 percent) charged by many lenders. After carefully completing the application, return it promptly to the financial aid office. They will fill out their part and transfer it to your lender for process-

---

Key Characteristics of PLUS Loans

- Loans must be repaid
- Banks, credit unions, savings and loans act as lenders, as well as the federal government through the Direct Loan program
- Insured by lender and re-insured by the state and federal government
- Interest rate is variable. Three-month Treasury Bill rate plus 3.1 percent adjusted annually every July 1; cannot exceed 9 percent
- Unsubsidized; accrues interest while student is in school
- A 4 percent fee is charged each time a payment is made
- Apply as soon after January 1 as possible

ing. Final approval is given by the lender, and it usually takes between five and ten business days to process the application.

Eligibility for PLUS Loans

Here are some points to consider for parents to determine their eligibility:

- Have a legal dependent enrolled in school at least half-time
- Be the legal guardian or natural or adoptive parent of the student receiving aid
- Not have defaulted on any previous student loans
- Undergo a credit check to determine approval rating
- Parents and dependent students must be U.S. citizens or eligible noncitizens

PLUS borrowers who are not eligible for deferment can apply for forbearance as long as they are willing to make loan payments but cannot afford to do so. Contact the organization carrying your loan for more information.

Disbursement

After your parents sign a promissory note, the lender sends a check by computer, made payable to both your school and the parents. This speeds up the entire disbursement process and saves recipients from waiting for loan payment by mail. Payments will be made to parents at least twice during the year, and if the lender agrees, borrowers may receive them every week or month. The total amount of each disbursement will never be more than half of the entire amount of the loan and it will always be paid in equal installments.

Payment Terms

Loans first disbursed after October 1, 1992, have a variable interest rate set each year in July, with a 9 percent cap. The organization carrying your loan must notify you of the new rate. If you have a PLUS Loan that was disbursed to you before that date, contact your lender for the current interest rate. Along with the interest and principal payments, parents must also pay a 4 percent origination fee for loans disbursed after the above date. This fee and the insurance premium (up to 3 percent) collected by the lender will be deducted from each disbursement in equal amounts.

There is no thirty-day waiting period for first-time PLUS Loan borrowers. Payment is received immediately according to the school's financial aid disbursement methods.

Payment Plans

Ten-year standard repayment begins 60 days after the final disbursement for the year. As with Stafford Loans, several repayment plans are available, including the Standard, Extended and Graduated

> **Beware:** With the PLUS program, *there is no grace period before repayment begins* because interest starts accumulating immediately. Parents have only sixty days from when the loan is first disbursed to begin making payments.

Repayment Plan. The Income-Contingent Repayment Plan is not available for Direct PLUS Loans, however. With FFELP PLUS Loans, repayment arrangements are made with the lending institution. FFELP PLUS Loans can be repaid over a period of 10 years, with a minimum annual payment of $600. If the loan is sold during the process of repayment, borrowers will be notified by both the old and new organizations and given new payment instructions.

Deferment of PLUS Loans

Parents have the option of applying for a deferment with the PLUS Loan program. Deferments apply only to the principal balance of the loan, not the interest. If granted deferment, borrowers will most likely have to continue making monthly interest payments. Some organizations carrying loans will allow borrowers to postpone interest payments until deferment ends, but this increases the amount of the principal balance. To apply for deferment, you must contact the agency that is carrying your loan. Eligibility for postponement depends on the current status of the loan and the date it was first disbursed.

For loans first disbursed on or after July 1, 1993, deferment is granted for a child's study in a graduate or fellowship program. In addition, up to three years of deferment may be granted for parents' economic difficulties or inability to find full-time employment. The loan must not be in default to be eligible for deferment. An application is obtained from the company carrying the loan and resubmitted every twelve months.

Forgiveness of a PLUS Loan

The repayment of a PLUS can be canceled or forgiven, but only under very specific circumstances. If your parents are deceased, have become permanently disabled, or have filed for bankruptcy, contact the company that carries your loan for cancellation details. Remember, any questions you have concerning repayment, deferment, cancellation, or interest rates with your PLUS should be directed to the organization carrying your loan and not the Department of Education.

Repayment of Loans

Loans must be repaid. You must never default on a student loan. Defaulting is morally wrong as well as legally wrong. It is morally wrong because not repaying a loan from a revolving fund can deprive a future college student of access to low-cost aid. You have, in effect, stolen money that did not belong to you. Defaulting is also legally wrong and the defaulter can end up in court.

Student loan repayment can be a 10- to 30-year financial commitment. If you start missing payments—even one—your loan could be in delinquent status, and if you miss a payment for more than 270 days, your loan goes into default. Delinquency can adversely affect you in many ways. If you're having difficulty making regular monthly payments, contact your lender or service provider immediately to make other arrangements to avoid further delinquency and, much worse, default.

If you expect repayment troubles, your lender can help. If you are temporarily unemployed, disabled or struggling, many lenders will work with you. You can be assured that most lenders will try to help you in any one of several ways. For example, deferment allows you to postpone payments. Forbearance is an agreement with your lender to postpone payments when you are not eligible for deferment. Loan forgiveness programs, in which the borrower's loans are paid off in exchange for volunteer work or military service, offer an option for easy repayment. Even if you are employed, changing your payment schedule or consolidating your loans may help simplify your life and reduce your monthly payments.

Loan Repayment Plans

Borrowers can select from several loan repayment plans to assist them in repaying their loans.

- *Standard repayment loan plan*: Most students use the standard repayment loan plan. Payments are always the same. With the Standard plan, the student will have monthly payments of at least $50 and can repay the loan for a period of up to 10 years, depending on how much has been borrowed. The borrower pays the level principal and interest throughout the loan repayment period. The advantage of using this plan is that payments will end in ten years. The disadvantage of this plan is that these payments will consume a proportionally larger part of a borrower's income when he or she is just beginning a new career.
- *Extended plan:* The Extended plan (which is not available with FFELP Stafford Loans) is a good option if you have a bigger loan that you think will be difficult to pay over 10 years. The Extended plan allows you to

pay back the money over a period of up to 30 years. The monthly payments are lower, but the added interest will mean you will end up paying more in the end.

- *Graduated repayment plan*: This plan allows a borrower to reduce payments in the early years of repayment, after which, usually every two years, they will gradually increase. The monthly payments for the Graduated plan increase about every two years, and by the end of the repayment cycle you will be making monthly payments of up to 150 percent that of the Standard loan. This loan is still repaid within the standard ten-year period. The advantage to this payment plan is that the borrower's income will likely increase accordingly. A disadvantage to this plan is that the borrower will pay more interest over the life of the loan.
- *Loan consolidation plan*: The Loan Consolidation plan allows a borrower to combine all eligible loans into a single monthly payment currently at a fixed rate. The advantage is that the borrower will have more time to pay off the loan. A disadvantage is that longer repayment periods may result in paying a lot more interest over the life of the loan. Not all loans may be consolidated. You must check with your lender to understand eligibility.
- *Income sensitive plan*: This plan allows a borrower to make loan payments according to monthly gross income. With the Income-sensitive plan, just as the name implies, payments are based on your income, as well as your family situation. The borrower must reapply annually in order to establish the monthly payments, which are adjusted to reflect changes in income. The advantage is longer repayment period of up to 25 years. A disadvantage is that the borrower will pay a lot more interest because the repayment period is a longer. This very flexible plan takes into account your ability to pay, and if by the end of 25 years there is still a balance due, the unpaid amount will be forgiven. However, the federal government could hold you responsible for paying the taxes on the amount that isn't repaid.

Up-Front Fees

When you are considering a repayment plan, remember to consider the total cost of the loan. Also, consider up-front fees, sometimes called origination fees and insurance fees, which may add up to 4 percent of the principal amount of the loan. These fees are deducted prior to loan disbursement to the college.

Consequences of Loan Defaults

Defaulting on a loan can have serious consequences. Here are some of them:

- Defaulted loans are reported to national credit bureaus and can remain on your credit report for seven years, which can mean not being able to obtain a credit card, car loan or mortgage.

- A defaulted loan may be turned over to a collection agency. They often charge collection fees as well as attorney costs, all of which become part of your debt.
- A defaulted loan will make you ineligible for additional financial aid, deferments or loan consolidation.
- A defaulted loan can cause you to lose income tax refunds, and federal and state tax refund amounts may be applied to student loan debt or withheld.
- Holds may be placed on your college records.
- Your wages may be withheld and your possessions may be seized .A defaulted loan can lead up to wage garnishments of up to 10 percent of your net wages.
- A defaulted loan may jeopardize employment by city, county, state or federal agencies, or cause termination if you are already employed.
- If you need a license to practice in your profession, it may be revoked, canceled or not renewed.
- A loan, whether or not in default, cannot be discharged in bankruptcy in most cases.
- The entire amount of the loan, including interest, may be due immediately.
- You may not be eligible for revised payment schedules or additional deferments.

Consolidated Loans

Students and parents can simplify their repayments of government loans by combining one or more loans into a consolidated loan. Although it may sound strange that you can "consolidate" just one loan, this is an actual option in which you can switch from one repayment plan to a more flexible repayment schedule. Consolidation loans are a good strategy, since it is easier to keep track of one payment per month, and because you can often get a lower interest rate. Another benefit is that sometimes you can get a consolidated loan even when you are have defaulted on another loan.

Borrowers always have the option of loan consolidation when the time comes around to start paying back loans. A consolidation loan program enables you to combine several educational loans into one new bank loan from a single source and take more time to repay the debt. If interest rates are lower when you consolidate than they were when you originally took out the loans, this can be not only a convenience but a financial advantage to you.

The best way to find out about consolidation loans is to either talk to your school's financial aid office, or to contact the Loan Origination Center's Consolidation Department at (800) 557-7392 for direct loans, or the consolidation department of the private lender you borrowed from if you have an FFEL Consolidation Loan.

Who Is Eligible for Consolidated Loans?

Anyone who is in need of consolidating a federally backed student loan can apply for a consolidated loan, but there are some restrictions, depending on the type of loan. To receive a Direct Consolidated Loan, you must have at least one loan that comes directly from the federal government. If you do not have any direct loans, you will then need to contact an FFEL (Federal Family Education Loan) lender. You will probably want to start by contacting the lender from whom you originally borrowed to find out about their FFEL Consolidation loan program.

Key Characteristics of Consolidated Loans
• Consolidated Loans must be repaid
• Lenders are participating private lenders and the Department of Education
• Insurance: insured by the federal government, or through a private lender with the backing of the government
• Interest rate: for direct loans, the interest rate is variable, but it cannot exceed 8.25 percent for the consolidation of a Stafford loan, or 9 percent for a PLUS loan; FFELP Consolidated Loans have an interest rate that is the average of the rate of the loans being consolidated rounded to the nearest eighth of a point, with a cap of 8.25 percent
• Deadlines vary: You can apply for these loans during grace periods, after you have begun repaying your loans, or during forbearance or deferment of a loan

The amount of the loan is equal to the total amount of the loans being consolidated. Combined loan amounts must equal $7,500 or more to consolidate. You can receive a Direct Consolidated Loan after you have begun repayment of a loan, or during a grace or forbearance period. If you are still attending school, you must be registered as at least a half-time student. If your school does not participate in the Direct Loan program, you must at least have one Direct Loan to repay.

You can consolidate any of the following loans:

- Federal Stafford Loans, unsubsidized and subsidized, including Guaranteed Student Loans (GSL)
- Direct Stafford Loans, unsubsidized and subsidized
- Federal Supplemental Loans for Students (formerly Auxiliary Loans to Assist Students/ALAS and Student PLUS Loans)
- Federal Perkins Loans, formerly National Defense/National Direct Student Loans (NDSL)
- Health Professions Student Loans (HPSL), including Loans for Disadvantaged Students
- Federal Insured Student Loans (FISL)
- Federal PLUS Loans

- Direct PLUS Loans
- Federal Consolidation Loans
- Consolidation Loans
- Nursing Student Loans (NSL)

Loan consolidation can offer you many benefits to help manage your education debt. Here are a few of them:

- Lower monthly payments
- A single monthly loan payment on one bill
- Low, fixed interest rates
- No application fees or credit checks
- A variety of flexible payment plans that allow you to design a repayment plan that best suits your financial needs
- Special borrower benefits that can lower the amount of interest paid over the life of the loan
- No penalties for prepayment, so you can repay your loan early at any time
- A personal loan counselor who can answer your questions and help you through the application process

The Downside to Consolidation

Although consolidation can truly simplify and help many students manage their monthly payments, there are some cases when consolidation may not be right for you. If you are close to paying off your student loans, it may not make sense to consolidate or extend your payments. Also, not all programs offer the same borrower benefits. Make sure you choose a reliable program that offers good borrower benefits and reliable service. Remember that by extending the years of repayment for your loans, you may be increasing the total amount you have to pay in interest. Be sure to discuss your options with a loan counselor before you select a payment plan.

Disbursement

After contacting the Loan Origination Center, you will receive an application form in the mail. Approval of the loan generally takes 90 days after the return of this form. The Loan Origination Center will check your eligibility and do a credit history if you apply for a Direct PLUS Consolidation Loan. They will certify that you have a loan with the original lender. You will then receive a letter in the mail welcoming you to the program and outlining the repayment terms, which will differ from student to student depending on the types and amounts of loans being consolidated and the current interest rates, which are updated quarterly.

7

The World of Grants

Distribution Patterns of Foundations,
Corporations, and Federal Funders

Understanding the distribution patterns of funders can help you seek money to further your performing arts goals through grants. The agenda of foundations, corporations, government agencies, private individuals, and nonprofits vary widely.

Corporation and foundation grants can be an important element of a performing artist's fundraising strategy. One of the advantages of including foundations and corporate giving programs in a financial-aid seeking plan is that they are primarily structured to make charitable contributions. Relying on just one funding source may be detrimental to your grant-seeking efforts. The old adage of not putting all your eggs in one basket certainly applies to raising sufficient funds. Create a healthy mix of foundation, corporate, and federal grant applications.

Foundation Philosophy

A foundation is an organization formed either as a nonprofit corporation or charitable trust. Its main purpose is to make grants to unrelated organizations or individuals for scientific, cultural, religious, or other charitable purposes. A private foundation derives the majority of its funds from one source—an individual, a family, or corporation. A public charity or foundation, however, receives its funds from many sources and must continue to raise funds from a variety of sources in order to keep its public status. Both individuals and organizations qualify to apply for grants from foundations.

There are several types of foundations: independent, community, operating, and family. These foundation types differ in their character, intent, creation, structure, and revenue streams. Understanding their similarities and differences makes you a more effective grant writer.

Independent foundations. The majority of foundations in existence today are independent foundations. Independent foundations are private entities set up to distribute grants to tax-exempt organizations. These types of foundations are funded by individuals or families in two ways: (1) Endowment, where the income earned from investment of the principal is used to make grants; and (2) Periodic contributions, where living donors contribute to the fund, using the foundation as a pass-through for their giving.

The best-known independent foundations are the "Big Daddy" foundations like the Ford Foundation, the Rockefeller Foundation, the Guggenheim Foundation, and the Hearst Foundation. They have been set up by major philanthropists and wealthy business people who created foundations to do good things in society. They give away large sums of money every year. Private foundations are usually administered by attorneys or bank trust departments.

Independent foundations are often named after the original donors. In most cases they stipulate giving categories. They are very specific about how they want the monies allocated. Independent foundations range from small operations with one full-time or half-time staff person to large, well-established foundations employing hundreds. They can range in size from a very small original gift, such as a $10,000 endowment, to those with hundreds of millions of dollars in assets.

Community foundations. Community foundations are locally or regionally focused. They accumulate their assets through a number of donors, establishing an endowment that is managed independently. A community foundation uses the income from the endowment to make grants. Nonprofits with local interests are more likely to receive funding from a community foundation than individual performing artists because the competition is less. Furthermore, there is a more direct link between the donor's local interests and the community-based organization applying for a grant.

Community foundations are a great example of strength in numbers. Usually established by one or two donors in a community, these foundations broaden their effectiveness by approaching other successful individuals and getting them to contribute to the foundation's corpus through direct donation, legacy gifts, or annual donations.

Operating foundations.
Operating foundations are classified by the IRS as such because they spend at least 85 percent of their income supporting their own programs. They generally do not make grants but exist to conduct research and programs. Oper-

> **Stat fact:** The Foundation Center Survey conducted in March 2007 lists the Greater Kansas City Community Foundation as the No. 1 U.S. foundation in total giving. Their total giving at the end of the 2005 fiscal year was $140,702,000. The New York Community Trust followed a close second, with total giving of $136,970,963.

ating foundations are legally separate from other types of foundations and enjoy a more favorable tax status. They raise funds, are governed by a board of directors, and employ professional staff to direct and carry out programs.

Family foundations. Family foundations are generally established by one or two donors, typically an entrepreneur, siblings, or a married couple. They have been founded to ensure that future generations continue to practice philanthropy. They are set up so that the endowment upholds values that the donors believe are important. Most founders are successful entrepreneurs who want to use their fortunes to support the communities in which they and their families live. For example, a philanthropic family living in Detroit may set up a family foundation to help rehabilitate youth addicted to drugs in their community. In return for their generosity they receive substantial tax benefits from the federal government.

Corporations

Corporate philanthropy is about giving money away. Clearly, businesses must see a benefit to their giving. Many corporate grant makers have developed philanthropic strategies in line with their business values. Corporations may also look for opportunities to expose potential customers to their products or services. Sometimes with corporate funders there may be hidden, vested interests in their philanthropy, which they may or may not disclose readily.

Corporate philanthropists realize that a good contribution program can accomplish many things:

- Social and civic responsibilities fulfillment
- Strengthening the communities in which they operate
- Good relationships with the surrounding community
- Improved customer relations
- Better employee morale
- Increased business and profits

~~• Changing the image of a product or service that the corporation pro-~~
duces

Corporate philanthropy is sometimes referred to as "enlightened self-interest," as they often engage in philanthropic activities where they have their own agenda. For example, a computer manufacturer may donate computers to local schools as a business strategy to promote its brand.

Corporate foundations are separate, legal organizations subject to the same rules and regulations as other private foundations. Corporate foundations are developed by businesses to carry out the corporations' charitable giving activities. These private foundations are legally separate from the corporations with which they are affiliated, yet their distributions are usually dependent on the company's' profits. In order to fund the foundations corporations take a portion of their profits and put it into a dedicated fund for philanthropy. The corporate foundation can legally support areas of strategic interest as long as the corporation does not profit directly from its foundation's grant making.

Profit-making businesses, usually large corporations, establish corporate foundations to enable them to support projects in communities where they operate manufacturing plants, retail outlets, and other direct business. They are mostly interested in helping organizations where their employees live. For example, Cessna may establish a funding program in Wichita, Kansas, to pay for their employees' children's college education. Their missions may state that they want to improve the quality of life for all citizens in the communities where they operate as a means of improving their own employees' lives.

Types of corporate giving. Corporations offer assistance in different forms. Here are some of them.

- *Cash* is a common form of corporate philanthropy. Direct cash donations vary from a few thousand to several million dollars.
- *In kind services*: Some corporations like to donate employee time and talent. Examples include printing or accounting services. A recent trend has been to combine cash grants, in-kind contributions, and employee volunteer services when seeking to help a nonprofit. Volunteers can provide valuable services that would otherwise tap into an organization's resources.
- *Executive loans*: Large corporations may have programs where an executive's time is loaned to a nonprofit.
- *Matching gifts*: Many corporations match their employees' giving to a certain dollar amount, thereby leveraging additional dollars for the charitable organization. Today, companies are beginning to match volunteer hours with cash, making it even easier for employees to support the organizations they care about.

• *Product Donations*: Corporations gain from donating new or used products. They get certain tax advantages and, in the case of used products, can save money in the storage and disposal of these products.

Government Funding

Federal government grants are where the money is and where the work is. Federal government grants are meant to launch big programs. That is why awards can range from very small grants of less than $10,000 to grants of several million dollars. Government funders have the responsibility of giving away taxpayers' money. As with other areas of government spending, many checks and balances have been set up to protect these public funds. Government money originates from the local, state, and federal levels. Such grants are often issued in the form of contracts, which are essentially a delegation of government responsibility to a third-party organization. The government will often give what's known as multiyear grants, which provide a predictable source of funding for several years in a row. Rules surrounding government funding are more strict than rules surrounding foundation or corporation grants.

Local, state, and pass-through funds. Government grants are tax dollars redistributed to programs in the community. As such, they can be made by any entity that collects taxes: federal, state, and even local city or county governments. Overall, the government grant-seeking process is similar to the process in the foundation and corporate world, perhaps just a little bit more intense.

• *Local government funds:* Local governments are the city, township, county, regional coordinating body, or other such mediums. Local governments rarely have grant opportunities and those that do, provide only limited programs. Local governments are more likely to issue requests for proposals that are actually for work they wish to have completed.
• *State government funds:* Grants from the state are among the easiest to apply for and to receive. The state is close enough to communities to have an understanding of what is going on and the problems they are having. It is large enough to provide grants in sufficient amounts to address the problems that have been identified.

Applicants can find state grant opportunities in nearly the same way as they find federal government grants: by going from department to department. Most states have a website that lists departments. Pages within each department contain information about their funding programs.

• *Pass-through funds:* State or federal governments occasionally will provide pass-through funds to a nonprofit organization in individual communities. In pass-through funds the local agency usually receives some compensation for reviewing the grant proposals, distributing the grant dollars, and ensuring that all reports and evaluations are submitted on time to the grant agency. The pass-through agent is likely to be your local government, one of the local nonprofits, or your community foundation.

Request for Proposals (RFPs). Grants are awarded to nonprofits in three typical situations: (1) as a response to a Request for Proposals (RFP); (2) in a response to a broad agency announcement (BAA); and (3) as a submission for funding made to a philanthropic organization, also known as "cold calling." When it is an RFP or BAA an organization receives a request for proposals that clearly outlines the types of projects the funder is seeking and the requirements for each project.

When the grant maker rather than the grant seeker wants to initiate a project, the dynamic of the relationship between the two is very different. For the grant maker the purpose is to address a problem by investing in experimental solutions. For the nonprofit executive it is an opportunity to secure new money.

In both approaches it is the task of the grant writer to examine the criteria for eligibility and determine whether the organization meets the criteria for eligibility established by the grant maker. The strategy is to emphasize how a specific grant request can help fulfill the funder's own mission. Whether it is an application submitted as an RFP or as a cold call, the grant proposal is formulaic. Applicants must follow the instructions and the outline provided in either the RFP or the funder's guidelines. The proposal elements are the same for an RFP as they are for any other grant proposal.

The first thing to read in the RFP is the purpose of the legislation and fund. What does the funder hope to accomplish with its money? If the stated purpose matches the purpose or mission of your program, good. Next, look at the list of qualified applicants. Often, the organization qualified to apply is very specifically defined. For instance, some grants call for the applicant to be a community arts organization; others for a local education agency. If your organization does not qualify, don't apply. Save yourself time, energy, and resources, and move on to an RFP that is likely to fund your request.

If your organization meets the RFP requirements, consult the deadline. Is there enough time to complete an application or will it be done at the eleventh hour? See the level and degree of difficulty required by the grant narrative. This will help you determine if there is enough time to complete the application.

Next, consider the funding allocation, average amount of awards, and probable number of projects. When the average grant award is several hundred thousand or million dollars, you can be sure that hundreds of qualified organizations will apply. If the department expects to award only twenty new grants each year, you must calculate the odds of your project's being one of the recipients.

Often, RFPs are issued for programs that require a certain local match and they will let you know what qualifies as a match or not. Match requirements vary. For instance, a 40 percent local cash match means that you have already made commitments for part of the money needed for a project before you can apply for the remaining. If the RFP states that in-kind money qualifies, you can gather a portion of the request match in donated space, staff time for coordinating or attending meetings, utilities, existing furnishings and computer equipment, and other items that are part of your organization's budget.

It can take a while to locate different departments and agencies that issue RFPs. So be sure to bookmark sites that you know you will want to return to again and again. Also bookmark sites where you downloaded an RFP, so you can check it again and again throughout the writing process. Check the website where you downloaded the RFP once or twice during the month you are writing. You will find the latest breaking news such as an extended deadline, clarification of the RFP based on questions from others, or changes in the level or funding since the RFP was issued.

Where do you find RFPs? RFPs are published by each federal agency and can be found on their individual websites. You can also go to your local congressional representative's office and ask for time to review the office copy of the *National Register*. The *National Register* contains all proposed grant opportunities for the upcoming year, regardless of which federal department is using them and regardless of whether it is secured funding or the actual levels of funding listed. The *Register* is published or updated annually, but is not distributed. Instead, a one- or two-page announcement is mailed to pre-established mailing lists approximately 90–120 days before the grant deadline. The announcement contains a brief description of the program, its *National Register* number, the requesting department, a list of legal entities that may apply, the URL of the full RFP, and an application or a telephone number so you can request an application package. It also contains information about any grant-seeker workshops or conferences that will take place and where they will be held.

Each RFP contains the following information:

- Purpose
- Issuing agency/department
- Criteria for the program

- Total grants available and range of prospective grant awards
- Eligibility criteria for applicants
- Statements that must be signed by the applicant
- Deadline
- Mailing instructions
- Outline of proposal content
- Points available for each section of the narrative
- Rubric (a chart of judging criteria and scoring) or other selection criteria for judges
- An application kit containing budget forms, cover sheets, and assurances
- Appendices/documents, resources call for reviewers, etc.

Grants for Individuals

Individual applicants qualify to apply for funding on their own merit, without the backing of an institution. Private foundations and family trusts are more likely to award grants to individuals than the federal government. Their awards may be small, but are easier to get than federal government grants. Individuals qualify for grants ranging anywhere from $500 to $100,000 or more.

Grants to individuals are awarded for various purposes. Here is a list of common causes:

- College tuition
- Publishing books
- Conducting research
- Emergency funding
- Starting a performing arts school
- Humanitarian work in developing countries

Application Checklist for Individuals

The level of difficulty and length of individual grant applications vary with each funder. Some may require a simple letter of inquiry while others may be more complex. Here is an example of an application checklist required by a federal funder:

Application Checklist:

Include the original (unbound, one sided) 30-page narrative and 12 collated copies in this order:

1. Signed application cover sheet
2. Statement of significance and impact

3. Table of contents
4. List of project participants
5. Narrative
6. Budget forms
7. Appendices
8. History of grants
9. List of evaluators

Plus

1. Two copies of the suggested list of evaluators
2. Resumes of principal project personnel
3. Videos demonstrating the existing research
4. One extra copy of the list of project participants
5. SASE (self addressed stamped envelope) to confirm receipt of application
6. SASE for any materials that you want returned

Label each accompanying document with the applicant's name, address, and e-mail address.

What Types of Grants Are Available?

To do effective research you need to know what types of grants are available. Once you determine the type of grant that best suits the client you are working for, you can funnel your research process with a sharper focus.

Here are some common grant types:

- *Project grant*: A project grant supports a particular project or program of an individual or organization. For example, it could pay a university to conduct research on asthma or to organize a summer music festival in the community.
- *Operating grant*: An operating grant is a grant made to an organization or individual to cover operating expenses for an ongoing program or project. This type of broad-based, unrestricted grant can cover anything from rent to the electricity bill to staff salaries or artists' fees. In other words, anything needed to keep the project going.
- *Restricted grant*: A restricted grant covers one specified part of a project, such as the fee for a musical score for a theater production being presented by an arts council.
- *General purpose*: A general purpose grant is a broad-based grant, not restricted to any particular purpose, to assist with the ongoing work of an organization. These are generally given only to organizations. An example is a $50,000 grant given to the Red Cross to support its work in developing countries.
- *Start-up funds or seed money*: Start-up funds or seed money are kinds of grants made to help an organization or individual start a new program or project. Seed money can cover salaries, operating expenses, and other

expenses necessary to start a new venture, such as a new performing arts center.

- *Challenge grant:* A challenge grant is an award that will be paid by a contributing organization if the grant seeker is able to raise a specified amount of funds to match the grant in question. For example, a foundation will give $30,000 to a nonprofit if the nonprofit also raises $30,000 through another grant.
- *Matching grant:* A matching grant is similar to a challenge grant. A funder gives money to match funds granted by another organization. For example, the Ford Foundation may decide to match a $70,000 grant by the Hearst Foundation to help fund a particular research program.
- *Regrant program:* A regrant program is an arrangement whereby a private foundation or a government agency gives funds to a nonprofit organization, which in turn administers a grant program with these funds, soliciting proposals and giving grants, usually on a local level.
- *In-kind contribution or service:* An in-kind contribution or service is a contribution to an organization or individual that might consist of materials or equipment, property, or free services of some kind. This is sometimes called a noncash grant.
- *Technical assistance:* Technical assistance is aid in the form of free consulting services that are offered to nonprofit organizations and sometimes to individuals. It may include fundraising or budgeting assistance, financial or legal advice, computer training, etc. Corporations may offer technical assistance as a part of their funding program.
- *Fellowships:* Fellowships are grants for educational studies or research, usually at the graduate or postgraduate level. They are always granted to individuals, though the funds may be channeled through a sponsor. The term "scholarships" strictly applies to undergraduates, although it is sometimes used loosely for both undergraduate and graduate grants.
- *Awards and prizes:* Awards and prizes are grants given on a competitive basis, for specific accomplishments or achievements. Awards and prizes are typically given to individuals.

Grant Proposal Elements

Regardless of length and funder, grant proposal basics are the same, and the information included in each section is integral to any successful funding request. The order of the proposal components may vary, depending on the funding organization and the type of grant that you seek.

The main components of a grant proposal are:

- Cover letter
- Abstract
- Table of contents (TOC)
- Need statement
- Goals and objectives

- Methodology
- Evaluation and dissemination

Cover Letter

A cover letter is an opportunity for you to make an inviting introduction to the grant maker about your organization and also about your project. The cover letter is the first piece in your proposal package and your first opportunity to create a lasting impression. It serves as your proposal's formal introduction. It should ideally be 1 to 2 pages long.

Some funders ask applicants to fill out their customized cover letter. When a standard form has been provided, applicants should not write another cover letter on their own. The template provided by the funder is sufficient.

Writing tips for the cover letter. Being aware of the following can help you to write eye-grabbing cover letters.

- *Write short sentences that are pertinent and substantial*
If you make your sentences very long you are getting too narrative. This is not recommended. Stay to the point. Don't digress and get into too much detail in your initial introduction. Your cover letter needs to give substance to your project. Don't be shallow, cute, or too personal.

- *Highlight the key points that have been fleshed out within the proposal*
If your cover letter is being accompanied by a narrative section, then discuss the main points that are being disclosed. In essence, it is a précis of your narrative, summing up the key points, and inviting the funder to make an investment in your project.

- *Submit a clear and readable letter*
Make your cover letter easy and simple. Don't be arrogant and demand money with a sentence like, "It is in your best interest to award our organization this grant. No other performing arts organization can conduct this project as well as we can." Funders don't tend to be too impressed with such arrogant language.

- *Address the letter to a specific individual and not "The Grants Officer"*
It is important that the cover letter be addressed to a specific individual at the foundation and not addressed "To whom it may concern." Generally, the individual contact information is listed on the funder's website. Be sure to correctly spell the person's name. If you do not have a name, call or e-mail the foundation and find out who is in charge of the grants program. Address the person by the last name with the proper salutation. For example, if the person's name is Dave Rodell, address him as "Mr. / Dr. Rodell," instead of "Dave."

- *Sign at the bottom*
If you are sending a hard-copy application always remember to sign the

cover letter. If you have completed a fifty-page grant application and mail it out without signing the cover page, it may get disqualified. This is especially applicable with federal funders.

Sample cover letter guidelines. Here is a sample application sheet provided by a federal funder:

Application Cover Sheet

Individual Applicant
Full Name:
Mailing Address:
Phone (W):
Phone (H):
Fax:
Field of Expertise:
Citizenship:
Institution:

Sample cover letter. The type of information to be requested in the cover letter depends on the grant narrative, the amount of funding requested, and the length of the proposal. Here is a sample cover letter that has been individually crafted to a funder:

Diana Ippstein, Foundation Officer
Suite 405
Tannet Building
Los Angeles, CA 00000

Dear Diana Ippstein,

I would like to apply for a grant from the Meyer Foundation. I am an individual applicant, seeking assistance to publish a book.

I am a food writer and have had hundreds of articles published in American, European, and Asian magazines. I am also the author of the book *Start your own Food Business*, published by *Health Food*, New York Press. As the editor of the *2007 Organic Food Directory* I write, review, and edit food and spa articles for the Organic Food Association in California.

I would like to self-publish a book titled *Healing Foods*. I have to pay copy-editing fees, production and layout costs, and marketing-related expenses. The total amount that I need to accomplish these is $3500.

Thank you.
Sincerely Yours,
Sheila Branson

The Abstract

An abstract is also called a summary, program summary, or executive summary. It is often the first thing a reader sees and may be your most important marketing tool. Usually the abstract is written last. The abstract summarizes the proposal. This summary helps the reader follow your argument in the proposal itself. The abstract defines your entire project on a single page, or sometimes in 300 words or so.

Keep your abstract basic. For example:

"The Good Samaritan Shelter requests $5,000 for a two-year, $50,000 job training program for homeless women in Georgia. Training will be offered at four rural shelters and will include basic clerical skills, interview techniques and job seeker support groups."

The abstract usually contains the following elements:

- Identification of the applicant
- Qualifications to carry out the project
- The specific purpose of the grant
- The anticipated end result
- The amount of money requested
- The total project budget

Tips for writing the abstract. Decide what the key points are in each section of the proposal and include the key points in the summary. Stress the points in the proposal that you know are important to the funder.

- *Start with an arresting sentence*

Remember, this is the first sentence your reviewer is likely going to read. Make it interesting and colorful. Don't start the opening sentence of the abstract by raising a question.

- *Establish credibility*

In brief, tell the funder about your organization and why it can be trusted to use funds effectively. The funder needs to be assured that philanthropic dollars will be used wisely.

- *Write short sentences*

Eliminate wordiness in the abstract. It needs to be brief and the sentences pungent. You have to convince the funder about your project in a short word count. This is not the place to be writing a novel.

- *Show the immediacy of the problem*

Give some statistics or paint an effective visual painting of the need to address the issue you are projecting. Indicate how your project is going to make a positive difference in society.

- *Stay within the word count specified in the guidelines*

Some funders ask you to write a 100-word abstract. Stick to the word count. Don't think the funder is going to be impressed if you write a long abstract describing how wonderful your project is. You can get eliminated early in the application process if you do. You need to conform to the rules set forth by the funder.

Sample abstract. Here is a sample 70-word abstract. It was submitted by an individual applicant who sought funds to conduct a photographic documentary:

Introduction
Building Bridges: A Photographic Documentary on Inter-Cultural Relationships Across America

Intercultural relationships are becoming a sign of our times. With globalization and modernism there have been large-scale migration patterns leading to cross-cultural marriages. "Building Bridges across America" will be a photographic exhibition covering inter-cultural marriages across America. The purpose of my project is to promote understanding and peace between different cultures. Through photography I want to create awareness and enhance our understanding of the similarities between people of different cultures.

Table of Contents

A table of contents (TOC) is typically used when your grant proposal is eight pages or longer. It makes it easier on the reviewer for two main reasons. First, a table of contents clearly shows you have included all the information the funder requested. Second, it shows a map of a complex document.

The TOC is an optional element in the grant proposal. If your proposal is short or is not divided into different sections, you may not need a TOC at all. For example, if the guidelines state, "Write a 15-page narrative describing your research project," you may not need a TOC. You are not dividing the narrative, as it is a single essay.

Tips for writing a table of contents. A table of contents is fairly straightforward. Pay attention to the following when you include one in your grant proposal:

• *Include the TOC at the beginning of the proposal package*
If you are including a TOC it should be introduced right at the onset of the proposal. This will give the reviewer an indication of the elements that have been fleshed out within the proposal and where to find them.

• *Paginate*
A TOC is difficult to use if the pages are not numbered. Most computers have page number insertions. The common format is to insert the page numbers on the lower right hand side of the page.

• *Make sure the page numbers correspond to the headings*
Once the proposal has been written, see the page numbers and the titles corresponding to them. If there is an incorrect page number the reviewer may be misled.

• *Include the TOC on a separate page by itself*
Don't include any other information such as contact information, cover letter, or abstract where the TOC has been printed. Devote a fresh page to the TOC.

Sample table of contents. Not all TOCs will have the following elements. Some may have fewer headings. Choose the headings according to the guidelines:

Table of Contents

Title	*Page number*
Project problem	2
Project fit with foundation objectives	3
Project population	5
Plan of work	7
Methodology	8
Possible limiting factors	10
Timetable	12
Project results	14
Dissemination plan	15
Follow-up and continuation plan	17
Line item budget	18
Summary of institutional budget	20
Appendix A: Institutional background	22
Appendix B: Qualifications of project personnel	24
Appendix C: Tax exempt letter	26

Problem or Need Statement

The need statement clearly defines the project for which funds are being requested and is also known as the problem statement or situation description. It performs three purposes. It tells the funder (1) the need for the project; (2) the problem at hand; and (3) the urgency and significance of the project.

The need statement is at the heart of the entire case for support. It indicates why the particular need or project should be of interest to the funder. It establishes that the applicant understands the problems and therefore can reasonably address them. The need statement studies the following questions: "Why is the project necessary? What is the issue and why should we care?" Do not assume that everyone sees the problem as clearly as you do. The need statement is where you are given the chance to make a compelling case as to why your project or program is needed. Like a good debater, you must assemble all the arguments and then present them in a logical sequence.

The need statement provides vital information not only on who you are and what you do but on the contribution you/your organization has made.

Need statements are aimed at assuring the carefully targeted reader that the proposed project is the place to wisely invest philanthropic dollars. When identifying a problem you must convince the funding source that the issues you want to address are important not only to the advancement of the organizations, but would benefit the funder's mission as well. Funders typically look for projects that benefit not only the applicant, but the broader community as well.

Tips for crafting successful need statements. Here are some guidelines for writing effective need statements. They are not hard and fast rules but some suggestions that can get your application a step closer to funding.

• *Don't describe the problem as the absence of your project*
You need to show that your project addresses the root cause of the situation and not just a superficial approach. "We don't have enough beds in our battered women's shelter" is not the problem. The *problem* is increased levels of domestic violence. More shelter beds is a *solution*.

• *Relate your problem to the interests and priorities of the funder*
Explain the consequences and results of the issues and needs that are being discussed within the proposal. Define the local or national problem to be addressed and why you are qualified to address it.

• *Provide some perspective*
Acknowledge other individuals or organizations working in your field. You don't want the funding source to think that you are not aware of the projects or that your project is a duplication and therefore unnecessary. Show how yours is different and what unmet needs your project will meet. Connect with others; don't isolate your project as superior.

• *Describe the target population to be served*
Describe your population, their issues and needs. Explain why you have you chosen this specific target population. If possible, cite specific cases of interest in the proposal. Including testimonials also adds credibility to your need statement.

• *Quantify your need*
Provide facts or statistics supporting your project. Unsupported assumptions will not create a compelling case for your specific needs. Ground your need statement in fact, not opinion. Information that is too generic or broad will not help you develop a winning argument for your project.

• *Weigh the gravity of the problem*
Determine whether it is reasonable to portray the need as acute. Every need statement does not have to pose a life-threatening situation. What is important, however, is to persuade the funder that the problem you are addressing requires attention or that the solution that you are proposing offers hope for improvement.

• *The need to be addressed should have a clear relationship to your mission and purpose*
The need that is described in the proposal should be consistent with your scope to respond to that need. You need to prove that you have the qualifications and skills to complete the proposed project successfully.

Sample need statement. Here is a sample need statement submitted by an individual applicant.

Roads to Sobriety

"Roads to Sobriety" will be a research project examining the crippling effects caused by alcoholism in families in Sri Lanka. Alcoholism is a major problem in Sri Lanka. One of every three families has an active male alcoholic whose drinking interferes with family peace. It also obstructs community development.

The Foundation for Mental Health wants to study the issue of alcoholism and how it can be addressed at the local community level. During previous studies conducted by a team of medical professionals and social service workers it was concluded that the majority of health professionals are misinformed about alcoholism. They encourage alcoholics in the fallacy of controlled drinking. Topics addressed will include alcohol treatment, prevention, and education.

As a result of the proposed project, the Foundation for Mental Health hopes to initiate an alcohol rehabilitation center in Sri Lanka. It will provide hope for thousands of families crippled by a loved one's drinking and show that life can be enjoyed without the bottle.

Goals and Objectives

The goals and objectives define the solution that is being proposed to address the problem described in the need statement. They are the outcomes of the planned program.

The goals and objectives offer a clear picture of the results of implementing your program and identify how the problem(s) will be addressed. A goal is ultimate whereas an objective is immediate. They address the question: How would this situation look like if it were changed?

Goals and objectives are usually written after the need statement has been completed and tie directly into the need statement. Goals, also referred to as work plan or specific activities, represent long-range benefits. Goals are where you want to be when the funds are used up. A goal signifies an "end." Grant application narratives must have goals to show the funder that you have a vision for solving the problem. Your project goals represent the idealized dream of what you want to accomplish. The goal describes the general impact you hope to have on the problem you have defined, without necessarily indicating the magnitude.

Goals project the "big picture" vision of what applicants wish to accomplish. They are usually presented in terms of hopes, wishes, or desires. Typically, goal-oriented words include appreciate, understand, advocate, analyze, illustrate, participate, integrate, and recommend. A goal is a broad-based statement of the ultimate result of the change being undertaken, a result that is sometimes unreachable in the short term.

Tips for writing clear goals. Identify project goals that are within you or your organization's competence and expertise. The goals must fit the mission and scope of your organization. Here is a general example of a goal: "Sober Living' is a nonprofit organization that identifies with the high rate of alcoholism among retired senior citizens in Madison County. Its goal is to reduce the numbers of senior citizens alienating their lives from society and confining themselves to the bottle." Here is another example of a goal: "Rose Foundation is a small nonprofit organization that will create jobs for unemployed youth in Garfield County."

Notice that the above goals do not specify the magnitude of the reduction, the time frame for achieving the goal, or the expected outcome. They indicate a general direction of impact. Despite the vague nature of the goals they are realistic for a community agency to achieve. An unrealistic goal for a small nonprofit in Madison County would be to minimize alcoholism among senior citizens throughout the United States, or for Rose Foundation to create jobs for unemployed youth throughout the United States.

• *Provide concrete examples showing previous experiences in related areas*
Let's assume your nonprofit organization is asking for funds to deliver nutritional counseling to pregnant women. Provide concrete examples of any previous work that you have carried out in this field. This gives an indication of your capacity to carry out the proposed project.

• *Give a clear picture of where you will be when you are done achieving the goals*
Explain what your organization plans to do about the problem. What are your overall goals? You might say: "The goals of this project are to increase the understanding among Colorado middle school students about the impact of smoking on their health, and to reduce the number of students who smoke."

• *Describe the population that will benefit from the project*
Include all relevant parties in the target population. Give details, includ-

ing: Who is the target audience, and how will you involve them in the activity? How many people do you intend to serve? How will you ensure that people actually participate in the program? Some projects have two audiences: the *direct participants* (the musicians in the community band, the kids doing summer clean-up in the parks) and the *indirect beneficiaries* (the music lovers in the audience, the people who use the parks). If so, describe both.

Objectives. Objectives are steps that lead up to the goals. An objective is a major milestone or checkpoint on your route to a goal. They are much more narrowly defined than goals. Like goals, the objectives are tied to the need statement. Objectives have to be attainable and serve to keep goals realistic. They are also known as outcomes or impact of activities.

Your objective section is the intellectual heart of the proposal, because you indicate precisely what you intend to change through your project and what you would accept as proof of project success for your target population. Use action words in the infinitive form, such as "to analyze, to advocate, to anticipate, to decrease, to increase, to motivate, to categorize, to construct, to design, and to illustrate." When sponsors fund your project they are literally "buying" your objectives.

Types of objectives. The two main types of objectives are process objectives and outcome objectives.

• Process objectives

"Process" refers to a series of actions directed toward a particular aim. A "process" produces change or development. Process or implementation objectives are those that you discuss what you plan to do. You can tell you have written a process objective if you started with words such as "to provide, to develop, or to establish." A process objective is abstract in its wording.

• Outcome objectives

An outcome objective states a quantifiable result of the project. "Outcome" refers to the way that something turns out in the end. Outcome objectives deal with program impact. Look for words such as "to increase" or "to decrease." They imply some sort of measurable change.

Tips for writing objectives. Here are some tips for writing effective objectives:

• *State objectives in terms of outcomes*

Give numbers when possible, and create a concrete picture of what the situation would look like once you address the need at hand. The objective section shows that you can produce definite outcomes. Include objectives that comprehensively describe the intended outcomes of the project.

• *Demonstrate that your objectives flow logically from the statement of need*

The objectives stem directly from your need. If there is a need to address the use of illegal drugs among teens, your objective should be to reduce the growing use of drugs in your community.

- *State the time by which the objectives will be accomplished*

Give an exact date as to when the project is going to take place, instead of saying something like, "The project will be completed around mid 2006." List your specific objectives in expected chronological order of achievement if you are submitting a phased proposal.

- *Objectives should clearly identify the population group being served*

If you are working on drug use among youth, identify the age group: is it 12 to 18, 18 to 25, etc.? Are you targeting specific groups of people?

Sample goals and objectives. The following is an example of goals and objectives submitted by an environmental organization wanting to research the feeding patterns of leopards.

Researching the feeding Ecology and Reproductive Behavioral Patterns of Leopards

Goal #1: To study the feeding patterns of leopards

The aims are to gather accurate information about what leopards eat. This could help in future conservation efforts. I will study the scat of leopards in order to get an idea of their feeding patterns. The objectives will address the following:

1. Are hair fragments, skin fragments, fish scales and bird feathers found?
2. If so, what types of animals do they belong to?
3. What are the main forms of prey found in the scat?

Goal #2: To study the reproductive behavioral patterns of leopards

The aims are to find out about the reproductive patterns of leopards. By knowing the seasons, weather conditions, and population factors affecting the reproductive behaviors of leopards can help in getting better results in the future breeding of leopards. The objectives will address the following:

1. Is there a higher frequency of mating during a certain time of the year? For example, is there a higher frequency of mating during the rainy season than during the dry season?
2. What is the gestation period of leopards?
3. Till what age do cubs follow their mothers?
4. How much litter do leopards typically give birth to? Do all the cubs survive?
5. What is the average life span of leopards?

Methodology

The methodology section of a grant proposal tells who is going to do what and when it will be done. It addresses the question: What can the organization or individual do to change the existing situation? The methods are the action plans to reach the eventual outcome that has been discussed in the proposal. It tells how the project activities will accomplish the objectives.

Typically, each objective is accompanied by one or more methods. For proposals with many objectives, it is a good idea to include a timeline showing when each method

> **Smart tip:** The methodology section is also known as statement of work, activities, approach, strategies, or procedures. Methods are closely linked to goals and objectives of a proposal. The objectives tell reviewers *what* you propose to do, whereas the methods section tells *how* you are going to achieve the objectives.

will start and finish. In simple terms, give the funder a clear picture of all the important steps you will take to accomplish each objective that you have indicated in your goals and objectives section.

The methods prove to the reviewer that your organization has the qualifications, credibility, and capacity to carry out the proposed project. The methodology section usually requires a fairly detailed account of the activities that will take place during the project. It is the place for applicants to prove their case to the funder that what was promised in the objectives can be carried out with efficiency.

The methodology section of a grant proposal addresses three basic components: how, when, and why.

- *How:* This is the detailed description of what will occur from the time the project begins until it is completed.
- *When:* This is the order and timing for the tasks. The timetable tells the reader "when" the project is going to take place.
- *Why:* You may need to defend your chosen methods, especially if they are new or unorthodox.

Tips for writing the methodology section. Paying attention to the following can help you to polish your methodology section.

- *Explain why you chose a specific methodological approach*

Each project requires a specific kind of method. Identify all project data that will be collected for use in evaluating proposal outcomes. For example, the methods used by an actor for a Broadway musical by Kurt Weill may be different from what a surgeon would use for a groundbreaking brain surgery.

> **Smart tip:** The nature of goals determines what methods are best to employ. Grant reviewers look very carefully at the appropriateness between goals and methods.

Some methods used by artists include:

- Still photography
- Videotapes
- Publications
- Digital photography
- Music recordings
- Face-to-face interviews
- Photographic archives

Common methods include:

- Survey research
- Formal intensive interviewing
- Participant observation
- Library research
- Archival research
- Aerial photography
- *Describe the major activities for reaching each objective*

Describe what you are going to do. Tell the funder about the project's "output." Be sure your proposal doesn't promise an unrealistic level of service. Unrealistic objectivities can go against your proposal.

- *Indicate the key project personnel who will carry out each activity*

Who is going to do the work and what are their credentials? Attach current resumes of key people. Some funders ask for the name of a project director, the person most responsible for the project. If there is more than one person organizing the event, give those names.

- *Show the interrelationships among project activities*

Describe your target audience, and how you will involve them in the activity. Some projects have two audiences: the direct participants and the indirect beneficiaries. If both audiences are included, describe both. For example, introducing an alcohol rehabilitation center can help to bring alcoholics back to sobriety. The direct beneficiaries are the alcoholics undergoing treatment. The indirect beneficiaries are their spouses, children, co-workers, and parents.

- *Include a time and task chart*

This is also known as the work plan and tells when the project will take place. Some funders will ask for the project start date and project end date. If the project is long, i.e., over a year, consider including a timeline of the different phases.

Sample methodology. EcoAsia a nonprofit organization, applied for funding to develop an eco-friendly fishing net to trap crabs in Sri Lanka. Instead of writing the crab classification system within a paragraph the applicant conveyed it in a more attractive form by creating a diagram:

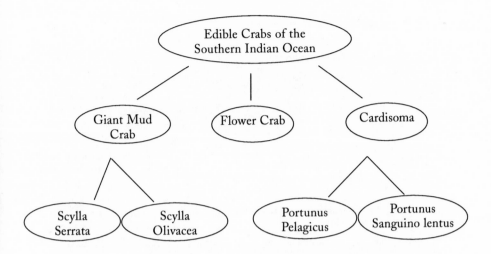

Prior to departing to the field my principal research assistant and I will prepare a sample questionnaire to interview 100 fishermen engaged in crab fishing. Our principal guide will be McAllester's suggestions for conducting face-to-face interviews in the field. I will ask the questions and my assistant will record them through a portable mini cassette player. At the end of the day we will transcribe the interviews and enter them into the computer in the Word program.

The choice of questions will target crab fishing methods, risks involved, and the kinds of shellfish caught in nets. Some sample questions include:

1. About how many crabs do you catch per day?
2. What types of crabs do you catch the most? How can you distinguish one from the other?
3. Do you sell all the crabs that you catch? Is there a larger demand than the production of crabs?
4. What are the main features that distinguish one crab species from the other?
5. How much do you earn per day?
6. Do you use any chemicals to catch crab? How does that affect the crab population?
7. What types of bait are used?

Budget

The budget introduces an estimate of how much your project or program idea is going to cost. It is the financial plan you have for the project estimated in the language of dollars. Proposal budgets may be fairly simple or quite complex. Usually, the greater the amount of money requested, the more detailed the budget gets. Typically the budget for private foundations is quite simple. Usually government funding sources require considerable detail and provide standard budget forms that must be used by prospective applicants. Refer to the funder's guidelines for information on acceptable expenses and instructions on how to present the budget. Keep in mind the funder's grant range as you develop your program and prepare the budget. To request an amount outside the range is an indication that you have not researched the funder thoroughly.

> **Smart tip:** The budget section refines your grant proposal with numbers. A well-crafted budget adds greatly to the proposal reviewer's understanding of the project. The budget may be simple as a one-page statement or your proposal may require a more complex presentation, such as a spreadsheet including projected support and revenue and notes explaining various items of expense or revenue and detailed cost computations.

A budget may include various components. Not all proposals require all of these components and the level of detail will vary from funder to funder and from project to project.

The following are some of the technical elements of a budget:

- Project or program budget
- Budget detail or justification
- In-kind distribution budget
- Matching funds
- Fringe benefits
- Direct costs
- Indirect or overhead costs

- *Project or program budget*
This refers to the income and expenses associated with the special project for which you are seeking funding. Include an estimated income and expense statement.

- *Budget detail or justification*
This is also known as budget narrative. It includes details on certain income and expense items presented in the budget.

- *In-kind distribution budget*
In-kind services are also known as estimated donated goods. Not all costs of the project will have to be paid in cash. Donated goods and volunteer time are important to many nonprofit ventures. In-kind support is non-cash, institutional assets that would have a cost attached to them if it were necessary to go outside the institution to purchase them. If, for example, you receive a donated computer or have a volunteer receptionist, the costs of the program will be reduced.

- *Matching funds*
Some funding programs have a matching requirement, i.e., grantees must

commit institutional resources according to a formula determined by the funder as a condition of receiving a grant. The matching requirement can be found in the funder guidelines. A funder may require cash, in-kind support, or a combination.

• *Fringe benefits*
A fringe benefit is an employment benefit such as a pension, a paid holiday, or health insurance, granted by an employer that has a monetary value but does not affect basic wage rates. It is an additional benefit that participants will receive during the project. The fringe benefit rates vary according to each organization. For example, in a university the fringe benefit rate is typically 28 percent during the academic year for full-time employees, and 8.0 percent for graduate students, faculty/summers, and part-time.

• *Direct costs*
Direct costs include personnel and the tools they will use to carry out the project. Personnel costs can include salaries, benefits, and consultants' fees. Direct expenses include the following: program staff salaries and benefits, supplies, equipment, program-related travel, program-related rent, and printing costs.

> **Smart tip:** Direct project expenses are non-personnel expenses you would not incur if you did not do the project. They can be almost anything: travel costs, printing, space or equipment rental, supplies, insurance, or meeting expenses such as food.

• *Indirect or overhead costs*
Indirect costs are the ones that are essential to all programs of the agency but are difficult to assign in specific amounts to any one program. They are costs that are shared by the programs of an organization such as the cost of the audit, the executive director's salary, general liability insurance, security, grounds, housekeeping, depreciation, and the copier lease. Overhead expense is common in government proposals.

Tips for writing the budget. Here are some tips to writing successful budgets.

• *Start early*
Get an early start in preparing your budget. Think about the day-in-day-out activities associated with your project. If there is an assessment phase at the end, leave sufficient time in your project timeline and resources to undertake the assessment.

• *Estimate the budget period*
Decide how long a period of time the proposal covers, and develop a budget for that length of time. If your proposal is for a six-month project the budget should demonstrate income and expenses for a six-month period; if your proposal is for a two-year project the budget must show two years worth of income and expenses.

• *Present a balanced budget*
Generally, federal funders expect to see a balanced budget for the project, one in which income and expenses are equal or approximately equal. Most funders are reluctant to support programs that will end the funding period with either a large deficit or a major surplus of cash.

Sample budget. Here is a sample of a basic budget submitted by an individual applicant to a private foundation. The grant request was to host a photographic exhibition:

Estimated Cost of Expenses

50 film rolls @$8:	$400
Film roll processing costs:	$500
Camera equipment:	$3,000
Stationery expenses:	$250
Postage costs:	$250
Travel expenses to research site:	$500
Total requested:	$4,900

	Cash Required	In-kind Donations	Total
Expected Revenue			
Foundation grants	$75,000		$75,000
Government grants	$60,000	$60,000	
Corporation grants	$25,000	$25,000	
In-kind donations	$22,000	$22,000	
Expected Expenses			
Salaries:			
Program coordinator	$35,000	$35,000	
Administrative asst.	$20,000	$20,000	
Contract personnel	$27,000	$5,000	$32,000
Program Services	$9,000	$9,000	

Smart tip: In-kind contributions are usually shown as both income and expense at the same levels. If, for example, you receive $3000 worth of donated food from local merchants, you also "spend" or use $3000 worth of donated food. If a volunteer teacher contributes $5,000 worth of her time, you also pay $5000 in teaching expenses. Remember that if you are showing in-kind contributions in your budget, they should be reflected as both revenue and expense.

Evaluation

The evaluation determines whether its money was well spent or not. From an applicant's perspective it gives an indication as to whether or not the program is going well. With increasingly tight budgets, funders want to know that their dollars are not being wasted. This can only be proven when grant recipients are committed to evaluating their progress and outcomes. Most funders require award recipients to provide written reports on how the goals and objectives were met.

Measurement tools or evaluation tools are what you use to collect the data or information that will show if your project reached its objectives or not. Information can be collected using

> **Smart tip:** The evaluation section is usually written after the need statement, goals, objectives, and methodology have been written. However, an evaluation plan should be a consideration at every stage of the proposal's development.

surveys, pre and post questionnaires or tests, musical recordings, statistics, or oral interviews, among other sources.

The evaluation section carries three components:

- Data collection
- Implementation
- Use of evaluation results

1. *Data collection* includes the following:
   a. How and when will you collect the information?
   b. What do you want to find out?
   c. Where will you get the information or data that you need?
   d. Who has the information that you need?

2. *Implementation* includes the following:
   a. What resources are needed to make sure the project has been implemented?
   b. Can an existing evaluation tool be used?
   c. Who is responsible for seeing that the evaluation is carried out?

3. *Use of evaluation results* include:
   a. Who will use the results?
   b. How and when will the findings be presented?
   c. What qualities does your program have for it to be successful?

There are different types of evaluation: Internal, external, outcome, process, qualitative, impact, quantitative.

- *Internal evaluations*

An internal evaluation can be done using someone within your organization. An individual within your organization has great intuitive knowledge of your program and is less likely to be seen as an intruder. On the other hand, the internal evaluation may be biased because of involvement with certain program aspects. There is a great deal of subjectivity involved in internal evaluations.

• *External evaluations*

They come from outside the organization and often have a fresh perspective and can see things previously unnoticed. Outside evaluators usually have high professional and scholarly competence. On the other hand they may be perceived as a threat by the staff and may require extra time to understand the program rationale. Using external evaluators offers considerable objectivity.

• *Outcome evaluation*

Outcome evaluations examine the end result of an intervention. This is also known as the summative evaluation. The goal here is to document the extent to which the project did what it was designed to do. Outcomes are the benefits, changes, or effects that occur to the target population due to participation in the project. Outcomes are usually expressed in humanistic terms.

• *Process evaluation*

Process evaluations generate information that will improve the effectiveness of the project during the grant period. They systematically examine internal and external characteristics associated with the delivery and receipt of services. This may include evaluating structure, the environment and settings in which services occur.

• *Qualitative evaluations*

Qualitative evaluations are rooted in direct contact with the people involved in a program and consist of three kinds of data collection: interviews, direct or field observation, and review of certain documents. Qualitative evaluations are most appropriate if your questions involve either:

1. Gaining insight into how the patterns of relationships within the program unfold
2. Understanding participants, staff or community feelings or opinions about a program

• *Impact evaluation*

Impact evaluation generates information to measure the overall worth and utility of the project beyond the grant period. It focuses on the project's larger value such as long-term fundamental changes in participants' knowledge, attitudes, or behaviors. You can demonstrate impact at several levels: the target population, the community at large, and beyond.

• *Quantitative evaluation*

Quantitative evaluations translate experience into units that can be counted, compared, measured, and manipulated statistically. Quantitative evaluations are most appropriate if your questions involve any of the following:

1. Understanding the quantities of particular aspects of a program
2. Determining if a cause-and-effect relationship occurs
3. Comparing two different methods that are seeking to achieve the same outcomes
4. Doing follow-ups at the post project period

Tips for writing an evaluation. Evaluation is an important component of the program development process. It is not a separate activity, nor an add-on function after a program has been completed. How a program will be evaluated must be determined prior to the program's implementation. Here are some tips for writing evaluations:

- *Describe why an evaluation of the project is needed; its purpose*

Project evaluations are conducted for various purposes. Here are some of the main reasons for evaluating:

1. To see if the program did what was expected
2. To see if the methods and objectives made an impact on the identified need
3. To maintain control over the project
4. To guide adjustments to the program that would make it more effective
5. To find out whether the program did what was expected
6. To determine if the methods specified were used and the objectives met
7. To determine if an impact was made on the need identified in the problem statement
8. To obtain feedback from the target group
9. Identify the type and purpose of your evaluation

Identify the evaluation results and how they will be analyzed. The main components of evaluation results are:

- People involvement
- End results
- Activities
- Practicing change
- Changes in knowledge, attitudes, skills, and aspirations
- Reactions

1. People involvement includes the following:
   a. How many people participated?
   b. Who participated in the project? How did their participation make a difference?
2. *End results include the following:*
   a. What is the long-term impact of the program?
   b. How have participants, their families, and communities been helped by the results of changes in practices, knowledge, attitudes, skills and aspirations? To what degree?
3. *Activities include:*
   a. What resources were involved in project implementation?
   b. What techniques and methods were used?
4. *Practicing change includes the following:*
   a. Have participants applied knowledge and learned skills into any new projects?
   b. How have the changes affected the community? Any tangible results?
5. *Changes in knowledge, attitudes, skills, and aspirations addresses the following:*

    a. How has the project changed the awareness, understanding and/or problems of the people and communities impacted by the project?

    b. Have participants changed their interest in ideas or practices that were part of the program content?

    c. Which ideas of change are progressive in nature? How are they beneficial?

    d. Have participants learned new skills?

    e. Do their performances show any improvement?

6. *Reactions*

    a. How did participants react to the program? Were they satisfied?

    b. Were their expectations met or not met?

    c. Demonstrate that an appropriate evaluation procedure is included for every project objective

- *Provide sufficient detail to demonstrate the technical soundness of all data collection instruments and procedures*

Describe the information that will be needed to complete the evaluation, the potential sources for this information, and the instruments that will be used for its collection. Identify and justify procedures for analysis, reporting, and utilization.

Dissemination

Dissemination refers to the distribution of information. Evaluation is closely tied to dissemination. Funding sources frequently pay for disseminating the results of your grant through one or more of the following mechanisms:

- A final report mailed to others in your field
- A quarterly journal mailed to others
- A newsletter mailed to others in your field
- Sponsorship of a seminar or conference on the topic
- Participation in national conferences to deliver results of the project
- A film or tape presentation on the project
- A slideshow presentation
- A CD or DVD

Dissemination is the method by which you tell others about your project. As grants become increasingly competitive, the dissemination of project outcome results takes on increasing importance. Project dissemination offers many advantages, including increasing public awareness of your program or project, soliciting additional support, locating more clients, alerting others in your field to new ideas, and adding to the stockpile of existing knowledge.

Tips for writing a successful dissemination. Here are some tips for writing successful disseminations:

• *Include why dissemination activities are important for your project*

For example, if you are conducting a research project on shark bites, producing a video about where they happen the most can serve as a warning for beach enthusiasts and what to avoid in the water.

• *Clearly identify the intended results of the dissemination effort*

If you are planning a film production, explain how it will be distributed, produced, and shared with consumers. Show specific results and final products. Succinctly describe any products to result from the dissemination effort

• *Specify precisely who will be responsible for dissemination and why they are capable of carrying it out*

Let's assume there is a television documentary on a specific topic. If a leading scholar in your university department is participating in the project, prove why he is qualified to promote the findings of the research project in the television documentary series. Identify key personnel who will be responsible for dissemination.

Discuss internal as well as external project dissemination and key figures involved.

Evaluate the effectiveness of the dissemination efforts and products.

Sample evaluation and dissemination. Here is a sample evaluation and dissemination. Funds were requested to conduct a research project researching Native American music and publishing a book.

Disseminating the Research Findings of Native American Music

The final products of the project will be a book, articles, and a website. The research team has secured a publisher who has expressed an interest to sign a contract for the book titled *Healing Through Native American Music*. Crown Publishers has agreed to publish it and market it at the national level. The book will also be made available in bookstores, libraries, universities, hospitals, and educational institutions throughout the United States. The research findings will also be submitted to magazines such as *Smithsonian*, *Journal of Ethnomusicology*, and *National Geographic*. A project web site will be created titled "Native American Music and Healing." The website will make it possible for scholars throughout the world to gain access to the research findings.

Applying for Grants Online

More and more funders are using the Internet to post their guidelines and accept applications. Within the next ten years the majority of funders are likely to make it mandatory to apply only online. Just as handwritten grant applications are now vintage, during the next decade applications sent via regular mail in hard-copy format are likely to become obsolete.

Being Internet-savvy places you at a distinct advantage in applying for grants. More and more funders are seeking "paperless" means of accepting applications. It is also cheaper than mailing out hard copies of applications.

Electronic inquiries are becoming more and more common as people are becoming facile at communicating via computer, Phones, cell phones, and Youtube. Many federal and state grants are becoming available for electronic completion and submission. Although e-mails can be very informal, resist the temptation to be casual in your exchange. Maintain a professional approach and be concise. Write the e-mail as if you were writing a physical letter to the funder.

Smart tip: There are some drawbacks of using online inquiries and applications. There is no record of the submission being received, unless the funder acknowledges in writing that the application was received. Another disadvantage is that there may be unreliable connections to the server. Federal funders especially send applications for peer reviews. With e-mails, it may be hard to do this.

Some funders post applications on their websites. Applicants have to register by creating a username and password in order to access the online form. The format for online applications varies. Typically, once you have registered you can start typing online and save the information at short intervals, so that the next time you return to the application, your previous material is still there. If the material is not saved the work may be lost. Some funders limit the number of characters you can use in the application. You may also want to print what you have done or copy and paste it into a word-processing document so you don't lose your work.

When sending e-mail submissions, confirm the address where it is being sent.

If all you can get is a general e-mail address, call the foundation and get the grant manager's direct address. Once you have one person's e-mail address at a funding source, you can generally use the same formula to reach another person within the same organization. For example, both Dave Bret and Jane Dawson work at Charity Foundation. If Dave's e-mail is dave@charityfoundation.net, it is highly likely that Jane's e-mail is jane@charityfoundation.net.

Subject lines can determine whether or not the reviewer actually reads your e mail inquiry. Make sure the subject line relates to the content of the message. If it does not, change it. With computer viruses on the rise, it becomes even more important to have a strong subject line. "Hello" in the subject line is not likely to get a quick response, if any. A subject line such as "International grant request for a performing arts project in Cambodia" is more likely to be opened.

The content of your e-mail is important. It conveys information about your project and gives cues about the person and organization requesting support. Your competence with the language is the first cue. If you misspell words and use incorrect phrases, the reader may assume either that you are uneducated or that you do not have the expertise to communicate effectively. Some funders may even feel insulted by such errors.

Within the body of the e-mail, describe your project. The challenge is to describe your project in a few paragraphs. Sometimes, applicants are asked to send the project information in an attached Word format document and not in the body of the e-mail. Make sure you include the most important points:

- The need being addressed
- The clients served
- Project description
- Projected outcomes
- Program duration

The most important statements should appear early in the e-mail. Details can follow in subsequent paragraphs. Remember to include a web address at the bottom that will directly link the funder to your organization's website. This will be helpful if they need additional background on your agency. Use attachments if you need to send supporting information. In general an attachment that is larger than 50kb may be hard to download; consider breaking it into sections.

Sign the e-mail with your full name and make sure your contact information (including e-mail address) is in the body of the e-mail. Many e-mail programs allow you to set up a default signature to be included at the end of every message. That means every e-mail is accompanied by your contact information. The signature can tell as much about you as the message itself. Include these things:

- Full name and title
- Name of organization
- Address
- Phone number
- Fax number

Smart tip: Formatting tips for e-mail exchanges

- Avoid being casual
- Write to a person, not to an office or department
- Address the person by name in the body of the e mail. If you don't know the person, use Ms., Mr., or Dr.
- Use a font that is easy to read
- Bold important headings for emphasis
- Don't use emoticons or e-mail slang e.g. LOL (laugh out loud) or a smiley face
- Use proper grammar
- Run a spell check

- E-mail address
- Your organization's website address

> **Smart tip:** Read your e-mail a few times before you hit Send. Save copies of all e-mail exchanges in a folder with the funder's name on it.

Resource Centers and Libraries

There are several resource centers and libraries dedicated entirely to information about funding sources. Having access to them can increase your chances of winning a grant. Knowing where to look for resources is a critical part of grant seeking. Hunting the right places can also save you a lot of time.

Associated Grant Makers

Associated Grant Makers is a resource center for philanthropy. The research library has a reference collection of publications and other information on foundation and corporate grant-making and nonprofit management including national foundations, corporate giving, IRS 990-PF forms, journals, newsletters, fundraising manuals, and proposal-writing guides. Its mission is to support the practice and expansion of effective philanthropic giving. AGM is a community of foundation staff and trustees, corporate grant makers, donors and philanthropic advisory services that builds a connection with nonprofit leaders. It is a warehouse of learning both for grant makers and grant seekers. Its events calendar offers grant-related activities offered every year.

Contact:
Associated Grant Makers
55 Court Street, Suite 520
Boston, MA 02108
Phone: (617) 426-2606
E-mail: agm@agmconnect.org
Website: http://agmconnect.org

The Foundation Center

Founded in 1956, the Foundation Center is dedicated to serving grant seekers, grant makers, researchers, policymakers, the media, and the general public. The center's mission is to support and improve philanthropy by promoting public understanding of the field and helping grant seekers succeed.

The Foundation Center provides education and training for the grant-seeking process. Other tools to help grant seekers succeed are:

- *Foundation Finder*: Allows users to search by name for basic financial and contact information for more than 70,000 private and community foundations in the U.S.
- *Grant maker websites*: Four distinct directories of annotated links to grant maker websites organized by grant maker type allow users to search or browse summaries of the collected sites.
- *Sector Search*: A specialty search engine that indexes every page of the most useful nonprofit sites on the Internet.
- *990-PF Search*: A searchable database of the 990-PF tax returns filed with the Internal Revenue Service by all domestic private foundations. Users can locate and download via. pdf (portable document files) the tax records on more than 60,000 private foundations. By looking at sections on the tax records that list giving patterns, award amounts, board members, and so forth, you can help decide if a foundation is a good match with your needs: www.fdncenter.org/funders/grantsmart/index.html

Contact: The Foundation Center
79 Fifth Avenue, 16th Street
New York, NY 10003-3076
Phone: (800) 424-9836; (212) 620-4230
Website: www.fdncenter.org

The Grantsmanship Center

The Grantsmanship Center is primarily a training organization for grant writers. The Center sponsors workshops on writing grant proposals; publishes a funding newsletter, The Grantsmanship Center Magazine, available free to qualified agencies; and sells reprints of articles related to proposal writing and fundraising. *TGCI* magazine provides information on how to plan, manage, staff and get grants for individuals and organizations. TGCI also publishes magazines that can be useful for grant writers.

Contact: The Grantsmanship Center
P.O. Box 17220
Los Angeles, CA 90017
Phone: (213) 482-9860
Fax: (213) 482-9863
E-mail: info@tgci.com
Website: http://www.tgci.com

Grant Types by Field

Grants are awarded in a variety of fields, ranging from arts to home-land security. Classifying them into one single category is impossible as funding fields vary. Sometimes, your project idea may belong to more than one grant type. This broadens the number of places you can look for aid.

Art Grants

Forget the starving artist. You can become a thriving artist if you know the right places to look for grants. Artists qualify for various awards, scholarships, and research grants. Whether you are a comedian, actor, or jazz pianist, there are grants out there for you. Turn to Chapter 16 for a listing of places that award art grants.

Education Grants

Private foundations, federal funders, family trusts, community foundations, corporations, and individual families offer a wide variety of programs for higher education. Grants are awarded both for individuals and organizations. Areas of funding include:

- College tuition
- International projects and travel
- Career advancement
- Research and professional support
- Cultural preservation
- Start-up costs for small businesses
- Disaster relief
- Emergency living expenses
- Medical and scientific research

Turn to Chapter 16 for a listing of places that award education grants.

Emergency Grants

The loss of a job, hospital bills, death of a parent, and natural disasters are all examples of sudden and unforeseen circumstances that can throw one's financial stability out of control. In the world of grants these are known as "emergency" or "general welfare" expenses.

Performing artists who need assistance with their living expenses have help. If you are out of a job, are in a transition phase, or are disabled to work, you may have difficulty paying your mortgage, paying medical bills, food costs, and other daily living expenses. Such financial struggles can affect your career as well. Specific grants are awarded to cover such emergency living expenses. These are usually one-time grants and are set up to help you to become self-sufficient later on.

Some of the categories for emergency living expenses include:

- Health insurance
- Hospital bills
- Loan and debt payments
- Disaster relief from events such as tornadoes, hurricanes, floods, and tsunami
- Monthly rent/mortgage
- Payment of medical bills
- Addiction recovery expenses (rehabilitation for alcoholic treatment; substance abuse treatment; psychotherapy, detoxification, sober living counseling)
- Food and clothing
- Physical therapy
- Child care, babysitting expenses
- Insurance
- Utility Bill Subsidies

Supporting documents for emergency grant applications include

- Resume
- A copy of your most recent bank statement
- A copy of your most recent tax return
- Copies of bills for which assistance is being requested
- A copy of mortgage/rent payment
- References who can testify on your behalf

Turn to Chapter 16 for a listing of places that award emergency grants.

Academic Competitiveness Grants

A new federal law has created a student aid grant program called the Academic Competitiveness Grant (ACG). First-year undergraduate students are eligible to receive up to $750. Second-year undergraduate students are eligible to receive up to $1,300.

- The ACG eligibility criteria are listed below:
- To be eligible for an ACG each academic year, a student must:
- Be a U.S. citizen
- Be Federal Pell Grant eligible
- Be enrolled full-time in a degree program
- Be enrolled in the first or second academic year of his or her

program of study at a two-year or four-year degree-granting institution
- Have completed a rigorous high school program of study (after January 1, 2006, if a first-year student, and after January 1, 2005, if a
  second-year student)
- If a first-year student, not have been previously enrolled in an undergraduate program
- If a second-year student, have at least a cumulative 3.0 grade point
  average on a 4.0 scale for the first academic year

At the time that you complete your application, FAFSA on the web will
predetermine if you are eligible to answer the ACG questions. You may also
contact the financial aid office at your school for assistance regarding ACG.

Federal Pell Grants

Pell Grants are designed to help low-income students pay for college.
A Federal Pell Grant is gift aid from the federal government. When they
first started, Pell Grants were called basic Opportunity Grants-to provide
college access for low income students. This program is specifically
designed to help undergraduate students finance their education for up to
six years of study without burdening them with a repayment plan. Nothing needs to be repaid to the government and there is no interest or fee to
pay.

Pell grants are often described as the "foundation" on which financial
aid packages are built. Generally, Pell Grants are awarded only to undergraduate students who have not earned a bachelor's or professional degree.
In some cases, you might receive a Pell Grant for attending a post-bac-
calaureate teacher certificate program. Students can receive Pell Grants
for their undergraduate study until they complete a baccalaureate or their
first professional degree (such as pharmacy or dentistry). Grants usually
do not have to be repaid. There is no charge to apply for a Federal Pell
Grant.

Federal Pell Grants help about 5.4 million full- and part-time college and vocational school students nationally. Students with family
incomes up to $50,000 may be eligible for Pell Grants. However, most Pell
awards go to students with family incomes below $20,000.

The maximum Pell Grant award for the 2007–08 award year (July 1,
2007 to June 30, 2008) is $4,310. The 2008 maximum grant is $4,600, the
largest increase in the program's 30-year history, and increases to $5,400
by 2012. The maximum can change each award year and depends on program funding.

Financial need is determined by the Department of Education using a standard formula, established by Congress, to evaluate the financial information reported on the Free Application for Federal Student Aid (FAFSA) and to determine the estimated family contribution (EFC). The size of your grant is determined by a scale linked to your need. A Pell Grant is paid to the college, which then credits the student's account. Be sure to send your application to the address on the form as soon after January 1 as possible. Missing the deadline means missing out on financial aid. Federal application processors generally want all forms in by the end of February.

All applicants requesting federal aid dollars will receive an SAR, telling them (1) whether they may receive a Pell Grant, (2) their Pell Grant Index number, (3) their EFC number, and (4) if they have failed to fill out the form correctly.

Once the FAFSA has been completed and filed, the progress of the application can be tracked by calling the Federal Student Aid Information Center toll-free at (800) 433-3243 between 9 A.M. and 5:30 P.M. (Eastern Standard Time), Monday through Friday. You also can check the status of your FAFSA online.

The actual award a student receives depends on a number of factors including:

- The price of attendance
- The family's financial situation
- Family size
- The student's estimated family contribution (EFC)
- The cost of attendance (as determined by the institution)
- The student's enrollment status (full-time or part-time)
- Whether the student attends for a full academic year or less

> **Smart tip:** Key characteristics of Pell Grants
>
> - No payback is necessary
> - Source: Federal government
> - Deadline: Application must be received no later than the last workday of June

Here are some requirements that Pell Grant applicants must meet:

- Your Pell Grant Index (PGI) number must be low enough to meet required need standards, as determined by the government; the number is found on your SAR
- You must be attending school no less than half-time
- You must be working on your first undergraduate degree

- You must meet all application deadlines
- You must be a U.S. citizen or eligible noncitizen

Apply for a Federal Pell Grant by completing a FAFSA Application. These are available at high schools, colleges, vocational schools, libraries, community and state agencies, through the website below, or by contacting:

Pell Grant
Box 84
Washington D.C. 20044
Phone: (800) 433-3243
http://www.ed-gov/programs/fpg/index.html

Federal Supplemental Educational Opportunity Grants (FSEOG)

Federal Supplemental Educational Opportunity Grant (FSEOG) is gift aid from the federal government. Preference is given to Pell Grant recipients with exceptional financial need, i.e., those with the lowest EFC. The size of the award is from $100 to $4000 annually (as of 2006–2007) for undergraduate study. The actual award is determined by the college.

FSEOGs are used to enhance educational opportunities for low-income students. They are also available to students with a high need. Unlike the Pell, which any eligible student receives directly from the government, FSEOGs are in a category called campus-based aid. That means each school's financial aid office gets an annual lump sum to distribute under certain rules, as it desires. Most schools deplete their FSEOG funds early, so apply early.

> **Smart tip:** Key characteristics of FSEOG
>
> - No payback is necessary
> - Campus-based program
> - Source: Government provides money to schools for grants
> - Deadline: Usually around January 1; actual deadline is set by the school.

Here are some eligibility requirements for FSEOG:

- You must be attending a school that awards FSEOGs
- You must show a high degree of financial need, as determined by the school
- Most recipients are full-time students, but those attending school half-time or less may also receive a grant
- You must be working on your first undergraduate or graduate degree
- You must be a U.S. citizen or eligible noncitizen

National Science and Mathematics Access to Retain Talent Grants (SMART)

A new federal law has created a new student aid grant program called the National Science and Mathematics Access to Retain Talent Grant (National SMART grant). Third- and fourth- year undergraduate students will be eligible to receive up to $4,000 per year.

To be eligible for a National SMART Grant each academic year, a student must:

- Be a U.S. citizen
- Be Federal Pell Grant eligible
- Be enrolled full-time
- Major in mathematics, science , technology, engineering, or a critical foreign language
- Be enrolled in the third or fourth academic year of his or her program of study at a four-year degree-granting institution
- Have at least a cumulative 3.0 grade point average on a 4.0 scale

You may contact the financial aid office at your school for assistance regarding the National SMART Grant.

8

Congratulations! You Have Been Awarded Financial Aid

Sealing the Deal: Acceptance Letter

If you have received a financial aid award, you are usually informed in writing, and in some cases, by e-mail or telephone. Once you receive your award letters, you should review them carefully to determine if it is financially feasible to attend the college of your choice. You need to evaluate the aid package. Compare how much in loans and how much in free money (scholarships and grants) each college is offering. While you are reviewing and comparing the different aid packages, it is important that you respond to each college's deadline date. If you don't respond by the deadline, there is a risk that a college may withdraw its offer. Responding to an aid letter does not officially commit you to attend that college. Most colleges subscribe to a National Candidate Reply Date of May 1 for tuition, room, and board deposits. Many colleges will give a reasonable extension beyond May 1. You need to check with each college for its extension policy.

Financial aid award offers can vary significantly from college to college. When reviewing aid offers, consider both the amount of your family contribution and the amount offered in self-help aid, e.g., loans and work programs. If an institutional grant is offered, it is important to ask how it can be renewed.

Award letters vary in format but most contain the following items:

- A statement of the expense budget developed. This varies based on factors like whether you plan to live on or off campus.

- Your estimated family contribution, as calculated under the federal methodology and the institutional methodology.
- The amount of your need.
- A description of how all or part of that need is to be met, listing each aid source and dollar amount.
- A suspense date by when you must return the award letter.
- Information on available procedures for "appealing" any information in the award letter with which you disagree.

In responding to the award letter, you have some choices:

- Accept the aid package as presented by the college
- Accept portions of the aid package and decline others
- Decline the aid package entirely
- Appeal the decision if you feel that additional aid is needed

Keep working continuously. Even after you get aid, if you are in need of funds for the following year, keep working. It is this continuous process that is going to keep you flowing, rather than applying once and having great expectations for the rest of your life.

Sample Acceptance Letter

Always acknowledge your acceptance in writing. In the event of your accepting an award, send a brief note through regular mail, printing your signature on it. In some cases, an e-mail is sufficient too. Here is a sample letter of acceptance:

Dear sir,

It is with great pleasure that I accept the scholarship that I have been awarded. I would like to accept the aid package specified in your award letter dated June 5, 2008. I am sending copies of the documents you have asked me to sign.

Thank you very much for awarding me this scholarship. I know it will make a difference in my college career.

Yours Sincerely,

Brent Eisner

Appealing the Aid Package

The success of an appeal with a college will depend on numerous factors, e.g., the academic qualifications of the student, how competitive the college is in attracting new students, and the willingness and ability of the college to provide more institutional aid dollars. A few colleges may have an appeal policy that includes meeting or matching aid offers from other colleges.

Since different schools may assess financial need differently, aid packages can vary widely for the same student. If your top pick doesn't offer you as much aid as other comparable colleges, you may be able to get a better deal, if you play it right. To get more aid, you need to know how the game works. Most colleges will consider adjusting an aid package if they are given legitimate documentation. You have to make a case for additional aid and your case should be based on documented financial circumstances.

Keep in mind that the best financial aid package is not necessarily the largest aid package, since aid awards include not only grant and scholarship money which you never have to repay, but also loans and work-study programs. When you receive your student aid reports, look over them carefully. Don't just look at the bottom line of what each school is offering, but study the awards and loans that make up each package. You should check whether or not the proposed aid package truly covers all your anticipated expenses. A school may claim to offer you 100 percent of your requested assistance, until you see that the numbers don't cover books, fees, transportation, and living expenses. For example, a university may offer you what seems to be a large package containing $15,000 in aid, but if you find that much of the assistance is in the form of PLUS or unsubsidized loans, the sweeter deal may be from the college that gives you $10,000 that is mostly grant money and subsidized, low-interest loans.

Keep in mind that the aid process is a business transaction. Reviewers are rationing the money out to meet the college's needs and recruit the students they want to get.

The best package is the one in which you have to pay the least out of pocket and where you have to borrow the least to finance school. The biggest key to success, whatever your circumstances, is to understand how a school determines your estimated family contribution (EFC). That way, you can best highlight how your circumstances differ from the norm or why they are worthy of reconsideration.

It is possible to have the financial aid office adjust your EFC or the cost of your college education. College and university aid offices take into account special circumstances under which the student or family runs into some unexpected financial difficulties (such as medical bills, disabilities, etc.) that affect the amount the family is able to contribute. If you feel you qualify for these unusual circumstances, contact your financial aid office immediately.

Some of the reasons for negotiating an aid package include:

- Your financial situation has recently changed (if true, this is the one reason that will almost always get you more aid)
- You do not believe the school has taken all your expenses into account

> **Smart tip:** When you submit an appeal to the financial aid office, ask when you will receive a response. If the answer is "not before the school's candidate reply date," which is usually May 1, ask for an extension beyond that date.

- The school is using your scholarship money or high-interest, unsubsidized loans to count toward your package
- You simply feel that what you can bring to the school (academic excellence, athletic ability) is worth the school's extra effort
- Costs have not been considered on the financial aid forms, including medical expenses, tuition for a young child in private school or for an older child in graduate school
- The financial aid determined was based on a year that was unusually profitable; you typically don't earn as much as you did in the year that was reported
- There is an unusual financial situation in your family. Be sure to organize material that you want to present to the office, e.g., medical bills, receipts, etc.
- Data is incorrect on the aid application or has changed significantly since original data was submitted

The first step in the negotiation process is to contact the school's financial aid office. But don't call until you have compared all the offers you have received since it is better to make your request with all the necessary information in hand.

Wait a few days after receiving an acceptance letter from a school before calling its aid office. Typically the financial aid office is swamped right after offers are sent out. Once you have a contact in the aid office, be somewhat discreet. Don't treat the aid officer like a used car salesman just waiting to haggle.

A better approach would be to say that you are very interested in attending but financing is a concern and you are a little confused how the school arrived at its decision given x, y and z about your circumstances. Only then might you mention that other schools were able to offer you more and ask politely if there is any chance the school could improve on its offer.

You should never approach an FAA with a snobbish attitude that you deserve more than you are getting. Always be friendly and reasonable, and explain your reasoning honestly. If you are a straight-"A" student or a talented athlete, you will, of course, have a better chance of winning the argument. But even an average student can negotiate a better deal in the right situations. Here is an example of a good versus a bad approach:

> *Bad approach:* "We have too much credit card debt to afford our bills and a college education, Can't you take our financial problems into consideration?" Remember, financial aid administrators rarely consider bad debt a reason to grant you more funds, except in some cases where unusual hardships are involved.
>
> *Good approach:* "I have calculated what we truly need to pay for all our college expenses, and the package you have offered does not seem to take all these factors into consideration. Can we realistically address these issues and see if the package can be adjusted?"

You can contact the aid office either with a phone call or through writing. Before you contact the school, gather all the supporting ammunition you can in front of you. If you have received a better offer from a comparable school, have it in front of you when you call and be prepared to send a copy of the rival award letter to the school with whom you are negotiating. They will probably ask to see it. You will want to attach copies of more favorable aid offers from other schools.

At no time—either on the phone or in writing—should you indicate that you will accept a school's offer of admission regardless of the aid officer's decision. The more they figure you are desperate to attend, the less likely it is they will improve your package, because they figure you'll go anyway.

The FAA is not the only person you can talk to, however. Colleges and universities typically have award committees that determine aid packages. To circumvent the financial aid office, contact the school's admissions office and request the name and address of the chairperson who heads the financial aid committee. Also, find out what day the committee is scheduled to meet next. Then send a letter of appeal to the chairperson before the meeting.

Sample Letters Asking for More Aid

Sample letter #1: Negotiating a bigger package

July 1, 2008
Bryan Kingsheart
123 Main Street
Worcester, MA 01603

Susan Hanson, Financial Aid Administrator
XYZ College
199 Main Street
Anywhere, CA 91023

Dear Ms. Hanson:

I have recently examined the Student Aid Report for XYZ College, and there are some items I wish to address. First of all, I would like to reject the PLUS loan, as it does not offer a very favorable rate. Please also reduce the $2,600 unsubsidized Stafford Loan to $1,500.

I also noticed that the package you have outlined here does not take into consideration some of the necessary expenses of college, including books, fees, and travel costs.

I am very impressed with the academic reputation of XYZ College, but I have also been considering Xavier University, which has presented me with a package that includes some of the expenses mentioned above. I would like to discuss my package further with you, and explore what other financial aid opportunities might be available to me at XYZ College.

Please contact me at your earliest convenience. Thank you for your time and consideration.

Sincerely,

Bryan Kingsheart

Sample letter #2: Requesting assistance with negotiation

October 1, 2008
Sandy Bonderman, Scholarship Administrator
The Center for Youth
Downing Street
Wichita, KS 00000

Dear Ms. Bonderman:

Thank you so much for awarding me the PDQ Scholarship for Academic Excellence. The $7,000 scholarship should go a long way toward helping me pay for my college tuition. I have recently run into a problem, however, and I would like to request your assistance.

I wanted to use your scholarship to attend XYZ University, but the financial aid office there used it instead to reduce my financial aid package. As you know, the intention of the PDQ Scholarship was to assist talented students with financial need such as myself.

Therefore, I would like to ask if you would be willing to write a letter of appeal to the university's financial aid administrator, Mr. Tony Hart. If you explain the intention of the scholarship to him, he may reduce the amount of loans in my package rather than the amount of school grants. This would be a very beneficial use of the scholarship money you have granted me. I will also be writing to Mr. Hart about this matter.

Thank you so much for your help. Please contact me if you have any questions, or if there is anything else you would like to know before pursuing this further.

Sincerely,

Susan Breson

Sample letter #3: Change in financial status letter

October 1, 2008
Robert Aniston, Financial Aid Administrator
University of Montana
100 University Drive
Billings, MT 00000

Dear Mr. Aniston:

Thank you for the recent offer of a financial aid package for attending Summerfield University. Unfortunately, since the time I submitted data about my family's finances on the FAFSA and FAF forms, our financial situation has changed dramatically.

ABC Company has had to lay off many of its employees, including my father, and we do not know when he will be able to return to work. Because of this, my family will not be able to contribute nearly as much as they expected toward my college education at this time.

I would greatly appreciate it if you could make adjustments to my financial aid package to address this change. Please let me know if there is any additional information you will need in order to complete the necessary paperwork, and thank you for your prompt attention to this matter.

Sincerely,

Seth Stephens

9

The Alternate Aid Route

There are many offline funding sources that offer financial aid. They may not be well known and sometimes are not advertised online. Explore these offline sources to defeat the competition. Here are some ways to help you get started.

- Your high school guidance office or college academic department
- Your church, synagogue, or temple
- American Legion, Jaycees, etc.
- Local government offices
- The chamber of commerce
- Your employer
- Clubs, athletic teams, academic societies, and other organizations you belong to
- Clubs, unions, professional associations, and civic groups that your parents belong to
- Civic and public service organizations
- Your local library where scholarship announcements are often published
- Your local funding information center
- The Boy Scouts and Girl Scouts of America
- Associations, particularly those representing your field of interest
- Area businesses and organizations offering scholarships
- State educational agencies
- College admission offices
- Ethnic or racial groups
- Local professional organizations

- Professional organizations such as American Medical Association or American Bar Association
- Hobbies or interests such as rodeo, fishing, or bowling
- Service organizations such as Lions and Rotary Clubs
- Insurance companies
- Local professional sports teams

IRS Publications on Alternative Funding

The IRS publishes several documents that provide useful information on alternative aid types. Here are some of them:

- Publication 970 (.pdf), Tax Benefits for Higher Education: www. irs.gov/pub/irs-pdf/p970.pdf
- Form 8863 and Instructions (.pdf), education credits (Hope Scholarship and Lifetime Learning Credits): www.irs.gov/pub/irs-pdf/ f8863.pdf
- Tax Topic 605, Education credits: www.irs.gov/taxtopics/tc605.html
- Frequently asked questions and answers from the IRS, Education Tax Credits: www.irs.gov/faqs/faq-kw52.html

College Installment Loans

This plan usually has three monthly payments per semester. Usually there is an administrative fee depending on the amount financed. Sometimes, a default penalty is charged if the total amount is not paid in full by the due date. Generally no interest is charged for this installment plan. Both full- and part-time students are eligible to use this plan.

The advantage of this plan is that it spreads out-of-the-pocket costs over the semester with a minimal processing fee and no interest on the unpaid balance. The disadvantage of this plan is that late payments may result in the cancellation of this option and/or may prevent you from registering for the next enrollment period.

Cooperative Education

The federal government sponsors thousands of students who take jobs in the armed forces, the Treasury Department, the Department of Health and Human Services, the Department of Agriculture, the General Services Administration, the Department of Justice, the Department of Labor and many other agencies.

The scheduling of work and school is flexible. Some students opt for parallel study and work, in which they attend school in the morning and work in the afternoon, or vice versa. The other option is to alternate semesters—one at work, then one at school.

AmeriCorps

The National Community Service Trust Act of 1993 established the AmeriCorps program, in which students can finance some or all of their college education in return for agreeing to perform specified community service. AmeriCorps volunteers receive a living stipend of about $7500 a year and get the opportunity to accrue educational awards of $4725 a year that can be used to pay tuition costs or repay student loans. Applicants must be U.S. citizens who are at least 17 years old and are high school graduates. AmeriCorps volunteers typically work in underprivileged areas of American cities and rural districts in four fields: education, public safety, human services, and the environment. Check the AmeriCorps website at http://www.americorps.org.

College Board

The College Board program offers Extra Credit loans to cover the full cost of your child's education. The minimum loan is $2000. The loan's interest rate floats at 4.5 percent percentage points over the 90-day Treasury Bill rate, adjusted quarterly. There is a 3 percent loan-origination fee, and the student has 15 years to repay.

Another loan that is part of the College Credit program is called the Extra Time loan, which is designed to pay for a single year of education expenses. It has similar features to the Extra Credit loan, except that you have the option of monthly payments of interest only while a student is enrolled, or monthly payments of principal and interest after the education is complete. For more information on these loans, visit http://www.collegeboard.com

College-Sponsored Long-Term Loans

Some colleges provide long-term loans to students and/or parents. Generally these loans have a reasonable interest rate. Also, some colleges will offer loans to students who demonstrate financial need and to students with no financial need if they need to borrow in lieu of the parental contribution. Usually these loan programs use institutional resources, which may be limited. Also, the maximum loan amount will vary from college to college.

The advantages of this plan are that it has long-term low interest, and no administrative fees. Usually, repayment begins six months after graduation or after the student leaves the college. Also, there are usually deferment provisions during periods of at least half time study. The disadvantage of this plan is that some colleges will require a cosigner.

College-Sponsored Payment and Loan Programs

Usually colleges will offer some institutional payment plans to assist students and parents in paying college expenses. Here is a sample institutional plan:

1. *Ten or twelve monthly payments to the school (beginning July or August):*
These monthly payments are not loans. They allow families to spread out the cost over the academic year. Usually, the last payment for the semester is due by the last month of the semester. These plans allow for the whole academic year to be spread over both semesters. There is usually a $50–$75 annual fee that could include life insurance. Sometimes a college will charge an additional fee for late enrollment. Also, no interest is charged on the unpaid balance. This payment plan is usually available to all full- and part-time students, and both undergraduate and graduate students.

The advantage to this plan is that it spreads out-of-the-pocket costs over the academic year with a minimal processing fee and no interest on the unpaid balance.

The disadvantage of this plan is that late payments may result in the cancellation of this option and/or may prevent you from registering for the next enrollment period.

ConSern

ConSern Loans for Education lend up to $25,000 each year per child at the 30- or 90-day commercial paper rate plus 4.6 percentage points, adjusted monthly. ConSern charges a 4.5 percent origination fee and allows you to repay a loan over as long as 15 years. These loans are designed for employees of companies that have adopted the ConSern program. For more information on how to qualify, call ConSern at (800) 767-5626 or go to http://www.consern.com.

The Hope Scholarship Tax Credit

Married taxpayers (filing jointly) with adjusted gross income (AGI) of less than $85,000 and single taxpayers with AGI of less than $42,000 may claim the Hope Scholarship Tax Credit. There is a phase-out of the credit for those with AGI of $85,000 to $105,000 for married taxpayers, or $42,000 to $52,000 for single taxpayers. These numbers are periodically revised, so check when the time comes. The credit is not available to taxpayers with AGI above those respective amounts.

This $1,500 tax credit per student applies to tuition and fees for the first two years of post-secondary education. To claim a Hope Scholarship Tax Credit, the student must be enrolled at least half-time for at least one academic period, and must not have completed the first two years of undergraduate study. The credit cannot be claimed for more than two years for any one student. The amount of the credit is 100 percent of the first $1,000 of qualified tuition and fees, but not room and board The expenses must be paid by the taxpayer and the taxpayer must list the student as a dependent on his/her income tax return. Scholarships and grants (not student loans) reduce the amount of qualified tuition and fees that the taxpayer can claim in applying for this tax credit. Gifts, inheritances, and bequests count as income by the taxpayer "as paid" or "as income." Check IRS Publication 970, Tax Benefits for Higher Education, for the definition of modified adjusted gross income, and for the most up-to-date guidelines and income qualifications.

For a student's parents to claim a Hope Scholarship Tax Credit for tuition and fees, parents must also claim the student as a dependent. If parents do not claim the student as an exemption, the student can claim the Hope Scholarship Tax Credit. Finally, if the student has been convicted of a felony, the credit will be denied. You need to complete IRS Form 8863 with Form 1040 or 1040A to claim the tax credit.

Key Education Resources

Key offers private supplemental loans such as the Key Alternative Loan, which allows undergraduates enrolled full-time to share the cost of their education. Key also offers the Achiever Loan to parents with three different ways to finance college or prep school tuitions. This loan charges 4.5 percentage points over the 91-day Treasury bill rate adjusted quarterly. Fees range from 3 percent to 5 percent of the loan amount, depending on the repayment method.

The Key Career Loan is designed for adult students attending college part-time. Key also offers the Monthly Payment Plan, an interest-free budget plan administered through the school that allows families to make equal monthly payments to meet annual expenses. Key also offers several programs tailored to graduate students in specific fields such as law, business, medical, and dental schools. For more information call Key at (800) KEY-LEND or visit http://www.key.com.

The Lifetime Learning Tax Credit

This credit is available to college juniors and seniors, to students pursuing graduate and professional degrees, and for courses (even a single course) to acquire or improve your job skills. It is mainly intended to help defray college costs after the first two years, when the Hope Scholarship Tax Credit is no longer allowed.

Like the Hope Scholarship Tax Credit, the Lifetime Learning Tax Credit can be used only for tuition and fees. You cannot claim both the Hope and Lifetime Credits for the same student in the same year. The Lifetime Learning Tax Credit equals 20 percent of the amount of qualified tuition and fees up to $10,000 for a maximum credit of $2,000 per tax return for all eligible students. Note: This is a $2,000 limit per return, not per student. You don't get another tax credit for each additional child.

The family income limits, to qualify for the Lifetime Learning Tax Credit, are the same as for the Hope Scholarship program. The amount of the credit is gradually reduced based on your adjusted gross income. Check IRS publications 970 for the definition of modified adjusted gross income and for the most up-to-date guidelines or income qualifications. Colleges will issue an IRS Form 1098-T before January 31 of the next calendar year. You need to complete IRS Form 8863 with Form 1040 or 1040A to claim the tax credit.

Smart tip: Consult IRS Publication 970, "Tax Benefits for Higher Education," for specific rules on eligibility and claiming these tax credits. Visit the website www.irs.gov or call toll free at 1-800-TAX-FORM (1-800-829-3676 to obtain more information.

Comparison of Education Credits

Hope Scholarship Tax Credit	Lifetime Learning Tax Credit
Up to $1500 credit per eligible student	Up to $2,000 credit per *return*
Available only until the first two years of post-secondary education are completed	Available for all years of post-secondary education and for courses to acquire or improve job skills
Available only for two years per eligible student	Available for an unlimited number of years
Student must be pursuing an undergraduate degree or other recognized education credential	Student does not need to be pursuing a degree or other recognized education credential
Student must be enrolled at least half-time for at least one academic period beginning during the year	Available for one or more courses
No felony or drug conviction on student's record	Felony or drug conviction rules do not apply

Some Considerations When Claiming a Hope Scholarship or Lifetime Learning Credit

If you have three children in college your Hope Credit may be as high as $4500 but your Lifetime Learning Credit will never exceed $2000 per year. With the Lifetime Learning Credit, the student doesn't have to be enrolled at least half-time, and there is no limit on the number of years the credit may be taken. However, you may not claim a Hope Credit and a Lifetime Learning Credit for the same student in the same tax year. These numbers are periodically revised, so check when the time comes.

Both the Hope Credit and the Lifetime Learning Credit belong to the person who claims the student as a dependent, even if someone else pays the expenses. If no one claims the student as a dependent, the student may claim the credit, even if someone else pays the expenses.

Military Loans

The military offers a great way to save on college. For example, the child or spouse of a veteran who died or was seriously disabled because of military service may be entitled to an education benefit.

National Service Corporation

Students can pay off their government loans through work in the National Service Corporation. Such work may include positions in state or local government, as well as in educational, environmental, law enforcement, or social activities. Those entering the program could pay off as much as $5000 worth of student loans for every year of service, up to $10,000. For the latest information on all federal programs call (800) 4-Fed-AID.

Nellie Mae

Formerly known as the New England Education Loan Marketing Association, Nellie Mae offers the EXCEL and SHARE programs, which will lend from $2,000 or more to the cost of education minus the amount of other financial aid received by the student. The one-year renewable loans charge the prime rate plus 1.2 percent for the first year, plus an additional 1 percent in subsequent years; they are adjusted monthly. Nellie Mae charges a guarantee fee of 7 percent. You may repay both principal and interest on the loan or interest for up to four years while the student is still enrolled in school. Your child can repay the loan over as many as 20 years. For more information call (800) 367-8848 or visit the Nellie Mae website at http://www.nelliemae.com.

U.S. Armed Forces Reserve Officer
Training Corp (ROTC)

ROTC is an acronym for Reserve Officer Training Corps, the military's college-based program for officer training. This program can offer both college financial aid assistance and a post-college career in the Army, Navy, Marines, or Air Force. No monetary payback is required. High school students should talk to an Armed Forces recruiter or a guidance counselor during early spring of their junior year. College students can contact the ROTC office on their campus.

Eligibility criteria for ROTC include the following:

- You must be actively enrolled in a participating school
- You must pass stringent physical examinations
- You must achieve satisfactory scores on the college entrance examinations (for example, SAT or ACT) required by the school
- You must commit to active and inactive duty as required by the military after completion of school
- You must meet specific military selection criteria (such as character evaluation, passing a military written exam, etc.)
- You must meet other miscellaneous requirements set by each branch of the military

Potential applicants should speak to their guidance counselor or a local military recruiter about this program. Generally, college students must have at least two years of study remaining and should visit the ROTC building on or near campus to find out details.

Students in a ROTC program can expect to receive either a two- or four-year tuition scholarship; non-scholarship programs exist, too. Scholarships pay for your ROTC books and lab fees as well as some or all of your other college expenses. A monthly nontaxable stipend of around $100 is commonplace and helps cover some of your personal expenses. Depending on the size of the scholarship, post-college military commitment is usually four years of active duty and four years of reserve duty (time commitments vary). In all cases, ROTC students must complete military course work in addition to their regular academic course work.

Sallie Mae

Sallie Mae (formerly the Student Loan Marketing Association), which buys and receives federally insured educational loans made by lenders, has introduced several programs to reward borrowers who make on-time payments on their Stafford loans by reducing their interest rates. For more details on these programs, call the Sallie Mae Service Center at (800) 524-9100 or the College Answer Service at (800) 831-5626.

The Education Resources Institute (TERI)

TERI lends a minimum of $2,000 to the cost of education minus financial aid per year per child at the prime rate plus 1.5 to 2 percentage points, adjusted monthly with no cap. There are no fees and your child can repay as much as 25 years. TERI also offers the Professional Education Plan (PEP) for graduate students. For more information, call TERI at (800) 255-8374 or go to http://www.teri.com.

The Military

The entire college tuition, plus a monthly allowance, will be paid if a student attends one of the military academies, such as West Point for the U.S. Army, Annapolis for the U.S. Navy, or the Air Force Academy. Thereafter, a student must serve in the military for a specific number of years after graduation.

You should apply to the academies during your junior year in high school. If you would rather combine military training with education at a public or private university you can apply to the U.S. Army or Air Force, which run their own Reserve Officer Training Corps (ROTC) program, while the U.S. Navy and Marines operate a combined program. All ROTC programs offer both two-year and four-year terms. To enroll in ROTC you must be a high school graduate and be physically and academically qualified. After graduation and at least two years in the reserve, you must serve at least four years of active duty in the service for which they were trained. ROTC programs also offer various specialty training courses, such as for doctors, nurses, and engineers. These programs can give you a solid marketable skill, making it easier to get a job once you complete the military service. ROTC programs require that reservists attend both regular classes and ROTC courses while on campus. For more details about the ROTC talk to a military recruiter.

10

Around the Globe

Study Abroad Guide

Financial aid is given for performing artists interested in studying abroad. If you are in college, talk to your financial aid office to find out what kind of award programs are available for spending time abroad. Individual scholarships are available for students wanting to pursue research in a specific field. Private foundations award a variety of grants for research, travel, and performances abroad. Various student exchange programs are available as well.

If your study abroad program costs more than what you normally pay, ask your financial aid office to consider the higher costs and give you aid. If studying abroad costs less, you should expect the normal aid award to be reduced. Your financial aid office may require a budget for your study abroad program to ensure that you are not awarded too much aid; that is, more than the cost of your education.

Federal aid can legally be used to study abroad as long as the program you attend has been approved for credit by your home institution. Federal law allows the use of aid to cover all reasonable costs of study abroad, including round-trip transportation, tuition and fees for the program, living costs, passport and visa fees, health insurance, etc.

College students in the performing arts who are eligible for federal loans, grants, and scholarships may use their aid in overseas programs approved by their home universities, but the programs have to be for credit. You will find it easiest to use federal or state aid if you go on a study abroad program run by your school. Some study abroad programs have scholarships for their students. Your campus might provide scholarships if you go on an approved program or one run by your institution.

It is legal to use federal grants, work-study, or loans for study abroad, but you can only get aid from a school where you are enrolled in a degree program, and you must be enrolled at least half-time (or full-time in some cases) while you get the aid. You have to maintain enrollment at your "home" campus (where you plan to get your degree) and your home campus must agree that the credit earned abroad is "approved." Under these circumstances, your home campus can award federal aid even if you are going abroad on a program sponsored by another U.S. school or by a foreign institution.

A few scholarships are provided to U.S. students by foreign governments and there are increasing numbers of scholarships available to minority and nontraditional students. Information about these types of scholarships can be found by contacting your study abroad office.

There are a few scholarships specifically for undergraduate study abroad. One of the well-known undergraduate scholarships is provided by Rotary International. This service organization has a yearly nationwide competition for high school, graduate, and undergraduate students. Awards range from travel grants to full cost grants.

The U.S. government provides scholarships specifically for undergraduate and graduate study abroad. The National Security Education Program (NSEP) provides scholarships for study in nontraditional countries. Awards are made after a highly competitive national process. If you get a scholarship from NSEP, you will be expected to complete a service requirement. Your campus should have an NSEP representative who can give you more information about this program. Check with your study abroad officer for details.

Many state aid programs follow the same rules and regulations as the federal government. If your state does this you should be able to use state aid for study abroad based programs approved by your home campus. In some cases, state grants or scholarships may be restricted to use in that state.

Packing Your Bags for Travel Abroad

When planning your departure from the United States to study in another country, there is more to it than simply packing your bags and heading to the airport with the ticket in hand. The length of your stay means you will need to give consideration to things like your passport, any necessary visas, and what form of money you will bring. Some countries may require you to get specific medical injections or preventive pills.

Passports

U.S. citizens are required to have a passport for entry into almost any country, even Canada and Mexico. If your destination doesn't currently require a passport, it is recommended that you obtain one.

Passport fees fluctuate. Currently, the cost of a U.S. passport for an adult 16 years and older is $97. This includes the passport fee of $55, a security fee of $12, and an execution fee of $30. An expedited service is also available for an additional $60. If you are required to obtain any visas, you will need your passport even further in advance.

All first-time applicants must apply in person. Applications can often be obtained from your local post office. You may be required to present your passport for identification at various times when you are abroad. It is a good idea to keep it with you in a secure place. Should your passport be lost or stolen, immediately file a police report with the local authorities and contact the nearest U.S. embassy or consulate for assistance with a replacement.

Visas

With the exception of a short tourist visit, most countries require that you obtain a visa for entry into their country. A visa is simply a stamp or endorsement placed in your passport by a foreign government that permits you to visit that country for a specified time, for a specified purpose. If you are studying abroad, you will likely be required to obtain a special student visa. Unless your study abroad program is facilitating this process on your behalf, you will need to contact the nearest embassy or consulate of the countries that you will be visiting to find out what their visa requirements and/or processes are. Depending on the country, it can take several weeks to process your visa, so be sure to allow for plenty of time.

International Student Identity Card

The International Student Identity Card, or ISIC, is a basic travel card for students going abroad. The ISIC is issued to more than 5 million students each year by academic and student travel organizations in more than eighty countries around the world. The concept of the ISIC is basic: it provides a consistent form of proof of student status that is internationally recognized, regardless of the country you are in. It provides you with a variety of discounts, including special student air fare, international phone calls, local discounts at tourist attractions and restaurants and more. U.S. International Student Identity Cards also provide the cardholder with free basic medical and accidental insurance while traveling abroad, along with a toll-free hotline for travelers in need of financial or medical assistance.

Online Resources for Study Abroad

Getting an idea of what is available can make a difference in your quest for seeking a study abroad program. Here are some places to get started on study abroad programs.

- Service Civil International (SCI)
Description: Provides information on volunteer and work camp opportunities. An example includes the opportunity to work with children's theater groups in Kosovo.
Website address: www.sci-ivs.org
Contact information: 5474 Walnut Level Road
Crozet, VA 22932
Phone: (434) 823-9003
Fax: (206) 350-6585
E-mail: sciinfo@sci-ivs.org

- Volunteers for Peace
Description: Offers information on a variety of volunteer opportunities abroad.
Website address: www.vfp.org
Contact information: 1034 Tiffany Road
Belmont, VT 05730
Phone: 802 259 2759
Fax: 802 259 2922
E-mail: vfp@vfp.org

- Council on International Education Exchange
Description: Offers exchange, volunteer, and work opportunities throughout the world.
Website address:
Contact information: 7 Custom House Street, Third Floor
Portland, ME 04101
Phone: (800) 40-STUDY
Fax: (207) 553-7699
E-mail: contact@ciee.org
Website: www.ciee.org

- Institute of International Education
Description: Institute of International Education offers information on international study and volunteer opportunities.
Website address: www.iie.org
Contact information: 809 United Nations Plaza
New York, NY 10017-3580
Phone: (212) 883-8200
Fax: (212) 984-5452
E-mail: iieresearch@iie.org.

- The Rotary Foundation of Rotary International
Description: A worldwide organization of business and professional leaders

that provide humanitarian service, encourages high ethical standards in all vocations and helps build goodwill and peace in the world.
Website address: www.rotary.org
Contact information: One Rotary Center
1560 Sherman Avenue
Evanston, IL 60201
Phone: (847) 866-3000
Fax: (847) 328-8554
E-mail: Not available

• American Friends Service Committee
Description: Carries out service, development, social justice, and peace programs throughout the world.
Website address: www.afsc.org
Contact information: 1501 Cherry Street
Philadelphia, PA 19102
Phone: (215) 241-7000
Fax: (215) 567-7275
E-mail: Not available

• Global Volunteers
Description: Provides short term service opportunities on community development programs in host communities abroad.
Website address: http://www.globalvolunteers.org/
Contact information: 375 east Little Canada Road
Saint Paul, MN 55117-1628
Phone: (800) 467-1074
Fax: (651) 482-0915
E-mail: email@globalvolunteers.org

• CARE
Description: Works with poor communities in more than 70 countries around the world to find lasting solutions to poverty.
Website address: www.careusa.org
Contact information: 151 Ellis Street
Atlanta, GA 30303
Phone: (404) 681-2552
Fax: (404) 589-2651
E-mail: info@care.org

11

Working Along the Way

Work Study

Federal Work Study (FWS) provides part-time jobs for undergraduate and graduate students. It is a form of working your way through college with government help. Walk into any office on any campus and the student you see filing papers or answering phones is probably earning work-study money. College Work Study is a part-time job at the college or university you attend. It pays you money to offset your educational expense.

Work-study is a campus-based program. This program is administered by schools participating in the program. Each school gets an annual lump sum from the government to pay a percentage of a student's wages at campus or community jobs. The jobs are lined up by the college financial aid office and assigned as part of a student's aid package. Each job pays an hourly wage. Any student with a need is eligible for work-study. The higher your need, the more likely the financial aid folks will offer you a job.

Most work-study jobs must relate to the student's major and can be found on campus or with nonprofit organizations. The number of allowable work-study hours any student may accumulate is closely regulated by the financial aid office in an effort to avoid situations whereby the individual earns more than his or her established need. Your financial aid advisor can tell you how work schedules are set and what circumstances must exist in order for you to participate in the program. The federal government pays 75 percent of wages, while the employer pays the remaining 25 percent. Schools determine their own deadlines (usually shortly after January 1).

Eligibility for Work-study

Students applying for work-study must meet some requirements:

- You must be working on your first undergraduate or graduate degree
- You must show adequate financial need, as determined by the school
- You can attend school full-time, half-time, or less than half-time
- You must apply before application deadlines have passed
- You must find a suitable work-study job if the school has not provided one for you
- You must be a U.S. citizen or eligible non-citizen

Doing Odd Jobs to Finance Your Education

Temporary jobs provide a great opportunity for full-time students to make extra money during the summer. You can get cash for books, clothes, and other legitimate expenses. During the summer months, college-age applicants typically work 40 hours a week, and most temporary services pay at the end of every week. Office positions are most likely in word processing, typing, and filing, although light industrial work is also available. Temp services usually put applicants through a series of office skill tests and then send them out to jobs that match their qualifications. Also, look into signing up for an internship. You will receive college credit based on hours worked, and most internship jobs also provide a small salary or stipend. You can also do odd jobs at the community church, grocery store, bookstore and virtually any other place that has a need for help and is able to pay.

Sometimes a side job off campus may lead to a full-time career after graduation. For example, if you are working as a receptionist at a local dance school and doing some bookkeeping, it might be a stepping stone in your career after graduation, especially if you are a performing arts major.

Campus Jobs for International Students

International students (who have no permanent residency status) have many restrictions about work and earning money during their time in the United States. Legally, they are only allowed to work on-campus jobs, unless their visa requirements specify otherwise. Usually the on campus jobs for undergraduate students may not always be the office-space jobs given to work-study students. Often, however, international students are willing to work and perform tasks that may require physical labor and long working hours in order to make a few dollars a week. Cafeteria jobs, physical plant maintenance, and library work are some of the on-campus jobs offered to international students. Check with your campus regulations or the international students center for further information.

12

The Acting Connection

Contacting Agents

An agent submits actors for roles, coordinates their auditions, and then negotiates their contracts when they are cast for parts. It is essential to be represented by an agent if you want to work as a professional actor in Hollywood. Targeting the right agent is key. An agent acts as a middleman between you and anyone who wants to hire you for your acting skills. Your agent can greatly influence your acting career, so you need to find the best possible agent for you who meets your personal acting needs.

It is not uncommon for an actor to have more than one agent. Some actors have an agent for commercials and another agent for theatrical work. If you are in a major market like New York or Los Angeles you will probably have better luck targeting the commercial talent agents first. If you are in a small market the agents probably will all be full-service agents, so you will just target any that you can find.

One reason that you, as an actor, need an agent is that only agents (and managers) have access to the Breakdowns, a service that many casting directors use to list roles they are casting. Also, having an agent legitimizes you by showing that someone believes in your acting ability. Additionally, an agent can open some doors by using his or her connections, which hopefully will land you more auditions and ultimately more work.

No legitimate agent asks you for a fee. All you need is for an agency to think that you have strong potential to make money as an actor. Any legitimate agency makes money only when the actor works, with the compensation being ten percent of the client's earnings. This is regulated by the Screen Actor's Guild and is standard throughout the industry. Union-franchised agents can charge you 10 percent of your salary for a job they helped you secure. This 10 percent covers costs of sending you out on auditions, bringing casting directors to see you in showcases, advising you, counseling you, and submitting you for work regionally or nationally.

However, it can be somewhat difficult to actually find an agent to represent you, if you are a newcomer to Hollywood. The reason is that there are thousands and thousands of actors seeking representation. SAG members have a better chance than non-union folks, but even most of them have to work hard to attract an agent.

Don't be too quick to start approaching agents until you have some kind of experience. The more credits and experience you have, the better off you will be. If you want a good agent, then you have to prove that you are a good actor. It is the agent's business to seek out talented artists and help them develop their careers. It is the agent who can open doors and lead the performer through them, and who can give suggestions that advance a career.

After you have made the decision to go with a particular agent, you have to sign a contract with that agent before he or she will actively represent you. When you sign a contract with an agent you are agreeing that this particular agent will exclusively represent you. When you are signed, both you and the agency will sign a SAG Talent Agency Contract (either TV/theatrical or commercials), which will be valid for one year. However, after the first 151 days, if you have not worked for at least 10 days in the preceding 90 days, you may be released from a TV/theatrical contract.

Never sign any contract without reading and understanding it as completely as possible. Be especially careful if you are signing a contract with a non-union–franchised agency because if you have a problem you won't have the union to protect you. A union-franchised agent will likely use a standard contract that the agency has used before.

Places to Look for Agents

There are a group of agencies in Hollywood collectively known as "The Big Five." They are International Creative Management (ICM), Creative Artists Agency (CAA), the William Morris Agency, United Talent Agency, and Endeavor. There are other very powerful and well-respected agencies, but these five combine to represent the majority of the most powerful actors in the industry.

One way to discover potential agents is to contact unions to request lists of franchised agents. Working with a franchised agent is best because he or she has agreed to follow union guidelines for working with actors.

Contact the following unions for lists of franchised agents.

- Screen Actors Guild National Office, 5757 Wilshire Blvd. Los Angeles, CA 90036-3600
Phone: (323) 954-1600
Website: www.sag.org
- Actor's Equity Association National Office 165 West 46th Street, 15th Floor, New York, NY 10036
Phone: (212) 869-8530
Website: www.actorsequity.org
- American Federation of Television and Radio Artists National Office, 260 Madison Avenue, New York, NY 10016-2402
Phone: 212 532 0800
Website: www.aftra.org

Contacting the Gatekeepers—Cast Your Call

Casting directors are the people who actually cast movies, TV shows, theater and commercials. These are the people whom you ultimately want to meet. The best way to meet a casting director is to have an agent.

Casting directors do the following:

- Analyze a script in order to break down the roles to determine the types of actors needed
- Determining the auditions needed for certain performances
- Choosing several potential actors for each role

Agents must always maintain the favor of casting directors, as casting directors are the potential buyers of the agent's clients' services. Casting directors may work directly for a single production company, or they may freelance and work for several production companies on a temporary basis.

Although casting directors sometimes advertise open casting calls in newspapers, more often they print a list of roles available and the type of people they want for each role, such as a young housewife or a tall basketball player. Such websites only give you information about the company; they don't provide breakdown lists of available roles.

They then send this list of available roles to a company, such as the Breakdown Services (www.breakdownservices.com), which gets paid to distribute this list to various agents.

The best way to create your own opportunities to audition is to contact casting directors yourself. By contacting casting directors on your own, you can increase the chances of getting a particular role without having to attend an open casting call or through an audition arranged by an agent. The best way to contact a casting director is to mail your headshot and resume to him or her and ask for a general interview.

Prepare Your Cover Letter

Many actors try cramming their whole "hopes and dreams autobiography" into the cover letter, until it resembles a chapter from a novel. The agent hasn't the time, nor the interest, to be an editor. Any submission that takes more than 15 seconds to scan through and read will likely be filed in the trash.

Cover letters should be short and sweet. You are telling the agent that you are an actor and you want representation. You can also add a few brief items that might give the agent more information about your skills and training. Write a cover letter for every agent you are contacting. Address the agent personally. "Dear Liz" is fine, but "To whom it may concern" is not. Make sure you put the agent's name on the envelope as well as the agency name. If you do this, it is more likely to get to the agent's desk. Keep it clean, simple, and professional.

Mailing cover letters can be costly and time-consuming, but it can be successful too. Though agents receive tons of mail on a daily basis from new faces, many actors have obtained representation this way.

Sample Cover Letter

There is no strict way of writing a cover letter. Here is a basic one:

Sonoma Bryman
5555 Movers Road
Los Angeles, CA 00000
sonoma@movesroad.com
Phone: (310) 000-0000

Jeffrey Sydney
Sudoni Talent Agency
Los Angeles, CA 90028

Dear Jeffrey,

I am currently studying acting at the Young Acting Talent Center in Hollywood and I am seeking representation. I am fluent in two foreign languages: Spanish and Chinese.

I am actively auditioning each week for independent film projects and plays and booking roles regularly. Enclosed is a current headshot and resume for your consideration. Please contact me when you are ready for someone of my type.

Sincerely,

Sonoma Bryman

Here is another short letter:

Agency Fish
1234 Longstead Avenue
Los Angeles, CA

Attn: Ms. Mary Bryce

Please accept my photos and resume for possible consideration of future representation. I will contact your offices next week to verify your receipt of this package.

Thank you very much for your time,

Seth Birmingham

Audition Tips

The audition can open doors in an acting career. It can also be the source that paves the way for getting financial aid to pursue your acting goals. Although there are no set guidelines to follow when auditioning, here are some standard rules.

You need to be prepared for your first audition, and your subsequent auditions. Being well prepared will ensure that you won't be overly-nervous on the day and that you will turn all of your attention onto your performance. Bear in mind that most of the people there are equally as anxious as you, so you need to be calm, collected and positive. Always have your headshot and actor's resume prepared. An 8" × 10" headshot is standard, with your resume attached to the back.

You may be expected to do a cold reading. A cold reading is similar to a sight reading for classical musicians. This is where you will be given a few lines to practice until you are called to perform. Use this time to practice, not chat with other actors. If you are called to "slate," this means you are to give your name, contact details and agents details (if applicable) in front of the camera before your performance. Be sure to look directly at the camera when doing so, and lead directly into your performance when you are finished "slating."

Expect to see a sign-up sheet when you arrive. Make sure you complete it. Bring with you your Social Security number and your agent's contact details if this is a call for union actors. If you have been asked to prepare a monologue, you are expected to know your lines and will be given around two minutes to complete your piece in front of the casting agent/director.

Be courteous to your judges. Always say hello, smile, be friendly and be confident. Don't try to be too familiar and flashy with the judges. You are not here to have lunch with them, but to try to get a role. Exhibit a small amount of eagerness and excitement to be auditioning for them. Also, don't show that you are desperate. Sometimes, when you show that you are too interested, people seem to want to shy away. Let them see you believe in the role you are auditioning for.

Research any background information you can on the casting director or others you know will be behind the table, such as the producer, director, assistant, etc. Chances are you won't be engaged in much conversation, but it will be impressive to them if you actually get a chance to make a brief comment on the last film they cast, an actor they worked with, or an interview you read about them.

Your audition may be held in someone's personal office or studio. Respect your surroundings. You must also be respectful to the other actors attending the audition. Don't consider the other actors around you as your competition and become discourteous or rude. These actors may well end up being your co-stars. Always be friendly, cordial and most importantly, professional.

Arrive at your audition early. Give yourself 15 minutes before you are expected at the audition. Being late not only looks terrible and may mean you are excluded from this audition, but it will mean that you are not relaxed and could hinder your chances of success.

Dress appropriately. There is no specific uniform or way to dress, but a typical experienced actor will wear something that does not take the shine away from his talent. A good thing to mention is that you should wear something that reflects the role. Men will find that a light blue shirt and khakis are good. Are you auditioning for an office worker? Then wear a tie and a jacket with it. Be more casual without the jacket and tie if it is appropriate to that role.

Have fun. If you don't enjoy what you do, no one else will. It's a long journey and auditioning is part of the process and something you will be doing your entire career. Yes, even when you are a big celebrity, you will still have to fight (audition) for the lead in that Spielberg blockbuster.

Take Your Best Shot: The Performing Artist's Guide to Getting a Great Headshot

A headshot is a standard requirement for actors and other performing artists, such as musicians, comedians, and dancers. It is, put rather simply, a photograph taken from the shoulders upwards. A headshot is used for many reasons. Your headshot is used by casting directors, casting associates, talent agents, directors and producers. It is also submitted by musicians, dancers, puppeteers, circus performers, and comedians in situations, when they are asking for aid. While this chapter on headshots was written with the actor in mind, artists in other performing fields can use the information as well.

A professional-looking headshot is key for actors, pianists, violinists, comedians and everyone in the performing arts industry. Don't send Polaroids, Xeroxes, or other photos in place of a professional headshot. At a point where you might be seeking just movie extra work, then a standard photo will suffice. This can help keep the cost of your headshot to a minimum.

Start by sending out pictures, about twenty to thirty agents at a time. Hopefully you will get several callbacks. With your picture, attach a brief letter explaining a little about yourself and that you are seeking representation. Short, direct and polite notes are best because they seem most professional. Let some of your personality come out too, but don't go overboard.

Choosing a photographer can be a little tricky, as there are many con artists out there, waiting to prey on fresh beginners trying to embark on a performing arts career. Ask to see some of their work and get pricing information. Make sure you know exactly what is included in your shoot. Find out if you can select high-resolution images burned onto a CD. Make sure you get a release from the photographer if you are going to have the headshots reproduced yourself and ask if you can get small resolution files (.jpegs) for web use.

Paying attention to the following may increase your chances of breaking into the acting industry. Some agencies or casting directors might ask you to send the images digitally and not in the form of hard copies. In such cases, use your discretion. The requirements may vary according to your circumstances.

Choose the Right Photo Size

Most people in the acting industry use headshots that are 8 × 10 inches in size. However, with movie extra work, the casting associate or extras casting agency will sometimes just require a 3" × 5" photo. You may supply your actor's headshot in black and white or in color if you prefer, as this is fast becoming the industry norm. Some agencies might ask you to send the images digitally.

Selecting an Outfit

Choose the right outfit. Make sure it is well pressed and clean with no visible threads or stains. Make sure your attire fits properly. It should not be too tight and should lay well when you move. Avoid white or very light-colored shirts for your headshot. White draws the eye. Dark or mid-tones are better and will draw attention to your face. Don't use wild or big prints and absolutely no logos.

Be Well Groomed

Guys should be clean-shaven, unless they are going for the scruffy look. Don't make any drastic hair style changes or cuts right before your shoot. Hair should be in a style that is easily obtainable. Simple is better. Women and girls should generally wear hair loose and down for a headshot. You have to be able to look like your headshot when you go to a casting. Avoid Mohawks and too much funky hair color. You don't know whether it might work for or against you.

Work with Your Photographer

On the day of your shoot, arrive on time or early. Relax, and try to have fun. Listen to your photographer, and if you have any questions, or you don't understand his/her direction, ask. After the shoot, try to review the proofs with the photographer if possible. He or she can help you choose your best look. Some photographers have more patience than others to help you decide which photos to edit and which to reject.

Provide Contact Information

Write your name on the front of the headshot page. Include an e-mail address as well. E-mail is an easy way to contact actors and schedule an audition. If you are worried about privacy, create a hotmail account specifically for that purpose.

Send Your Headshot in an Easy-to-Open Envelope

Nothing is worse than trying to tear open 500 glued-shut headshot envelopes. The best approach is this: Buy clasp envelopes and clasp them. If you are worried about the contents falling out, or Peeping-Tom postal officials, place a small piece of tape over the flap.

Write a Brief Handwritten Note

You might be surprised how much difference a note can make. It is your chance to get a few additional seconds of the casting director's time, and to make your case for why he or she should call you in. Remember, with a handwritten note, you are not asking for the part here, but only for an audition.

Union Members

Many studios, producers, and directors exploited the desperation of actors in the early days of show business. Actors then banded together and formed unions to protect themselves. Various unions have increased pay for actors, protected actor's rights to work in clean and sanitary working conditions, restricted the time limits that actors can be expected to work each day, provided legal counsel, and even offered health and retirement plans.

You can look into the requirements for, and benefits of, joining professional associations and unions, international, national, regional, and local. You don't have to join a union to work as an actor, but the highest-paying and most prestigious acting roles almost always go to union members, so when you have reached a point where you can vie for those roles, joining a union is a wise thing to do.

Although a union's main job is to protect your rights and ensure that you are paid fairly, they also can offer a variety of other services that can make your quest for an acting career and financial aid much simpler. Many unions offer seminars and workshops to help their members find work. They maintain bulletin boards where actors can post classified advertisements. They also offer information on financial aid. Unions provide listings of libraries where members can borrow and study scripts. As a union member you may qualify for a whole range of additional benefits, including credit union membership, health insurance, pension plans, financial aid, and even access to a retirement home.

Some unions provide assistance in the event of an employer dispute. Others include free assistance with income tax preparation (SAG's VITA Program). A SAG-AFTRA credit union also offers members low-interest credit cards. There are also casting lines by SAG and AFTRA that list casting announcements, and bulletin boards in union offices with notices posted by other members regarding apartments or houses for rent, automobiles for sale, airlines tickets, and more.

Another important benefit of being a union member is health insurance for qualified performers. Union membership provides access to agents and casting directors through guild-sponsored seminars and showcases. Actors can attend these free events by preregistering in advance. The focus of some events is purely informational, while others offer actors an opportunity to showcase scenes or perform cold readings for industry people. In addition, another organization, the SAG Conservatory, offers classes and workshops, along with question-and-answer evenings with prominent casting directors in town. All of these events are free of charge.

If you are getting started in acting, you may not want to join any union right away because joining the union effectively eliminates you from working on nonunion productions. As a beginner you may want to get experience working in the numerous (but lower-paying) nonunion productions first.

Be prepared: when you decide to join a union, the cost to join may be fairly expensive, usually over $1,000. Also, after joining a union you must pay dues regularly, but the regular dues are much less expensive than the initial union membership dues. The regular dues usually run $100 or more, depending on how much you are actually earning as an actor.

In the world of entertainment the main union is the Associated Actors and Artists of America, also known as the Four A's. Within the Associated Actors and Artists of America are several branches that cover specific fields of acting. The three most popular actors' unions are:

- The Screen Actors Guild (SAG)
- Actors' Equity Association (AEA also known as Equity)
- American Federation of Television & Radio Artists (AFTRA)

The Screen Actors Guild (SAG)

There is a long history regarding the development of the Screen Actors Guild, commonly known as SAG. Since its formation in 1933 the Guild has grown to approximately 90,000 members and continues to act in the interests of all professional actors through a process of collective bargaining with producers. As an actor in Hollywood it is highly recommended that you, at some point, seek membership in the SAG if you want to have a career in television or film. Most feature films and television programs are union projects and can hire only SAG performers. Additionally, being a member of the union is important because it legitimizes you as an actor. SAG also maintains a list of agencies that have agreed to follow SAG guidelines for working with actors. Unfortunately for newcomers, getting into SAG is a difficult task, as certain requirements must be met.

SAG's eligibility requirements. Becoming a member of SAG is one of the biggest hurdles many newcomers face. You can't just show up and join. You have to become eligible. Once you are eligible, you then have to pay an initiation fee plus semiannual dues.

Following are several ways a non-union person can beat the system and become eligible to join, as there is no standard route or typical path to follow.

1. Being employed under a SAG contract

The most common way to join SAG is through a clause known as the Taft-Hartley Act, which allows non-union members to work up to 30 days on a union production. Officially, union productions can only hire union members, but because that would prevent new actors from ever breaking into show business, the Taft-Hartley Act gives a newcomer a way to become a union member.

In the event you are hired to work on a union project, then the Taft-Hartley Act will be applied to you. It states that a non union performer can be hired to work as a union performer and then work with that status for another thirty days, but after that time period that person must join the union if he or she wants to work "union" again. To join you simply need to have a letter from a producer of a SAG-signatory project that states that he or she plans to hire you for his or her particular production.

2. You have worked a principal role in another union

If you have been a paid-up member of an affiliated performers' union for at least one year and you have worked at least once as a principal performer in that union's jurisdiction, then you are eligible to join SAG. The affiliated performers' unions are: AFTRA (American Federation of Television and Radio Artists), AEA (Actor's Equity Association, AGVA (American Guild of Variety Artists), AGMA (American Guild of Musical Artists) and ACTRA (Alliance of Canadian Cinema, TV and Radio Artists). To join, you need to mail a copy of your principal performer's contract to the SAG membership office. Once your eligibility has been verified, you will be contacted to schedule an appointment.

3. You have worked as a SAG extra player for three days

You are not supposed to do union extra work if you are nonunion, but to be eligible to join SAG, nonunion people have to do union extra work for three days. There are several ways to accomplish this. A surprising number of professional actors today have been able to join SAG by working as union extras for three days at some point early in their careers.

American Federation of Television and Radio Artists (AFTRA)

As the name implies, the American Federation of Television and Radio Artists (www.aftra.org) covers anyone involved in television, radio, and broadcasting, which include entertainment programming, industrial programming, and educational media, such as software distributed on CD-ROM.

AFTRA governs television programs shot on video, such as sitcoms

> **Warning:** Don't ever sign up with a non–SAG affiliated talent agency or you may not be treated fairly. A non–SAG agent likely won't hear of the higher-paying union roles available, either.

and soap operas, as well as radio. Anyone can join AFTRA at any time. The initiation is a one-time fee plus semiannual dues. Many actors do this when they first come to Hollywood, but it is really not necessary. Even if you eventually want to join AFTRA, you can work on an AFTRA program as a principal or extra for thirty days without being a member. After that, AFTRA will hold any future checks until your initiation fee is paid in full.

AFTRA has an open-door policy. Make an appointment with the membership department of an AFTRA office, fork over the hefty initiation fee, plus dues for the first six months, and you are in. Simple as that. By virtue of the Taft-Hartley Act, an actor can work under the auspices of AFTRA for up to thirty days without joining the union. After the initial thirty-day period, the actor becomes a "must join" in the eyes of AFTRA, and indeed, "must join" before working again.

Actors' Equity Association (AEA)

The Actors' Equity Association (www.actorsequity.org), which is also known simply as "Equity," covers actors who perform in theater. Equity is the oldest of all the actors' unions (formed in 1919) and began as a way to counterbalance the power producers held over actors. Actors in theater often got paid marginal wages (if they got paid at all), were forced to endure horrible working conditions, never got paid extra for working on holidays, had to make or buy their own costumes, and could be forced to attend unlimited numbers of rehearsals for any length of time-all without any pay, of course.

An actor is eligible to join Actors' Equity Association after being a member of either AFTRA or SAG for one year and having performed a principal role within that union's jurisdiction. One can also become a member of Equity through the Equity Membership Candidate Program (EMC), which entails working for fifty weeks (forty if one passes a written test) at participating Equity theaters. Equity allows a one-year member of AFTRA who has worked for three days as an extra within AFTRA's jurisdiction to join Equity.

To protect its members, Equity forced producers to post sufficient advance funds to guarantee salaries and benefits, established minimum salaries and pay for rehearsal time, and even established rules forbidding producers to force actors to work in any theater that discriminated against audience members because of race, color, or creed.

> **Smart tip:** Working at a union's office, either as a volunteer or paid employee, is an excellent way to meet actors, writers, casting directors, and producers.

Like SAG, Equity has also established guidelines for how agents should treat actors. When looking for an agent, call your local Equity office and ask for a list of Equity-franchised agencies. A publication called the Ross Reports also lists agencies, so be sure to check both lists in case one list is more current than another. Then, contact those agencies only.

Warning: After you join Equity, never work on a non–Equity production, or else you could be fined and lose your Equity membership. Equity may allow its members to work in non–Equity productions that are sponsored by charities or religious organizations, but make sure that you get written permission first.

The three common ways to become a member of Equity include:

- Providing proof that you are wanted for a role in an Equity-recognized production company
- Working for up to 50 weeks in Equity productions (known as the Equity Membership Candidacy Program)
- Providing proof that you have been a paying member of an affiliated Four As guild (such as SAG or AFTRA) for at least a year and that you have had at least one role as a principal performer with that union

13

Investing Strategies

Art of Investing

The health of your financial status as a performing artist can affect the type of financial aid you can apply for and the aid you are likely to get. One of the first things you should keep in mind when filling out forms for federal aid or for your selected college is what factors are considered when the information you provide is evaluated.

Here are some things to note when applying for aid:

- *FAFSA submission*: The date of submission of the FAFSA should be considered carefully because the total amount of assets and marital status are reported as of the application date.
- *Avoid major purchases*: Beware of making big purchases prior to filling out your financial aid document. If you have been saving money for a big-dollar purchase, such as home repairs or a new car, you should buy it well before you submit the FAFSA. This purchase will reduce the assets reported on the FAFSA.
- *Base year income*: You should attempt to reduce your adjusted gross income and net worth for the "base year," which is the calendar year prior to requesting aid, e.g., calendar year 2007 for aid in 2008–2009. This can affect your financial aid.
- *Capital gains earnings*: You should attempt to minimize capital gains during the base year because capital gains are treated as income. More capital gains may mean less financial aid.
- *PLUS Loans*: After graduation, parents and graduate/professional students who borrowed through the Federal PLUS loan or alternative loan programs may want to convert these loans to a home equity

loan or line of credit in order to deduct the interest payments on their 1040 federal income tax return.

- *Your credit score*: Both private lenders and the federal government are interested in knowing if you are a good credit risk before they offer you a loan. Most loans and interest rates available to parents will be based on their credit report,

> **Smart tip:** A credit report can be ordered from one of the following credit bureaus:
> - Equifax: 1(800) 685-1111 or visit www.equifax.com
> - Experian: 1(888) 397-3742 or visit www.experian.com
> - Transunion: 1(800) 916-8800 or visit www.transunion.com
> - TRW: 1(800) 498-0965 or visit www.trwcredit.com

sometimes called a credit score. If you are planning to go to college, during your sophomore or junior year in high school your parents should check their credit status.

Borrowing Against Assets

If the total financial aid package for which you qualify is not adequate, or if you want to cut down on outside borrowing, you might consider your last option: taking a loan against your assets. You may have accumulated substantial equity in certain assets that you can borrow against at a lower interest rate than your other borrowing options.

The most obvious places to look for equity include the following:

- *Your company savings plan*: If you or your parents have participated in a salary reduction plan at work for several years, you probably have accumulated a substantial sum of money. Most employers will let you borrow against that money and have you repay the loan through payroll deduction. Interest rates charged on such loans are often quite favorable, at one or two percentage points more than the prime rate. However, borrow against your retirement savings only as a last resort. These plans are designed to provide long-term growth for your retirement years, not to pay college costs.

While you are investigating options at your company, ask the employee benefits department whether your firm provides college loans or scholarships to children of employees. Some companies, particularly large corporations, offer such loans at attractive, below-market interest rates.

- *Your home*: If you have paid down your mortgage and built up substantial equity in your home, you might be able to open a home-equity line of credit that charges only one to two percentage points more than the prime rate and allows you to repay it as quickly or as slowly as you wish, as long as you meet each month's minimum payment. Remember, however, your home is on the line. If you default, the bank will foreclose. You can open a home-equity credit line with a bank, savings and loan, credit union, or mortgage company.

Borrowing Against Retirement Plans

Qualified retirement plans and IRAs are most likely the largest cash resource available to parents. If you decide to obtain a loan from one of these sources, you need to discuss this borrowing with a qualified tax advisor or certified financial planner to determine whether there are any tax consequences.

Here are some suggested questions that need to be answered before you make the decision to borrow either from a retirement plan or an IRA account.

- Does your retirement plan allow you to borrow or withdraw money to pay for college?
- Is there a limit on the amount you can borrow? If yes, is all or a part of the distribution, taxable?
- Is there a 10 percent early distribution penalty?
- Is the interest rate competitive with other loans?
- What are the repayment requirements? Are they more or less favorable than other loans?
- How will an IRA distribution for college expenses impact your tax liability?
- Will you qualify for an education loan interest deduction on your federal tax return?

Traditional and Roth IRAs offer a tax deduction for contributions, and the funds may be used penalty-free for higher education. However, you are taxed on any withdrawals at your marginal income tax rate.

Under the current needs analysis, the value of your retirement plans is not considered an asset. Money that you save outside retirement accounts, including money in the child's name, is counted as an asset and reduces your eligibility for financial aid.

Therefore, it does not make sense to forego contributions to your retirement savings plans in order to save money in a taxable account for your child's college fund. When you do, you pay higher taxes both on your current income and on the interest and growth of this money. In addition to paying higher taxes, you are expected to contribute more to your child's educational expenses.

Beware: It is not recommended to use retirement plans for college expenses. They are not counted in the federal need analysis formula. If possible, use liquid assets such as cash in savings accounts first. This will reduce the amount of assets reported on the FAFSA. If you need money from your retirement fund, it is wiser to borrow from the retirement fund, if possible, and avoid any penalty from withdrawing money from the fund.

Tuition and Fees Deduction

As of 2006 a deduction of up to $4,000 for college tuition and related expenses is available for married taxpayers with AGI of less than $130,000 and for single taxpayers with AGI of less than $65,000. This is an above-the-line deduction, which means that you do not have to itemize your deductions to take advantage of this incentive. A deduction of up to $2,000 for college tuition and related expenses is available to married taxpayers with AGI as high as $160,000 and to single taxpayers with AGI as high as $80,000.

Reporting Your Home's Value

A common mistake people make is not accurately reporting their assets. This is especially true for such items as the value of a home, or of business assets such as equipment. While the federal government no longer considers home equity, most colleges will; and miscalculating the value of your home will cost you financial assistance.

Treatment of Home Equity and Other Assets

Your family's assets also include equity in real estate and businesses you own. Although the federal financial aid analysis no longer counts equity in your primary residence as an asset, many private (independent) schools continue to ask parents for this information when making their own financial aid determinations. Thus, paying down your home mortgage more quickly instead of funding retirement accounts can harm you financially. You may end up with less financial aid and pay more in taxes.

There are some important differences between filling out the government's Free Application for Federal Student Aid (FAFSA) and a college's financial aid form. For example, the government no longer considers the equity in your family's home when calculating the estimated family contribution (EFC). Many colleges, especially private schools, still do factor in home equity. This is why many financial advisors tell their clients it is a good idea to take out a home equity loan to reduce the family's perceived net worth.

If, for some reason, you did not want to be considered for nongovernment aid, then it might make sense to put more money into paying off your mortgage, where it will not count in the FAFSA calculations. But most parents and students want aid from all possible resources, so you still need to consider how home equity will affect your aid package.

Home Equity Lines of Credit/Home Equity Loans

Many families are in a position to pay some or all of college expenses by borrowing against the equity in their home. In taking out a home equity loan, the borrower will receive one lump sum payment and pay interest on the total principal borrowed. This loan is actually a second mortgage on the borrower's home.

The equity line of credit is flexible, lets you borrow what you need, and pays interest only on the amount actually used. The interest is usually a variable rate tied to the prime rate. Also, once the principal is repaid, it may be borrowed again.

Advantages include the following:

- One-time application (without having to renew or pay fees)
- Potential tax deductibility
- Funds are available when needed
- Funds are available to more than one sibling attending different schools
- Only pay interest on funds actually used
- Some lending institutions will not charge an application or closing fee
- Repayment up to 20 or more years depending on the size of your loan
- Various repayment plans, e.g., interest only initially, then regular repayment schedule

The following are some conditions for getting an equity line of credit:

- Borrower must be credit-worthy and have an acceptable debt-to-income ratio
- Borrower must be a homeowner (the home is collateral)
- Interest rate will vary with lender
- Interest paid may be tax deductible, but only if you itemize deductions on Form 1040. Check with tax advisor.

Your Life Insurance

With a permanent life insurance policy, you pay an annual premium to cover insurance expenses, plus an additional amount contributed to the cash value of the policy. The cash value grows tax-deferred. If you have amassed a large amount of cash value in the policy, you can usually borrow against it at a favorable rate to fund education expenses without owing any taxes. However, the amount you borrow from the policy

Smart tip: The Federal Trade Commission urges potential home equity borrowers to be aware of negative loan practices. Check out www.ftc.gov/bcp/conline/pubs/homes/eqscams.htm for additional information on negative loan practices.

reduces the death benefit, should you die before the loan is repaid. Again, consider this a last resort because such a loan will retard the growth of your cash value as well as lowering your death benefit by the amount of the loan.

Treatment of Assets in the Financial Aid Process

Generally, parental assets (not including equity in primary residence for federal methodology) are assessed up to 5.6 percent and student assets at 35 percent as of the date the FAFSA is completed. On July 1, 2007, the 35 percent assessment rate was reduced to 20 percent for dependent students and independent students with and without dependents other than a spouse. The key with assets is ownership. Check with your tax advisor to determine ownership of a particular asset.

Noncountable Assets

Noncountable assets also affect the financial aid package. As you continue to plan for asset reallocation, certain assets are not used in the federal need analysis formula. These assets are retirement plan assets, your personal residence, life insurance, annuities, and personal property (e.g., cars, boats, and snowmobiles). Also, consumer debt is not considered in the formula. For example, if the family has $50,000 in cash and $50,000 in consumer debt, the family net worth for aid purposes is still $50,000. Consequently, asset planning favors maximizing non-countable assets and increasing investment or business debt instead of consumer debt.

Taxable Accounts

A standard, taxable account has the most flexibility when it comes to education savings. Account earnings are taxed, but the earnings are the result of the sale of assets held for more than one year. They will likely be subject to a lower capital gains rate of a maximum 20 percent (15 percent through 2008).

Shifting Assets

Shifting one's assets with the idea of lowering the EFC can be a tricky business. If done cautiously and honestly, however, it can be an effective strategy. An important thing to keep in mind when managing your assets in this way is that many colleges and universities not only investigate a family's finances during the student's senior year in high school, but also during his or her junior and sometimes even sophomore year. Sudden changes in financial assets will draw a financial aid administrator's (FAA's) attention to the financial aid forms you have filled out.

One of the biggest mistakes many parents make is trying to hide their assets by putting money into an account under their child's name. While a child's income is taxed at a lower rate than a parent's, when it comes to financial aid schools will count 35 percent of the student's savings toward the EFC but only 5.6 percent of the parents' savings. There is an alternative, however. Money can be given to a student's grandparents or other relatives for safekeeping.

The law limits such gifts to $10,000 per year, but this can be a questionable strategy. First of all, the person who receives the gift, whether it is a grandparent or other relative, is not legally bound to use it to pay for junior's schooling. Also, the sudden disappearance of large sums of money from your assets will start bells ringing for any FAA who keeps an eye on your family's financial history.

For these reasons, it might be best to limit such family asset shifting to more modest amounts. If a grandparent is also willing and able to help pay for a grandchild's education, you might try combining some of your gift money with their contributions into a savings account under the grandparent's name, thus creating a larger fund that will earn more interest.

If you are planning to buy an expensive item, such as a car, a new computer system, or equipment for your business, do it sometime during the years that will be reviewed for EFC consideration.

If you anticipate owing the IRS money when you file your next tax return, calculate your taxes and make the payment before December 31, rather than waiting until April 15 of the next year. This way, the loss will be considered a reduction of assets.

> **Beware:** Some colleges go even further by asking you to provide information on the value of your car, your retirement plan, or your life insurance policy. Such questions do not inspire confidence that the school is working to offer you a large aid package.

Student Assets

Student assets may affect the level of financial aid. If there are assets and money in the student's name, use those funds because it will reduce the amount of future student assets reported on the FAFSA, which is assessed at 20 percent.

Plans

Section 529 Plans, also known as Qualified Tuition Programs (QTP), are among the best ways of saving for a college education. These are state-sponsored savings plans. Funds can be used for qualified educational expenses such as tuition, fees, room and board, books and supplies. Anybody can contribute to a prepaid tuition plan. This lets people give the gift of education to someone else.

The purchaser of a 529 program retains full ownership regardless of beneficiary. age. Typically, the owner is a parent or grandparent, and a minor child is the beneficiary. The money in the plan is controlled by the account owner, not the child, until the funds are withdrawn. This usually makes 529 plans a preferred choice for college savings over making an irrevocable gift to a child and putting it into a custodial account.

Investing in 529 Plans can affect the level of financial aid. Since it is a savings plan owned by the parents, it has a smaller impact on the federal need analysis formula. One owned by the grandparents is even better because it is not used in the federal analysis formula and has estate-planning features.

529 savings plans are mostly managed by well-known financial service companies. Most plans offer a variety of investment choices. However, not every plan offers every type of investment, and the fees charged by the various plans can vary widely.

In some 529 plans the distribution can be paid directly to the beneficiary. In others the choice is between having a distribution paid either to the account owner or directly to the school. When a distribution is paid to the school, it is seen as having been paid

> **Smart tip:** Only cash can be contributed to a 529 savings plan. If you want to move some of your current investments to a 529 savings plan, they need to be liquidated first. This will usually be a taxable event.

to the beneficiary. If the child dies or decides to not go to college, the plans can be transferred to another member of the family.

529 Plans have a unique feature that can make them an interesting part of one's estate planning arsenal. The account is treated as a completed gift for estate tax purposes. Although the owner retains control of the funds, the establishment of a 529 Plan account is treated as a complete gift to the beneficiary. As such it is no longer a part of the account owner's taxable estate. When you make a deposit to a 529 Plan, there is no tax impact at the federal level. Prepaid tuition plans are exempt from federal income tax, and are often exempt from state and local income taxes. Favorable state tax status may be limited to the state's own plan. Some states offer a full or partial tax deduction for contributions to the state's plan. Earnings and withdrawals, if used for qualified educational expenses, are exempt from federal taxes.

One potential problem with college savings plans, however, is that there is no guarantee associated with the investment. The money you place in the savings plan is subject to the regular market conditions of the day, and by the time your student enrolls in college, the amount in the account may not be enough to cover all expenses. However, if all goes well, you may end up with more money than you bargained for.

Each state has its own version of the 529 Plans, so make sure you do your research. Just because you live in a particular state does not mean you have to enroll in a 529 Plan for that state. Do some research to see what state offers the best benefits so that you get more for your money. If your state does not offer a tax-deductible plan, then it may be wise to look elsewhere. Likewise, spend some time on comparison. Which state offers the lowest fees? Which plan is the most flexible? Which states allow you to use an advisor? These are all very important questions to answer before you make a decision.

There are two types of section 529 Plans: prepaid tuition plans and college savings plans. Prepaid tuition plans let you lock in future tuition rates at in-state public colleges at current prices and are usually guaranteed by the state. College savings plans are more flexible, but do not offer a guarantee. Also, a group of several hundred private colleges offers a national prepaid tuition plan for private and independent colleges known as the Independent 529 Plan.

Prepaid Tuition Plans

Prepaid tuition plans are college savings plans that are guaranteed to increase in value at the same rate as college tuition. With prepaid tuition, you prepay college tuition bills years in advance. In most of the prepaid plans you contribute an agreed amount in exchange for future benefits. These programs allow you to buy future tuition at public state colleges at today's price. For example, if a family purchases shares worth half a year's tuition at a state college, these shares will always be worth half a year's tuition, even 10 years later, when tuition rates may have doubled.

The main benefit of these plans is that they allow a student's parents to lock in tuition at current rates, offering peace of mind. The plan's simplicity is also attractive and most offer a better rate of return on an investment than bank savings accounts and certificates of deposit. The plans also involve no risk to principal, and often are guaranteed by the full faith and credit of the state.

Currently, prepaid tuition plans are operated by state governments, with the tuition guarantee based on an enrollment-weighted average of in-state public college tuition rates. A few have separate plans for two- and four-year colleges and for room and board. If the student attends an in-state public college, the plan pays the tuition and required fees. If the student decides to attend a private or out-of-state college, the plans typically pay the average of in-state public college tuition. The family will be responsible for the difference, if any. Earnings are guaranteed by the state to match or exceed annual in-state public college tuition inflation. The cost of a plan can vary, depending on the age of the child.

Federal legislation passed in February 2006 allows prepaid tuition program distributions to be treated as an asset of the parents. Federal financial aid formulas count up to only 5.6 percent of parental assets when calculating the student's financial need. Consequently this investment will now have a limited effect on how much financial aid you will get.

Interest rates vary widely. You might take advantage of this program if you think the school's tuition will rise faster than the interest rate on the loan and if the interest rate is competitive to one you could obtain elsewhere, such as a home equity loan.

If you pay with a lump sum or a series of payments, your child is guaranteed up to four years (if you prepaid that many credit hours) at a state school when he or she reach college age, no matter what the tuition at that time. The price of college is deeply discounted; the younger your child, the steeper the discount. These plans can be a good deal if you are fairly sure that your child will want to attend college in your state.

Prepaid tuition plans do have some drawbacks. If your child attends school out of state, each program has different refund policies. Some states will refund the equivalent of current state tuition. Others will give back only your initial investment, plus a low rate of interest. Some will refund only your initial investment without interest and also hit you with a cancellation fee. In addition, the IRS has ruled that you must pay federal income tax on the difference between your initial investment and the cost of tuition covered by another state's prepaid tuition plan when your child enrolls.

College Savings Plans

College savings plans are more like IRAs or 401(k) plans. Most of these plans usually don't have any state guarantee, but they have more flexibility to accept various levels of contributions and offer at least the possibility of higher returns on investments.

529 State College Savings Plans allow you to save money for college through state-sponsored investment accounts. You can use the funds at most accredited public or private colleges or universities in the United States. Also, some plans allow you to use the money at accredited vocational and international colleges. The beneficiary of the program can be changed without penalty to certain other family members. Also, some states waive taxes for residents or let parents deduct a portion of the annual contribution.

In these plans your contributions are invested in mutual funds offered by the plan's program manager (like Vanguard, Fidelity, etc.). Some plans allow you to choose among different investments or investment portfolios. Most have ready-made investment portfolios tailored to age and risk tolerance, and these are professionally managed by the state or the program manager.

Coverdell Education Savings Account (formerly Education IRA)

Formerly known as the Education IRA, this account is similar to an IRA but it is used for education costs. Coverdell Education Savings Accounts are actually trust or custodial accounts. They can be opened at most banks, mutual fund companies, or brokerage firms. A maximum of $2,000 can be contributed before April 15 of each year (for the previous calendar year). These accounts let families put away $2000 per beneficiary per year and use the money tax-free to pay for qualified college expenses for the designated beneficiary. In addition to parents, grandparents, aunts, uncles, and friends can contribute to a Coverdell account. Coverdell's "parent-owned" accounts are counted as a parent's asset up to 5.6 percent in calculating the student's need. The account can be invested in almost any type of instrument, such as bank CDs, individual stocks and bonds, mutual funds, unit investment trusts, and exchange-traded funds.

In the account opening forms, two individuals need to be named: a beneficiary and a responsible party to direct the investments. The form usually designates the beneficiary's parent or guardian as the responsible party. The responsible party does not necessarily have to be a contributor to the account. Each contribution must be made before the beneficiary's 18th birthday (except for "special needs beneficiaries"). The funds in the account grow tax-free and can be withdrawn by the designated beneficiary at any time. If the withdrawal is for a use other than as a qualified education expense, then the income portion of the withdrawal is subject to income tax (at the beneficiary's tax rate) with an additional 10 percent tax penalty.

> **Smart tip:** Always talk with a person versed in the field, a lawyer, or financial advisor to determine which plan suits your specific needs.

Comparison of 529 and Coverdell Education Savings Accounts

There are some advantages and disadvantages involved in owning a Coverdell account instead of a 529 Plan. Here are some of them.

Advantages:

- The Coverdell Education Savings Account can be self-directed, with a wider array of investment products available.
- The Coverdell funds can be used for private elementary and secondary education, and not just for college.
- The tax-free status of these Coverdell plans will continue after 2010, while the tax-free status of 529 savings plans is currently scheduled to end at that time.

Disadvantages:

- Contributions to Coverdell Education Savings Accounts are limited to $2,000 per beneficiary per year.
- The age of the beneficiary is limited in a Coverdell account.
- The contributor relinquishes ownership of Coverdell funds.
- The effect on need-based financial aid eligibility is probably less favorable for a Coverdell than for 529 savings plans.
- There is less flexibility in changing beneficiaries in a Coverdell ESA.
- There is a 6 percent excise tax on excess contributions in a Coverdell ESA.
- The Coverdell ESA is not eligible for the state tax deductions available to some 529 plans.
- The Coverdell account has a limited life. No contributions can be made after the beneficiary reaches his or her 18th birthday, and the account must be liquidated by the time the beneficiary reaches 30.

Custodial Accounts and Trusts

Families that want to save money in the child's name have two main choices: custodial accounts and trusts. They are Uniform Gift to Minors Act and Uniform Transfer to Minors Act.

UGMA/UTMA

UGMA/UTMA accounts are custodial accounts opened on behalf of a minor. Custodial accounts under the Uniform Gift to Minors Act (UGMA) accept money. Custodial accounts under the Uniform Transfer to Minors Act (UTMA) also accept property. Both are irrevocable gifts to a child where a custodian is responsible for managing the funds until the child reaches the age of majority. UGMA and UTMA have one major drawback. Once the funds are turned over, the child can do whatever he or she wants with them.

Opening an UGMA/UTMA account is simple. All you have to do is open an account with a financial intermediary such as a bank, mutual fund company, or brokerage house and deposit the funds. One advantage that this account has over Coverdell and 529 accounts is that you can deposit securities into the account. You may want to do this in order to move appreciated securities into a child's account as a gift, so that when the securities are sold, the capital gains are taxed at the child's rate instead of the donor's rate. Currently you can provide a gift to your child up to $11,000 per year without having to consider gift taxes. Two parents can provide up to $22,000 per year.

There are disadvantages in UGMA/UTMA accounts. Once funded, the gift is considered irrevocable. Any withdrawals by the custodian are required to be for the benefit of the child. Interest income and capital gains are taxed at the minor's rate. Ultimately the balance of the account is turned over to the minor at age 18 or 21, depending on the individual state in which the account is opened. This may be a definite disadvantage to parents and grandparents who may watch in dismay as funds set aside for education get spent by the child elsewhere as soon as the age of majority is reached. UGMA/UTMA accounts have the additional disadvantage, when computing financial aid, of being considered the child's asset instead of the parents' asset.

Minority Trust

Under Section 2503(c) of the tax code, families can establish an inter vivos (living) trust for a minor, provided the funds are used solely for the benefit of that minor. The trust has one main advantage over a UGMA. The trustee has control over the funds until the "done" is 21 years old. One exception is the Crummey Trust, in which the funds remain under the trustee's control as long as the trustee chooses, with one caveat: The trust's recipient (presumably your child) may withdraw contributions made to the trust within a designated time frame following the contribution. If your child makes no withdrawals, the contribution is added to the principal. If your child does something really stupid with the money, you can simply stop adding to the trust.

Charitable Remainder Unitrust

To establish a charitable remainder unitrust, you donate a set amount of money (usually at least $50,000) to a college or a charitable institution, such as your alma mater or local art museum, but stipulate that from 5 percent to 10 percent of the value of the gift (or a portion of the income generated by the gift) be paid out each year as income to a fund for your college-bound student. At the end of a designated time frame the principal goes to the college or charity. Meanwhile, you, the donor (1) receive a substantial tax deduction, (2) build a college fund for Junior, and (3) give money to a favored charity. Many people choose to donate an appreciated asset for the trust to sell, because that way they avoid paying tax on the appreciation, yet they get to deduct the full market value of the item. You will need professional help to set up such a trust.

Introduction to Bonds

There are three important terms to know as you learn about bonds, in general: the par value, the coupon rate, and the maturity date. Knowing these terms will help you analyze the different types of bonds available and be able to compare them.

1. *Par value* is the amount of money the investor will receive once the bond matures. This means that whoever sold you the bond will return to you the original amount that was loaned, or the principal.
2. The *coupon rate* is the amount of interest that the bondholder will receive expressed as a percentage of the par value. The bond will also specify when the interest is to be paid, whether monthly, quarterly, semiannually, or annually.
3. The *maturity date* is the date when the bond issuer has to return the principal to the lender. Once the principal is paid, the debtor is no longer obligated to make interest payments.

Baccalaureate Bonds

Baccalaureate bonds are zero-coupon bonds (see below) issued by certain states to assist families saving for college tuition by means of added tax benefits.

They are actually ordinary zero-coupon municipal bonds. Only about 20 states issue baccalaureates. To use them you must be a resident of the state. They work like any other tax-free zero-coupon bond except that your state will give you a discount on the tuition if you enroll in the state university and pay with these bonds.

Zero Coupon Bonds and Taxes

Even though you do not receive any interest while holding your baccalaureate zero-coupon bonds, the IRS requires that you calculate an annual interest income and report this income each year. Usually, the issuer of your zero-coupon bond will send you a Form 1099-OID, Original Issue Discount, which lists the interest. You should report this interest like any other interest you receive.

For capital gains purposes, the calculated interest you earned between the time you purchased and the time you sold or redeemed the baccalaureate zero coupon bond is added to your cost basis. If you held the bond continually from the time it was issued until it matured, you will generally not have any gain or loss.

> **Smart tip:** Zero-coupon bonds generally come in maturities of from one to forty years. They are issued at deep discount and redeemed at full face value. Holders of zero-coupon bonds must pay tax on interest annually even though you don't receive it until maturity.

Treasury Bonds

Treasury bonds might be a good option in saving for college. Treasury bonds are sold by banks, brokers and dealers. The term for treasury bonds is 30 years. Bonds are sold in increments of $1,000, so the minimum purchase amount is $1,000. The price and yield for treasury bonds are determined at auction. Bonds are auctioned four times each year, in February, May, August, and November. The price may be greater than, less than, or equal to the face value of the bond. You can hold your treasury bond until it matures or you can sell it before maturity.

Two types of bids are accepted at auction:

- *Noncompetitive bids:* You agree to accept the interest rate determined at auction. With this type of bid, you are pretty much guaranteed to receive the bond that you want and in the full amount that you want.
- *Competitive bids:* You specify the yield you are willing to accept. However, your bid may be:
  1. accepted in the full amount you want if your bid is equal to or less than the yield determined at auction
  2. accepted in less than the full amount you want if your bid is equal to the high yield, or
  3. rejected if the yield you specify is higher than the yield set at auction

Treasury bonds exist in two formats. Older bonds are usually in paper format. But today, they can exist in electronic format, too. Paper bonds can now be converted to electronic bonds, making things a lot easier to manage.

Converting Paper Treasury Bonds to Electronic Form

If you hold paper treasury bonds, you might consider converting them to electronic form to manage them better. It is a simple process, and TreasuryDirect walks you through it step-by-step. Here are some points to consider in the conversion process:

1. Take a look at your treasury bond. Complete the assignment on the back of each bond by writing in "To the Secretary of the Treasury for conversion and deposit into Legacy Treasury Direct."
2. Include the account number in the assignment on the back of each bond if you are transferring into an existing account in Legacy Treasury Direct. If you don't already have an account, you can complete a form online to open your account.
3. Have everyone who owns the bonds to sign the bonds in the presence of a certifying individual of a financial institution. By the way, a notary public is not an acceptable certifying individual, so go to your bank.
4. Submit your bonds to the customer services department of TreasuryDirect.

U.S. Savings Bonds

Parents who purchase Series EE Savings Bonds and the new inflation-adjusted I Bond will not have to pay tax on the accrued interest, provided they use the proceeds for their children's education. To qualify, they must pay the money directly to an eligible institution, or to a state tuition savings plan. There is one catch, however. Your income for the year in which you plan to redeem your bonds includes all the interest the bonds have earned.

Bonds may be purchased anytime during the year, but to qualify for the tax exclusion, purchasers must be at least 24 years of age. In other words, families with income too high to benefit from the tax break may not have their children take advantage of the benefit by buying the bonds themselves.

EE Bonds

EE Bonds earn 90 percent of the average yield of five-year Treasury securities over the preceding six months. Rates are adjusted twice a year (May 1 and November 1). Series EE Savings Bonds are safe, low-risk savings products that pay interest based on current market rates for up to 30 years for bonds purchased May 1997 through April 30, 2005. You may purchase EE Bonds via TreasuryDirect or at almost any financial institution or through your employer's payroll deduction plan, if available. If you redeem EE/E Bonds in the first 5 years, you will forfeit the 3 most recent months' interest. If you redeem them after 5 years, you won't be penalized.

Here are some key facts to consider when buying electronic EE Bonds:

- They are sold at face value; i.e., you pay $50 for a $50 bond and it is worth its full value when it is available for redemption
- Purchase in amounts of $25 or more, to the penny
- $5,000 maximum purchase in one calendar year
- Issued electronically to your designated account

Here are some considerations when buying paper EE Bonds:

- They are sold at half their face value; i.e., you pay $25 for a $50 bond but it is not worth its face value until it has matured
- Purchase in denominations of $50, $75, $100, $200, $500, $1,000, and $5,000, and $10,000
- $5,000 maximum purchase in one calendar year
- Issued as paper bond certificates

Who Can Own EE Bonds?

Individuals, corporations, associations, public or private organizations, and fiduciaries can own paper Series EE/E Bonds. At this time, only individuals can open a TreasuryDirect account and own electronic savings bonds. Unlike other securities, minors may own U.S. Savings Bonds.

You can own U.S. Savings Bonds if you have a Social Security Number and you are a:

- Resident of the United States
- Citizen of the United States living abroad (must have U.S. address of record)
- Civilian employee of the United States regardless of residence

Inflation Bonds (I Bonds)

For people who worry about the impact of inflation on the value of their bonds, Uncle Sam has introduced Inflation Indexed Savings Bonds (I Bonds) which have yields pegged to the inflation rate. Inflation-indexed bonds (also known as inflation-linked bonds or colloquially as "linkers" are bonds whose principal is indexed to inflation. They are thus designed to cut out the inflation risk of an investment. Inflation-indexed bonds pay a coupon that is equivalent to the sum of the increase in an inflation index and the real coupon rate.

A common misconception about these bonds is that the interest rate changes with inflation. What actually happens is that the underlying principal of the bond changes, which results in a higher interest payment when multiplied by the same rate. For example, if the coupon of an annual bond was 5 percent and the underlying principal of the bond was 100 units, the annual payment would be 5 units. If the inflation index increased by 10 percent, the principal of the bond would increase to 110 units. The coupon rate would remain at 5 percent, resulting in an interest payment of 110 × 5 percent = 5.5 units. The only known exception to this is the Australian Capital Indexed Bond, in which the interest rate is adjusted as well as the principal.

These bonds are fairly safe, so purchasers can devote a greater percentage of the rest of their portfolio to high-yielding stocks without increasing their portfolio's overall risk.

Zero-coupon Bonds

A zero-coupon bond (also called a discount bond or deep discount bond) is a bond bought at a price lower than its face value, with the face value repaid at the time of maturity. It does not make periodic interest payments, or so-called coupons, hence the term *zero-coupon* bond. Investors earn interest via the difference between the discounted price of the bond and its par (or redemption) value. Examples of zero-coupon bonds include U.S. Treasury bills, U.S. Savings Bonds, and long-term zero-coupon bonds.

In contrast, an investor who has a regular bond receives income from coupon payments, which are usually made semiannually. The investor also receives the principal or face value of the investment when the bond matures.

These are bonds stripped of their interest coupons. Owners receive no income while holding the bonds. Instead, income compounds and reinvests semiannually. At some future date, investors receive a fixed sum that is much larger than the purchase price.

Zero coupon bonds may be long- or short-term investments. Long-term zero coupon maturity dates typically start at ten to fifteen years. The bonds can be held until maturity or sold on secondary bond markets. Short-term zero coupon bonds generally have maturities of less than one year and are called bills. The U.S. Treasury bill market is the most active and liquid debt market in the world.

Many families like to use zeros to save for college because they can time maturity dates to coincide with tuition bills. Also, they know exactly how much money they will receive when those bills come due, a certainty that for some families is more important than taking chances with a riskier portfolio.

HH/H Bonds

Series HH bonds, also called "current income bonds," were originally offered on January 1, 1980, to replace Series H bonds, which were withdrawn from sale. If a Series HH bond is redeemed before final maturity, interest ceases as of the end of the interest period preceding the date of redemption. If the redemption date falls on an interest payment date, interest ceases on that date. Series HH bonds have an original maturity period of 10 years and have been granted one 10-year extension of maturity with interest, bringing their final maturity to 20 years. Unlike EE bonds, HH bonds are current-income securities. You pay face value, and receive interest payments by direct deposit to your checking or savings account every 6 months until maturity or redemption. HH bonds can be used to supplement retirement income. The holder receives interest payments every six months since the date of issue.

> **Smart tip:** Denominations available for HH/H Bonds are $500, $1,000, $5,000, and $10,000. The minimum purchase is $500.

Series HH Bonds reach final maturity twenty years from date of issue. You can cash in HH bonds anytime after 6 months. Series HH bonds are not sold for cash. They are available in exchange for Series EE bonds, Series E bonds, and Savings Notes whose final maturity date is not more than one calendar year earlier than the issue date of the Series HH bond. The proceeds of matured Series H bonds can be reinvested in HH bonds.

Certificate of Deposit (CD)

A certificate of deposit is a promissory note issued by a bank. It is a time deposit that restricts holders from withdrawing funds on demand. Although it is still possible to withdraw the money, this action will often incur a penalty. For example, let's say that you purchase a $10,000 CD with an interest rate of 5 percent compounded annually and a term of one year. At year's end, the CD will have grown to $10,500 ($10,000 * 1.05). CDs for less than $100,000 are called "small CDs." CDs for more than $100,000 are called "large CDs" or "jumbo CDs." Almost all large CDs, as well as some small CDs, are negotiable.

CDs are similar to savings accounts in that they are insured and thus virtually risk-free. They are "money in the bank." They are different from savings accounts in that the CD has a specific, fixed term, often three months, six months, or one to five years, and, usually, a fixed interest rate. It is intended that the CD be held until maturity, at which time the money may be withdrawn together with the accrued interest.

At most institutions, the CD purchaser can arrange to have the interest periodically mailed as a check or transferred into a checking or savings account. This reduces total yield because there is no compounding. Some institutions allow the customer to select this option only at the time the CD is opened.

T-bills

U.S. Treasury securities are a great way to invest and save for the future. T-Bills are a short-term debt obligation backed by the U.S. government with a maturity of less than one year. Essentially, T-bills are a way for the U.S. government to raise money from the public. T-bills are sold in denominations of $1,000 up to a maximum purchase of $5 million and commonly have maturities of one month (four weeks), three months (13 weeks) or six months (26 weeks).

T-bills are short-term securities that mature in one year or less from their issue date. They are issued with three-month, six-month and one-year maturities. T-bills are purchased for a price that is less than their par (face) value; when they mature, the government pays the holder the full par value. Effectively, your interest is the difference between the purchase price of the security and what you get at maturity. For example, if you bought a 90-day T-bill at $9,800 and held it until maturity, you would earn $200 on your investment. This differs from coupon bonds, which pay interest semiannually.

For example, let's say you buy a 13-week T-bill priced at $9,800. Essentially, the U.S. government gives you an IOU for $10,000 that it agrees to pay back in three months. In such a case you will not receive regular payments as you would with a coupon bond. Instead, the appreciation and, therefore, the value to you comes from the difference between the discounted value you originally paid and the amount you receive back ($10,000). In this case, the T-bill pays a 2.04 percent interest rate ($200/$9,800 = 2.04 percent) over a three-month period.

T-bills are the most marketable money market security. Their popularity is mainly due to their simplicity. They are issued through a competitive bidding process at a discount from par, which means that rather than paying fixed interest payments like conventional bonds, the appreciation of the bond provides the return to the holder.

Treasury Notes

Treasury notes, sometimes called T-notes, earn a fixed rate of interest every six months until maturity. T-notes mature in two to ten years. They have a coupon payment every six months, and are commonly issued with maturities dates of 2, 5 or 10 years, for denominations from $1,000 to $1,000,000. Treasury notes can be bought either directly from the U.S. government or through a bank.

You also can purchase notes through a bank or broker. You can hold a note until it matures or sell it before it matures. To buy a Treasury note through the U.S. Treasury, you place a competitive or noncompetitive bid for the note. With a competitive bid, you specify the yield you want. However, this does not mean that your bid will be approved. With a noncompetitive bid, you accept whatever yield is determined at auction.

Treasury notes are extremely popular investments as there is a large secondary market that adds to their liquidity. Interest payments on the notes are made every six months until maturity. The income for interest payments is not taxable on a municipal or state level but is federally taxed.

> **Smart tip**: Use Treasury notes to finance education and supplement retirement income.

Treasury Bonds

Treasury bonds (T-bonds, or the long bond) have the longest maturity, from ten years to thirty years. They have coupon payments every six months like T-notes, and are commonly issued with a maturity of thirty years. This is a marketable, fixed-interest U.S. government debt security. The income that holders receive is only taxed at the federal level.

Treasury bonds are issued with a minimum denomination of $1,000. The bonds are initially sold through auction in which the maximum purchase amount is $5 million if the bid is non-competitive or 35 percent of the offering if the bid is competitive. A competitive bid states the rate that the bidder is willing to accept; it will be accepted depending on how it compares to the set rate of the bond. A non-competitive bid ensures that the bidder will get the bond but he or she will have to accept the set rate. After the auction, the bonds can be sold in the secondary market.

Mutual Funds

One of the best ways for small investors to play the market is via a mutual fund. By having your money pooled with that from lots of other investors, you gain the advantage of diversification and professional fund management. Mutual funds are usually categorized by investment goal. Here are some types of mutual funds:

- *Growth Funds* aim to increase the value of your investment rather than provide you with a large stream of dividends. Growth funds

generally invest in stocks and are best suited for people who plan to hold on to the fund for a longer period of time.
- *Income Funds* focus on providing investors with high current income (i.e. larger dividends). Income funds generally invest in corporate and government bonds, or stocks with good dividend paying records. They bring higher yields than money market funds but their share price can move up or down, making them a little riskier.
- Money market funds are very safe, and accordingly offer the lowest return. Money market funds generally invest in high-quality securities with short maturities (e.g., bank CDs, U.S. Treasury bills)

Other types of funds include hybrids of the above, for example, aggressive growth, balanced growth; and growth and income. Investors will also find specialty funds grouped by company type. Some examples include energy, environmental, health care, real estate, utilities, etc.

14

Resume Elements

The resume is the performer's business card, reference letter, portfolio, and certificate of professional standing, all rolled into one. It is the marketing tool that will get you work and financial aid. Putting it together, making it effective, and getting it out should be mandatory and should be given the kind of attention you would give to an audition for an important role.

In preparing your master resume, plan its structure. To do this, you will need to gather every crumb of useful information about yourself and your career. These informational elements will clarify your career goals to prospective employers—and yourself.

There is no standard format for the resume. When organizing your resume pay careful attention to its overall look. It should be pleasing to look at, well structured and easy to understand. Each resume is as individual as the performer it represents. Certain data, however, should always be included in a resume, and some information is better left out.

Personal Data

Personal data include pertinent awards received, professional memberships, offices held in professional associations, titles of publications authored, etc. The top personal data section should generally include your contact information, such as your name, contact phone number, union affiliations, and talent agent's name.

Vital Statistics

Important vital statistics include height, weight, and the color of your hair and eyes. This information is essential for an actor. You may include or omit items such as age, vocal range, and measurements. A general rule of thumb is to include information that will help make you stand out, or underscore a special ability.

Measurements need to be listed only in modeling or commercial resumes. For their own protection, many individuals in acting prefer to leave measurements to the costume designer after they have the role.

Many performers dislike putting an age range on a resume because they do not want to be typecast into a narrow bracket. They theorize that the casting person should decide whether they appear to be the appropriate age for a role.

Listing a vocal range is important if you can sing. If there is no mention of vocal range, and no musical credits on your resume, the assumption may be made that you cannot sing at all. Show anything you have done that may be pertinent to singing ability, including musical roles and training.

Experience

The body of your resume will describe your experience and list your credits. This section is usually organized by genre. Let's say if you are an actor, then it should be organized according to theater, film, television, and commercials. If you do more work in one area than another, it is a good idea to compile two or more different resumes, so that your "film" resume lists film credits first, while your "theatrical" resume lists theater credits first.

Training

The purpose of the training section is simply to show where and with whom you have trained. This will help those who see it determine the areas and extent of your training in acting, voice, dance, and related theater skills. If you have trained with well-known teachers, be sure to include their names. If, however, the names are not well known and their inclusion makes the resume look cluttered, do not list them. In such cases the type and duration of training should be sufficient.

Special Skills

The "Special Skills" section should list those talents that might be useful to show that you have a diverse rage of interests. Let's say you are in acting. Start with theater-related skills such as stage combat, acrobatics, the ability to play musical instruments, and accent and dialects. You can add to this list almost anything you do well, such as photography, graphic design, sign language, carpentry, or puppetry. These skills can also generate conversation at an interview or audition.

Preparing Your Master Resume Step by Step

The following steps illustrate a systematic approach to squeezing keywords while developing a resume. You can integrate any of the following steps into your own resume development process:

Step 1: Clarify Your Financial Aid Objective

An objective specifies your target market and/or job title. It is your call whether to include an objective. State the financial aid or the job that you are applying for. Not only is this brief and to the point, it includes yet another set of important keywords. An objective can provide a focus for organizing your resume's content.

First, make a list of all the titles you can think of that describe the kinds of aid you are seeking. Second, make a list of all the experiences you can think of that might impress judges. Third, organize your title list and work experiences list.

With these objective statements you can prioritize and organize the information you need to include in your resume that supports this objective.

> **Smart tip:** Your final resume may or may not contain an objective statement. However, it is important to develop your resume with a clear objective in mind so that you know how to organize and prioritize your resume's content.

Step 2: List Each of Your Job/Position Titles in Chronological Order

Make a list of each position or job title you have had, whether it was paid or nonpaid. If you are a professional in the performing arts, information about past employment is the backbone of any resume. It documents your employment history and provides specific information about the types of jobs you have had. Most importantly, it shows how they can be utilized for your benefit and how you can get aid.

Step 3: List Responsibilities for Each Position Held

Job responsibilities describe your work duties. This description reflects distinctive tasks that you have performed, or are held accountable for performing. Your responsibilities are synonymous with a description. Explain briefly the type of work you did. If you volunteered, mention that as well.

For each listed item include the following information.

- Position or job title
- Company/organization name
- Department/division
- Location (city and state)
- Dates employed

Step 4: List the Skills You Used for Each Job

Skills highlight your abilities, expertise, proficiency, and understanding of key areas that you develop as a result of your work experience and education. Job skills are specific and unique to your work experience, profession, and career goals. They indicate your level of proficiency in a given area as a result of carrying out your job responsibilities. If you are a dance student at a university, and have attended dance school in the past or have tutored, include that information under "Job responsibilities."

List the specific skills that are unique to your work experience, education, profession, and career goals. This list of skills will serve two purposes: to generate a list of accomplishments using these skills, and to develop your keyword summary.

Step 5: List Your Accomplishments That Illustrate Each Skill Used

By definition, accomplishments are experiences that you successfully completed as a result of using a particular set of skills that were required for a particular task. For example, if you worked as an intern at an orchestra, you can list the work you performed under the conductor.

Step 6: Write a Specific Statement That Quantifies Each Accomplishment

Job accomplishments answer the "so what" questions as a result of the tasks you performed in your job. They indicate the degree of benefit you provided to your employer as a function of how well you applied the skills you used in performing a certain task.

Qualifying or quantifying your accomplishments indicates to what degree a task was completed successfully.

Step 7: List Your Specialized Training and Education

Include your formal education and specialized training here. Formal education is characterized by the award of an accredited degree or certificate, and includes the following information:

- Degree or certificate earned
- Name of institution
- Location of institution (city and state)
- Major area of study; credits earned
- Date of completion

Specialized training includes training that was received at seminars, workshops, on-the-job training, and other in-house training programs for which no specific accredited degree or certificate was awarded. However, this training is important to professional development and indicates training that supports your job objective. You should include the following information about your specialized training:

- Name of training received
- Name of organization that provided the training
- Date of completion

Typically, if you have 15 or more years of experience, you can list your education toward the end of your resume.

Step 8: Extract Important Keywords and Summarize

Take a look at the keywords generated in the resume so far and highlight those nouns you think that someone might use as keywords to find your resume. Ask yourself whether these keywords adequately describe your work experience and support your job objective.

Step 9: Summarize Your Qualifications Relevant to Your Objective

The summary should be a concise statement highlighting three to five of your achievements in work, areas of expertise, qualifications, professional skills, and any other distinctive qualifications. It is best completed after outlining your skills profile, employment history, and education.

Step 10: Write the Actual Resume Text

Now you are ready to write the actual resume text. Remember to revise and edit several times before final submission.

Two Types of Resumes

There are two basic types of resumes used to apply for financial aid, job openings, college admission, and internships. Depending on your personal circumstances, choose a chronological or a functional resume.

Chronological Format

A chronological format is useful when the amount of time on each job (paid or unpaid) may be viewed as a strength, your work experience prepares you for your job objective, former job titles of employers are impressive, or you want to show your advancement in a company or a field of work.

The body of a chronological resume includes a listing of your work history, beginning with your most current job. Other sections may include a job objective; information on your education; a summary of skills; volunteer experiences; unions and other work-related associations; and community activities. Keep in mind that information near the top of the page gets read most carefully. It can be effective to state your job objective and/or your qualifications in a sentence or two before presenting your work history.

In the work history section list your latest employment first, then previous jobs according to dates. State your job title, employer, and dates of employment for each job. Under each job explain exactly what your duties and responsibilities were, what skills you learned, and what you achieved. It is important to use words that tell how much, how often, how well, and what results were produced.

Fundamentals of a good chronological resume. Here are the key components of a standard chronological resume:

- *Identification*: It is essential that a potential employer can reach you. The identification section should include your name, address, phone number(s), and e-mail address. If you are a college student, this section might also include a school address and a permanent home address.
- *Job objective*: A job objective is optional and should only be included for new college graduates and those changing careers. Otherwise, use your cover letter to show your career interests and job objective. If you do use an objective, make sure your objective explains the kind of work you want to do, and keep it between two to four typed lines.
- *Key accomplishments*: Think of this section as an executive summary of your resume. Identify key accomplishments that will grab the attention of an employer. This section should summarize your major accomplishments and qualifications. Use nouns as keywords and descriptors. For example, if you are a stand-up comedian, highlight some of your key performances, awards, or television appearances (if any).
- *Education*: This section should include school(s) attended (including years of attendance), majors/minors, degrees, and honors and awards received.
- *Professional Experience*: This section can also be labeled "Experience," "Work History," or "Employment." If you have a performing career, it

should include company name, your job title, dates of employment, and major accomplishments. List experiences in reverse chronological order, starting with your most current experience.

- *Accomplishments*: List your accomplishments in bullet format rather than paragraph format. Use action verbs when describing your accomplishments.
- *Affiliations/Interests*: This section is optional; include only if you have room on your resume for it. If you are affiliated with the Screen Actors Guild for instance, you can note it here.

Sample chronological resume.

Cynthia O Riley
456 North Undermountain Road
Weymouth, MA 02189
Phone: (781)555-5555
e mail: criley@weymouth.com

Profile:
Goal-driven achiever with strong organizational skills and detail orientation.
Creative problem-solver and performing artist, who can see the big picture while never losing sight of details that deliver results. Motivated team player with demonstrated talent for deploying research and organizational skills toward analyzing, upgrading, and streamlining complex marketing processes for improvement of opportunities.
Enthusiastic self-starter who can boost productivity, work in a team setting; and bring out the best in others. Savvy business artist who can cut costs, foster efficiency, and ensure profitability.

Education:
Bachelor of Arts
Tufts University, MA
Graduation Date: May 2003
Major: Music (Piano Performance)
Minor: Information Technology
Overall GPA: 3.89, Minor GPA: 4.00

Experience:
Tufts University, Chamber Music Ensemble, Piano Performer, October 2005–present
Assisting violinists, flutists, and clarinet players in semester recitals
Participating in weekly practicing sessions with peer students
Teaching assistant in piano performance

Greenwood University, Division of Information Technology, August 2006–August 2007
Manage team of five assistants in 30-desktop lab
Develop solutions for all aspects of lab usage

Ensure safety and security in the lab
Serve as key member of IT management solutions team

Awards and Honors
Syracuse University, Rose Award, given to the outstanding undergraduate
Junior in the Arts
Outstanding Marketing Senior Award
Beta Gamma Sigma—Business Honor Society
Dean's List
Who's Who Among American College Students
Phi Eta Sigma—Freshman Honor Society

Functional Format

The functional resume can be thought of as a "problem solving" format. The functional resume gives you latitude to "make sense" of your work history and match up skills and accomplishments that might not be obvious to the employer in a traditional chronological format.

The body of a functional resume highlights your major skill areas. Emphasis is placed on your skills, not on work experience. Job titles, dates, or names of employers may be left out. However, other sections may include a job objective, information on education, a summary of abilities, and memberships and other work-related associations.

Situations where functional resumes work the best. If any of the descriptions below apply to you, you may want to investigate the functional format:

- Those who have done volunteer work should emphasize this by pointing it out in the detailed listing of their job history.
- Workers who do not wish to show the length of their employment history (e.g., because of their age) can use a functional job format.
- College students or recent graduates may also benefit by using the functional resume. Choose your main skills and organize your extracurricular activities, volunteer work and studies around those skills.
- Military personnel applying for jobs in the civilian world should also use the functional resume. Potential employers are generally interested in your transferable skills rather than your military career.
- Those changing careers should consider this type of resume. When changing careers, the skills that you list need to be related to the position you are applying for. Look at tasks performed in your previous job from a different angle. If you were an air traffic controller and are applying to become a director of a music festival, make sure to show your prospective employer that you can work under pres-

sure and take up responsibilities. This is far more important than your knowledge of marine biology if you are an underwater diver.

- You have a "mixed bag" work history, with no clear thread uniting positions held.
- Those with gaps in their work history, such as homemakers who took time to raise and family and now wish to return to the workplace. For them, a chronological format can draw undue attention to those gaps, while a functional resume enables them to portray transferable skills attained through such activities as domestic management and volunteer work.
- Military transitioners entering a different field from the work they did in the military.
- Those who performed very similar activities throughout their past jobs who want to avoid repeating those activities in a chronological job listing.
- Job-seekers looking for a position for which a chronological listing would make them look "overqualified."

Sample functional resume. Although there is no standard format for a functional resume, here is a sample for you to follow.

Sophia Abington
5467 Sargasso Terrace
Paxton, MA 00000
Phone: (508) 452-0000
E mail: Sophia@paxton.org

Objective:
To contribute to your organization's success through the use of exceptional performing skills, managerial, and people skills.

Qualifications:
Solid managerial and administrative experience.
Exceptional versatility and adaptability.
Dedication and drive as a hard-working individual.
Superlative communication and team-building skills.
Ability to perform well in a pressured environment.

Professional Skills:
Interpersonal and teamwork skills.
Worked with international dance troupes in different settings
Interacted with a wide variety of personalities while scheduling meetings/appointments and making travel arrangements for dance teammates.

Sales and Marketing Skills:
Interacted with clients and utilized excellent organizational skills to arrange and coordinate special events.

Organized performing dance troupes for weddings, receptions, and holiday parties, as well as everyday lunch and dinner planning.

Delivered excellent customer service and conducted in-house sales promotions for a movie theater.

Oversaw daily dance performances at country club and five-star luxury hotel.

Managerial and Supervisory Skills

Proved multi-tasking abilities by scheduling and supervising staff, consisting of kitchen workers, bartenders, and food servers, while functioning as clubhouse assistant manager at country club and simultaneously serving as pool manager and swim instructor.

Served as right hand to lead managers of an entertainment company in an administrative assistant capacity.

Computer Skills:

Proficient in using personal computer skills such as Microsoft Windows, Microsoft Word, Excel, Access, PowerPoint. Additionally, use Word-Perfect, Lotus 1-2-3, Microsoft Publisher, ClarisWorks, First Choice and First Publisher for word processing, spreadsheet, and graphic design, including internal/external correspondence, reports, procedure manuals, and presentations.

Experience in Search Engine Optimization, such as using inbound links, keywords, and descriptive titles in websites.

Employment History:

Administrative Assistant, Blue Ribbon Technologies, Inc., Pasadena, CA, 4/98 to present.

Visiting dance entertainer, Lutheran Nursing Home, CA, 11/97—4/98.

Office Manager, City of Entertainment, Pasadena, CA 1/97—12/97.

Clubhouse Assistant Manager, Golden Bear Country Club, San Diego, CA, 2/96—8/96.

Education:

Assumption College, Worcester, MA

Groton School, Groton, MA, class of '94

> **Smart tip:** The functional resume is ideal if you are looking for a complete career change.

The Student Resume

The student resume is a short, biographical resume of your life. For most students, winning a scholarship or grant is not only a matter of luck. It is the result of tedious research, careful proofing of forms, requesting information early, and putting in the years it takes to have good grades. A resume can become an important part of this process. Your student resume needs to give a complete list of all your accomplishments, interests, and activities.

An exceptional student resume will add more integrity to the scholarship application package. Be sure to include all your activities and interests both inside and outside of school. Scholarships are not reserved for only "A"-grade students, even though your grades will be judged carefully. Other qualifications such as community service, volunteer work, and recreational activities are equally important. If you have not done much to help your community, join an organization or group. It is never too late.

Winning scholarship resumes ultimately leave such strong impressions because they create vivid portraits of the applicants. They do not just recite accomplishments. Rather, they depict the person behind all of the grades, extracurricular activities and awards. After all, judges award scholarships to people, not to resumes. But it is the resume that creates this image of the applicant. If a judge feels like he or she knows you, it creates a powerful, personal impression that helps your application become more outstanding.

> **Smart tip:** A good resume tells a story.

Basic Outline of a Student Resume

There is no standard format for writing a student resume. Each resume is as individual as the performer it represents. It may differ according to your field, the purpose for which the resume is being crafted, and other details. Here is a basic skeleton.

Contact information—Name, address, phone number

Objective: State clearly and concisely why you want to go to college and give your professional and occupational preference.

Scholastic record: Describe your scholastic record as fully as you can, including grades, standing in class, and awards and honors you have won.

Knowledge of foreign languages: State how many foreign languages you command. Indicate whether your knowledge is a result of lessons, or if you have learned them from your family, or if you have lived in another country.

College entrance requirements
Demonstrate that you can meet college entrance requirements by indicating how many units of each subject listed below you have taken. Also, indicate your SAT and/or ACT score.

English
Social studies
History
Algebra

Plane geometry
Trigonometry
Science
Chemistry
Physics
Other subjects
SAT
ACT

Hobbies:
List all hobbies and favorite interests.

Clubs and associations:
Give name and type of organization.

Extracurricular activities:
Describe all extracurricular activities and the extent to which they have absorbed your time. Activities both within school and outside of school are important.

Employment experience:
Full information on employment is vital. State the name of company, supervisor, duties, responsibilities, and length of time for each job.

Skills:
List your skills. Include the various computer programs that you are familiar with.

References:
Copy the most important paragraphs from each letter of reference you have in your possession. Retain the letters of recommendation to include in the complete packet or application.

Example of a Student Resume

Jane Dawson
165 Rosewood
Oregon, OR 00000
Phone: 666-66-6666
janedawson@jmail.com

Academic Honors:
National Honor Society
President Award
Class rank: 25/500 (top 5 percent), Marble High School; 3.9 GPA, SAT: Verbal 550, Math 650

Foreign language skills:
French, two years in high school
Mandarin, private lessons for three years

Extracurricular activities:
Varsity tennis team

Student Council president
Campus newspaper writer

Community/volunteer activities :
St. John's Church, Roseburg, choir
Baseball summer camp volunteer
Community orchestra usher

Work experience:
Summer 2008: parking lot attendant, Citiway grocery store
Spring 2008: part-time cashier, local grocery store
Summer 2007: pianist, nursing home in Oregon

References:
Music teacher: "Jane is a diligent and hardworking student."
Soccer coach: "Jane is a great team player."

Professional Resume for Actors

An actor needs a good resume that will clearly and effectively help sell himself or herself to potential agents, casting directors, directors, and producers. Consisting of a single page, and attached to the back of the photograph, your resume has precious little time to make an impact. It makes the most of your acting experience, training and special skills. The perfect-looking resume welcomes the eye of its viewer.

Resumes for an actor, however, are not the same as traditional "corporate" resumes. When organizing your acting resume, pay careful attention to its overall look. It should be pleasing to look at, well structured and easy to understand. Let's assume you are an actor and want to get the attention of a casting director. Imagine how many resumes casting directors receive. If yours is hard to read and digest, your credits and skills simply will not register with them.

A typical resume lists a job applicant's previous employment, experience, education, and so on. You don't need a typical resume. You need an acting resume. An acting resume focuses exclusively on acting and establishes your credibility as an actor by listing your acting experience and training. Your acting resume should promote you as an actor, show agents and casting directors that you are serious about being an actor, and demonstrate that you have the necessary training, skills, and/or experience to do the job if hired.

In the entertainment business, actors submit their headshots and resumes together. The resume is attached to the back side of the 8" × 10" picture, usually with staples. Paper clips, tape or glue that wrinkles the paper are not recommended. The resume will include several important things about you as an actor. First, it will list your acting experience, such as any film, television, theater, and commercial work you have done. It won't include non-acting employment, such as summer lifeguard jobs, congressional internships, or professional employment in any other field. Second, it will detail your education and training as an actor, which includes any high school, college and professional experiences. Finally, it will list any special skills that you have.

Tackling the Basics of Creating a Resume

Creating an impressive-looking acting resume isn't hard. You can choose from a variety of ways to put your resume together. But if the content and appearance of your resume are sloppy, hard to read, and disorganized, then you come across as a sloppy and disorganized actor. Make sure that your resume is easy to read, neatly organized, and loaded with experience that's especially appropriate for a particular role. Doing so makes you look your best.

A typical acting resume appears in black ink against a plain white background. It should fit on one side of a single page that measures 8x10 inches, so that it can fit neatly on the back of your head shot. That way, if someone is impressed by what she sees in your head shot, she can flip over and read about your experience as an actor.

Be sure to trim your resume to the exact same size as your head shot, so that the paper doesn't get torn or bent. Also, a resume that is larger than your head shot may be hard to file. It may be distracting to see the extra width and length of your resume sticking out underneath.

Standard Components of a Typical Hollywood Acting Resume

Here is a basic outline of what your acting resume should include.

Your name: This is the very first item on your resume. Many feel it should stand out, but not overwhelmingly. It can be a font size larger than the text or simply bolded or italicized. But whatever you do, don't make it one or two inches tall just to fill space.

If you have a fairly common name and are nonunion, you might want to check with SAG and AFTRA to see whether or not someone in the union already has it. The reason is that two people in a union cannot share names that are spelled or sound the same. Thus, if your name is Hank Smith and someone else in SAG is named Hank Smith, you are going to have to use a different name when you eventually join SAG. Therefore, it might be a good idea to start using a stage name now that you won't have to change down the road.

Union affiliations: Underneath your name, any union affiliations are listed, e.g., SAG, AFTRA, AEA, etc. If you are eligible to join a union like SAG but haven't joined, then write "SAG eligible." This helps to legitimize you in some people's eyes. If you have no union affiliations, then don't write anything. Keep in mind that most people won't be looking to see whether or not you are in SAG or AFTRA, except for some agents.

A contact number: You will need to include a telephone number where someone can contact you or your agent (if you have one). Instead of using a home telephone number, many actors opt for a voice mailbox for messages, which requires a monthly fee. The reason is that in the event your picture ends up in the hands of a pervert you wouldn't want to be harassed at home.

Vital statistics: Get ready to reveal some of your most closely guarded secrets. Casting directors need to know as many things about your appearance as they can to see if you are a possibility for a part. Vital statistics include height, weight, and hair and eye color. Parts are cast for people of all heights and sizes, so don't be self-conscious about whether you are the right size.

Film, television, and theater experience: These are all fairly self-explanatory categories. While there is no rule carved in stone about how these should be listed, most people with a lot of experience tend to separate each category and then list work under each appropriate heading. Others who are fairly new sometimes combine them into "Film and Television" and "Theater." Some may opt to leave out "Film and Television" completely if they have no experience in that area. In the Los Angeles–style resume, film and television appear before theater because that is the main industry there.

When listing your film, television, and theater experiences, include the following four items for each role:

- The name of the film, play, or television shows you were in
- The role you played
- The type of role you played (lead role, featured role, supporting role, or a recurring role)
- The studio name, television network, theater, or director you worked for

Be sure to include all experience, unless you have numerous jobs and plays to choose from. Most people generally list the most recent work first, especially for television and film. For theater, most list the prestigious work first (i.e., Broadway, off–Broadway, community, college, high school and so on). Also, if you have any industrial or training film experience, then either list it under "Film" or create a separate category for it.

Commercials: On 99 percent of all actor resumes, under the category of "Commercials" you will see something like "list available upon request" or simply "upon request" after this heading. This is because commercial agents don't want casting directors to be influenced by what you may or may not have done in the past. For example, unlike films and television shows, many ad agencies want fresh new faces, not someone who has been overexposed in ten commercials in the last year. Therefore, it is wise to say "upon request."

Even if you have experience in television commercials, never list them on your resume. If your resume says that you once did a commercial for Hertz rental cars, another rental car company, like Avis, may be reluctant to hire you for its ad campaign.

If you are seeking commercial representation and you have commercial experience, you should by all means mention it when you contact the agent. Either explain all your commercial experience in your cover letter, or make a special resume that lists the experience. This will help you tremendously.

Training: Here, you should list all professional study, college training, private coaching, and any weekend workshops or seminars that you have attended. If you have a degree, say so, even if it is in another field.

While training isn't absolutely essential, as several of today's great stars have never taken an acting class in their lives, it gives you credibility. It makes a casting director feel safer when calling you in. It also can make you a much better actor. If you don't have any training, then you should probably get some.

If you have been to any workshops or taken any classes, you should list them here. Be sure to include a description of what the class was for, the instructor, and the dates of training. Any type of training, workshop, or seminar that you have taken to improve your craft should be listed in this section.

Your acting experience and education: Initially you need to list every available acting experience you have had, just to fill up your resume. Eventually, as you gain more experience, you can choose the more impressive roles and eliminate the less important or trivial ones, such as your bit role as a butler in a community theater or your appearance in a play put on by your college drama department. Be sure to include information about your college education if your degree is in an acting or performance-related field such as drama, broadcasting, or public speaking.

Special skills: Finally, you should list any special skills that you have. This is the final category on your resume. You should fill this with every activity that you can do reasonably well. This category is most often referenced by commercial casting directors who need special skills for commercials.

If you are an avid tennis player, can juggle fresh eggs without breaking them, and know how to tap-dance, you should list all of these things. Many times it is possible to get a role not based on how you look or what training you have had, but instead because there is a need for a performer who has a specific skill. In the beginning, it is important to get any and all experience possible to add to your resume.

Below is a listing of useful skills that actors have. While you won't need to know how to do all of them, knowing just a few of them might help you to get a part someday. Use this guide to creating your own:

- Sports: martial arts, football, baseball, ice hockey, tennis, swimming, roller skating, Rollerblading, weight training, Frisbee, rodeo, etc.
- Arts: Dancing, musical instruments, singing, art, comedy
- Unique skills: juggling, contortionist, magician, card dealer, firearm expert, auctioneer, yoga, stilts
- Dialects: the more specific the better

The New York and L.A. Resumes

For the New York actor, it is often appropriate to list the theater credits first, followed by those of film, television, commercials, industrials, training, and special skills. There will be exceptions to this format, of course. For example, if you landed a principal role in a feature-length film right after graduating from acting school, you would be more likely to start your resume with the category "Film" rather than "Theater."

If you have many areas of work such as national tours, regional theater, dinner theater, or summer stock, break your credits down into those subcategories for easy reading.

In Los Angeles, where the emphasis is on film and television, the preferred format is to list film credits first, followed by television, theater and commercials, followed by training and special skills.

Sample resume in Los Angeles format.

Name: Sarah Burlington
Unions: SAG, AFTRA
Vital Statistics: Height: 5' 7"
Weight: 125
Hair: Blonde
Eyes: Brown

Film Experience:	Role	Production Company
The Giant Within	Anne (featured)	Touchstar Pictures
		(Bryan Carrington, Director)

Television Experience:		
Murder One	Guest Star	ABC
Dynasty	Guest Star	Fox
Friends	Guest Star	ABC

Theater Experience:		
Vanities	Joanne	Bryn Mawr Stage Co.
Candy Cane	Sheila	Sommerville Theater

Training:
Acting: Jude Nelson (two years)
Speech: George Swenson

Special Skills:
Piano, clarinet, oboe, aerobics, diving, gymnastics, tennis

> **Warning:** Some actors glue their resumes to the back of their head shots. Unfortunately, glue tends to lose its adhesiveness with age, which can cause your resume to separate from your head shot. To avoid this problem, use staples instead.

Electronic Resume

Getting your resume online can draw the attention of people who can steer you towards financial aid and boost your career. Sometimes funders, agents, and financial aid officers may request an electronic resume. At other times there may be sources who are browsing through the Internet, looking for resumes that merit attention. They may be able to give you financial aid. This method of receiving aid, however, is rare.

Using the Right Keywords in Your Resume

It is important that your resume contains "keywords" relevant to the positions you are seeking in order for it to gain visibility. Include a keyword in the objective. This allows a prospective financial aid reviewer or employer, searching hundreds of resumes for a specific skill or position objective, to identify the keyword and find your resume.

> **Smart tip:** E resumes gain wide exposure. The biggest advantage of posting your resume electronically is the potential for it to be seen by large numbers of individuals seeking skills that you possess.

In essence a keyword is what's "hot" in your particular field at a given time. Every industry has keywords, and it has become more and more important to include a few in your resume. It is a buzzword, a shorthand way of getting a particular message across at a glance. For example, if you are a pianist you might say you are looking for participation at classical music festivals. In this case someone searching for the keyword "classical pianist" will pull up your resume and know that you are interested in performance. You may need to conduct additional research to make sure you know what keywords are most likely to be used in your desired industry, profession, or situation.

Keyword summaries are more useful when developing a web resume than a traditional paper resume. They not only attract search engines that index web resumes by keywords, but they also provide a human viewer the opportunity to assess your skills and qualifications at a glance.

The keyword summary that you develop for each one of your financial aid applications will be kept in your master keyword list. From these, you will develop a master keyword summary for your resume, consolidating those keywords that overlap, and the ones that are applicable to the particular job you are applying for. The master keyword summary will include various keywords from your education, specialized training, and personal data sections as well.

Tips for Electronic Resumes

There are no specific rules for creating electronic resumes. Here are some guidelines to keep in mind when developing an e-resume.

- Use standard fonts
- Keep in mind that underlining, italics, and fancy scripts may not scan well
- Use boldface and capitalization to set off elements
- Keep information and elements at the left margin. Centering, columns, and even indenting may change when the resume is optically scanned
- Do not use any lines, boxes, or graphics
- Place the most important information at the top of the first page. If you use two pages put "page 1 of 2" at the bottom of the first page and put your name and "page 2 of 2" at the bottom of the second page.
- Use multiple keywords or synonyms for what you do to make sure your qualifications will be picked up if a prospective employer is searching for them
- Be descriptive in your titles
- Avoid tabs. Use your space bar

- Any special characters such as mathematical symbols must be avoided
- Word wrap can be disadvantageous in e-resumes. Use hard returns (the return key) to make line breaks

E-mailing Your Resume

At some point in your performing arts career you may need to e-mail resumes and cover letters to apply for financial aid, jobs, and educational pursuits. Some of these messages may be sent within the body of the e-mail itself, while others may be sent as an attachment. Before you decide to send your resume as an attachment, consider that many employers and resume listing services are requesting that you do not send attachments when responding to a job via e-mail.

> **Beware:** Don't paste your resume into the body of your e mail. There is a chance that it will come out looking very different when it reaches the reviewer. Lines could be broken, spacing could be completely different, etc. Instead, send it as a file attachment so you can be sure that the reviewer will see it exactly as you sent it.

An attachment is a separate but internal part of an e-mail message. When you send a message to somebody else, as a convenience you can "attach" a file to ride along with your message. Some e-mail programs don't support attachments at all. Furthermore, attachments can take up a lot of disk space, depending on what type of files they are and how many you receive at one time.

Some people receiving attachments might lose formatting because they are not supported by their client's software. As a result, they will see strange characters at the end of the supported text at the bottom of their messages. Try to keep it as basic as possible when sending attachments.

Sending Cover Letters as Part of an E-mail Message

In most cases candidates should submit a cover letter with their resume in the body of the e-mail message, but not as an attachment. If you know that your recipient uses attachments, place your cover letter in the body of your e-mail message, and send your resume as an attachment. This way you only include one attachment in the e-mail message itself.

Don't send a cover letter via e-mail with just the URL to your web resume. This is perceived as laziness and conveys your lack of effort. Instead, preface your resume with a targeted cover letter that is short, adds something fresh, and can be read within the first screen.

When you are writing the cover letter in the body of the e mail, avoid using all-capital lettering in your letter. On the Internet this comes off as shouting. Also avoid using emoticons and smiley faces in e mail exchanges. Emoticons are symbols used to convey body language taken for granted during face to face chatting. Not only do these come off as too casual, but you are assuming that everyone knows what they mean.

Creating Your E-mail Signature

An e-mail signature is very much like a signature block found at the end of business correspondence. You can include your name, phone number, e-mail address, and home page URL in your signature. Once you type in what you want in your signature, your e mail program will add it to the bottom of all of your outgoing messages. For email purposes it is text that is automatically appended to all of your outgoing messages. Many email programs can automatically append the contents of a signature file to the very end of each message you send.

An e-mail signature can serve multiple purposes. You can include information similar to that found on a business card, as well as something that gives insight to your personality, such as a quote that best represents your outlook on life.

Some e-mail programs will let you create several signatures, which you can invoke as needed. In Microsoft Outlook, for example, you can access the AutoSignature feature from the Tools Menu.

A general rule is to avoid making your signature more than four or five lines long, not to exceed 60 to 65 characters per line. Also, if you have a web resume, you should include its URL in your e mail signature. Not only does this allow interested people to link to it, but the URL to your web resume can be picked up by the major search engines that index newsgroups for this kind of information.

Smart tip: To create your signature in MSN:

Go to Tools, Options, Edit. You should see your signature information immediately in the "user" category.

Edit your signature and click OK when finished.

Web Resume

Web resumes are flexible, low-cost alternatives to the usual distribution process of resumes. Furthermore, they showcase your talents to the widest possible audience and allow you to be in several places at once 24 hours a day. Just as you "work a room" when attending a networking event, by integrating basic web page design with resume development principles, you can reach a broader audience working the web.

If you want to create a personal web page that serves as your resume, you will need to create your resume in HTML. This requires an understanding of basic web page design principles, HTML, the tools to create web pages, how to transfer your page onto the web, and how to monitor its effectiveness once it has been posted on the web.

A web resume is a web document containing hyperlinked, "clickable" text and images created in HTML. Whatever you can do on paper, you can do on the web with ease and creativity. Web resumes demonstrate accomplishments and expertise with a personal style that is lost in traditional paper resumes. With a web resume you can communicate as much information about yourself as needed to achieve your career goals. It provides a perfect opportunity to develop online portfolios of accomplishments, incorporating items considered taboo in traditional paper resumes-photographs, written testimonials, and personal paragraphs. The web now touches all areas of business and improves the way business is done by reducing cost and increasing revenue.

Rather than mailing your resume to several different employers, you post your resume in one location on the web, and recruiters actively look for it. This poses a two-pronged resume development challenge for the job seeker, leading prospective individuals or companies to your web site.

On the web, costs do not increase as the amount of information you communicate increases. With paper resumes size is a constraining factor, as they must be kept to one or two pages for the sake of the review process. Paper resumes beyond two pages reflect badly on the applicant because they are too wordy. Web resumes are different, since the job seeker can put on a large multimedia presentation for an employer and have him or her begging for more. Skilled users can make web pages that bring text, graphics, audio, and video together to showcase their skills.

Web resumes can be as large as you want or as small as you want. Visitors to Web resumes can choose to concentrate on what interests them. Links are important navigational aids that allow visitors to quickly and easily locate information. By clicking text or images, a series of actions is initiated. The two most common actions are to link to another part of the same web page or to link to another part of the web.

> **Smart tip:** The greatest advantage of the web over a paper resume is that information can be updated daily or as frequently as you like.

Changes to your web resume can be posted the day you make them. After you have added, deleted, or updated the information in your web resume, it takes only seconds to post your pages to the web using the File Transfer Protocol (.ftp). Compare this

> **Smart tip:** Hang out with nine losers and you will be the tenth loser. Hang out with nine winners and you will be the tenth winner.

to the time-consuming process traditionally associated with maintaining a current paper resume that could add days or weeks to getting it distributed in its updated form.

15

Cyber Aid

Promoting Your Talents on YouTube

YouTube is a cutting-edge trend that has exploded the possibilities for performing artists to get noticed by people who would otherwise be unlikely to give them some kind of financial aid. Performers from any part of the world now have an excellent avenue to display their skills. YouTube is a very public way of applying for financial aid, where review committees can watch your talents and skills in action before they make a decision on what type of aid to give.

Dancers, musicians, puppeteers, comedians, singers, and performing artists in virtually any discipline can display their performances online for millions of people to watch simultaneously. If you live in Russia and would like a Hollywood agent to watch a video of your act, YouTube now gives the space to do that. Clowns, jugglers, acrobats, comedians, and many other artists can show their performances to donors, investors, and agents in any part of the world. If a scholarship committee in California has asked an applicant in India to come in for a live performance to demonstrate Kathkali dance, instead of paying thousands of dollars for a ticket and undergoing visa hassles, the applicant can now make arrangements to record a performance via YouTube. YouTube is also useful for musicians who want to perform for millions of people at once, in the expectation that a potential investor may take notice.

> **Smart tip:** YouTube is an online video streaming service that allows anyone to view and share videos that have been uploaded by its members. It is a video sharing website which allows Internet users to upload and share videos that they have made. YouTube is free.

Performing artists who
produce videos that are rated
highly can get their videos on
the "Featured Videos" section
of the home page, thus increasing viewers.

> **Smart tip:** In order for your video to be considered for listing in "Featured Videos," write to editor@youtube.com.

Creating an Account with YouTube

When visiting the YouTube website to watch videos, you can do so without having to create a YouTube account. Despite not being required to create a YouTube account, you may want to look into doing so, as there are a number of benefits to being a YouTube member.

One of the many benefits to registering for a free YouTube account is that it is relatively easy to do. When you sign up, you need to provide a little bit of information about yourself. This information includes your name, the country that you live in, your ZIP Code, your date of birth, your sex. You will also need to create a YouTube username for yourself, as well as a password.

In addition to being able to rate or review videos, registering for a free YouTube account also gives you the option of sharing your videos with other Internet users. Nonregistered YouTube members are unable to upload and share any videos that they may have made.

To become a member of YouTube, go to the "Signup" page (http://www.youtube.com/signup), choose a username and password, and enter your information. Then click the "Sign Up" button and you are done.

There are several types of YouTube accounts: comedian, director, guru, musician, partner, politician, and YouTuber. In addition to performer information, musician accounts, for example can publish a schedule of show dates. The Groups feature allows users to share videos and have discussions on a common theme.

YouTube allows you to keep an address book. You can keep a contact list of your friends to easily send them private messages and share videos. In your address book you can create a separate section for agents, casting directors, producers, and so on.

Considerations When Making a YouTube Video

When it comes to making a YouTube video, one of the things that you will need is a video recording device. Popular video recording devices include camcorders, webcams, and cell phones with video recording capabilities. If at all possible, you will want to try to use a webcam or a camcorder, as these video recording devices often produce the best quality.

If you are interested in using your cell phone to help you make a YouTube video, you will need to make sure that your cell phone has video recording capabilities. You will find that most new cell phones do. For the best quality videos, you want to use traditional camcorders, particularly digital ones, but webcams are also nice, low-cost alternatives.

Once you have a video recording device, you can start to make your own videos. Popular videos on YouTube include video blogs, comedy skits, how-to videos, or travel videos.

If you are looking to make your YouTube video a hit, quality is something that you will want to take into consideration. Many YouTube video viewers dislike watching poor quality videos.

Editing is also something that you will want to take into consideration. YouTube actually encourages you to examine your video before uploading it to their site. If you notice anything that you would like changed, you are advised to edit your video before uploading it to YouTube.

It is also important that you think about and examine the content of your video, especially if you are planning on doing a performance video.

You will want to be cautious about offending any of your viewers, intentionally or not. Keep in mind that any performance means different things to different individuals. You are advised to use your best judgment.

Market Your YouTube Videos

As much traffic as YouTube brings you and your videos, you may be looking for more. Perhaps the easiest way to market your YouTube videos is to let friends, family members, or coworkers know that you have videos available for viewing on YouTube. For the best chance of success, you are advised to e-mail the direct links for your YouTube videos to those that you know.

It is advised that you post your own YouTube videos on your own websites, but if you know of anyone else who has a blog, you may want to think about giving them the needed HTML codes to have your YouTube video appear on their blog.

You can also market your YouTube videos on online message boards. Online message board marketing can be done in two different ways. For instance, there are many online message boards that let you discuss or share anything, in general, with other board members. You may want to think about posting links to some of your YouTube videos, especially if you think other members would enjoy watching them.

If you belong to an online message board or forum that allows you to have a signature, you will want to look into doing so. Your signature will always appear at the end of each of your messages. Therefore, the more active you are online, the more exposure your YouTube videos are likely to get.

Videos Available on YouTube

One type of YouTube video that is rapidly increasing in popularity is the video blog. While it may seem awkward to watch a video blog made by someone you have never met before, you may find video blogs to be quite entertaining. Blogging traditionally involves writing daily posts about your performing arts activities. Instead of writing down your words online, you are talking into a camera and then posting the video for the entire world to see. For your safety, you will want to avoid giving your real name, especially if you are showing your face on your video blog. It is advised that you do not mention your real name in any of your YouTune videos, but you definitely do not want to mention your address or any of your phone numbers. Do not divulge your personal information for your own safety.

Performing comedians have many outlets available to be exposed on YouTube, as comedy videos are extremely popular. For instance, there are some YouTube members that create comedy skits ones that are staged. There are also some YouTube members who happen to get candid videos.

It is also possible to find music videos available for viewing on YouTube, many of which are from contrasting music genres. For the most part, the music videos on YouTube are videos that local bands or musicians made themselves.

MySpace

MySpace, at www.myspace.com, is fast becoming a great resource in the entertainment industry. It is an online communication service that uses a combination of e-mail, photos, blogs, forums, user profiles, and more. Myspace.com is immensely popular because of its easy accessibility. It can broaden your horizons and allow you to share ideas of common interest. It is, in a sense, a vast community where you can socialize and network according to your

> **Smart tip:** With MySpace you are allowed to
> - Upload videos
> - Upload music
> - Create social network groups
> - Add music from your favorite artist to your home page
> - Manage your own personal calendar and more.

own style and your own schedule. MySpace also gives you the opportunity to interact with people of similar skills. It is free.

Performing artists can use myspace.com to display their work, which can then be referred to reviewers for financial aid consideration. Let's assume you are applying for a theater scholarship and want reviewers to get an instant look at your skills. Sure, you can send a CD of your performance. You can also refer them to your MySpace site, where reviewers can see your skills instantly.

MySpace gives musicians, comedians, filmmakers, and other artists the means to reach their established fan base and introduce themselves to a whole new audience. It is an easy, accessible, and entertaining way to broaden your horizons, share ideas, and record your own activities. It is especially valuable to new artists who are just starting out and trying to break out into the entertainment world. It can be invaluable if an artist's circumstances do not afford them the time or ability to promote their work in a traditional manner.

Whoever joins MySpace will have access to other members' profiles. This is a great way to locate people with similar interests and widen your networking circles. For example, there is a browse key that will allow you to scout out members according to specific criteria such as age, geography, occupation, etc. If you hit upon someone you want to contact, you can go ahead and e-mail him or her directly.

> **Stat fact:** There are more than 55 million MySpace members, two and one-half times the amount of traffic as Google, and it is ranked as the seventh most popular English-language website.

MySpace is a great way for those unfamiliar with HTML to have their own website. Users can easily create their own place on the web that is comparable to any site created with hours of inputting HTML code. MySpace profiles are far more manageable and offer an ease of use unmatched by traditional web design.

The Online Search for Financial Aid

No one will just hand the money to you. You have to seek it. Your first online stop for financial aid should be the websites of all the colleges where you are applying for admission or the college you already attend. College websites are often gold mines of scholarship information if you know where to look for it. First, check the admissions page, which often lists merit scholarships. Then, go to the student financial aid page, which may also list merit scholarships. Check the page for your academic department to discover if any scholarships for your field of study are mentioned.

The second step in winning scholarships is to hunt for the scholarships for which you are most qualified. There is no central place where scholarships are advertised; no book or database can claim to list all available awards. There is not one screen to click that will make all the scholarships appear on a list like magic. Therefore, you must use every resource to search for scholarships and create the most complete list possible of scholarships and financial aid contacts.

Most scholarship search services require you to fill out a personal profile listing your individual characteristics and accomplishments. The program then combs the database of scholarships to find those that you may be eligible for, according to the information that you provided in the profile. Therefore, you should be as accurate as possible when completing the profile in order for the program to result in the best list of scholarships for you. Read the instructions very carefully.

> **Smart tip:** There are several free scholarship databases available online. With more than $1 billion in scholarships, they are not easy to win and competition is fierce. Put as much time as possible into this endeavor. It will pay off.

The power of the Internet can help you discover the secrets of finding and winning scholarships. Do not expect it to be your only source, though. Use it as another tool to augment your search. Competition is tough, and the scramble for financial aid is brutal, but using the Internet will greatly improve your odds. Seek out as many scholarships as you can and apply, apply, apply.

Online Promoting

The Internet and the World Wide Web have created a new way of connecting with one another. Online promoting needs to become an important part of your financial aid seeking plan. In the long run, it can also save you money.

Here are some methods of using the Internet to gain more publicity for performing artists.

Posting Resumes Online

The medium for sending and receiving resumes has changed. Online resumes are beginning to replace the paper resume sent by mail. In the new online resume networking strategy you can now make your resume work for you 24 hours a day. On the Internet, electronic resumes have become a form of ongoing communication between performing artists and sources awarding financial aid.

An applicant can post a resume for a computer audience one of three ways. It can be sent via e-mail, via an electronic form (e-form), or by creating a web page. With the three posting methods you would think that all you have to do is to create a resume and randomly post it to many web sites. Random resume posting is hardly likely to bring any results. Targeting the right audiences is key. The challenge in posting is that you never really have an idea who will view your resume.

Electronic Mail

If you post your resume via e-mail, you should have a basic understanding of how e-mail works, where to get an e-mail account, and how to create a plain text version of your resume. You should also be able to use attachments, incorporate a cover letter, and take advantage of e-mail features such as using hyperlinks and creating an e-mail signature.

Search Engines

Search engines are the best online starting points to find relevant financial aid websites. First, go into a major search engine. In order to do this go to the navigator bar and type www.google.com or www.yahoo.com. You can type in the keywords relevant to your industry such as "Financial aid for actors." Browsing and searching are the most common activities on the web.

Media Sites

Media sites are online equivalents of newspapers and trade magazines. They allow users to purchase products, read product reviews, and download software. They also provide a forum to interact with like-minded people, depending on the focus of the magazine.

Search Engine Optimization for Beginners: How to Get Started

Search engine optimization (SEO) is the act of getting a website listed with search engines. Internet marketing can become a vital tool in your financial aid package.

Let's say a state arts council is interested in distributing several thousand dollars to promote a dance troupe, with the funds it has received from a government source. Most likely, the request for grant proposals will be advertised in the newspapers or online so that all dancers in the area or nationally are equally informed. The arts council may also go to Google or Yahoo and do a key word search on "Dance troupes in New York City." While they may not do their decision-making based on Google results, this step might be taken to get a sense of who is current in that field. You want to be in the top twenty results or so and SEO makes this possible.

About 70 percent to 80 percent of website traffic usually comes from search engines. If you are a performing artist with a website, it is important to rank high on the search engines because most people don't look beyond the first two pages and if your website is not seen there, then you are probably only receiving 25 percent to 35 percent of fair traffic and sales.

Crawler-Based Search Engines and Human-Powered Directories

The term "search engine" is often used generically to describe both crawler-based search engines and human-powered directories. These two types of search engines gather their listings in radically different ways.

Crawler-based search engines, such as Google, create their listings automatically. They "crawl" or "spider" the web; thereafter, people search through what they have found. If you change your web pages, crawler-based search engines eventually find these changes, and that can affect how you are listed. Page titles, body copy and other elements all play a role.

Human-powered directories such as the Open Directory, depends on humans for its listings. You submit a short description to the directory for your entire site, or editors write one for sites they review. A search looks for matches only in the descriptions submitted.

Changing your web pages typically has no effect on your listing. Things that are useful for improving a listing with a search engine have very little to do with improving a listing in a directory. The only exception is that a good site, with good content, might be more likely to get reviewed for free than a poor site.

Rich Web Content

Write good content. This is probably the single most important thing you need to do if you want to be found on the web. Even if your site is technically perfect for search engine robots, it won't do you any good unless you also fill it with good content. You can't expect consistent high rankings without good content. Good content brings return visitors.

Good content is text that is factually and grammatically correct, though that is not necessarily a must for all kinds of sites. Whatever your site is about, the content needs to be unique and/or specific enough to appeal to people. More specifically, it needs to be useful to the people you want to find your site.

Closely related to good content is fresh content. By adding new content regularly, you give visitors a reason to come back. Search engine robots will also visit your site more often once they notice that you update regularly, which means that any new content you add will be indexed quicker.

> **Smart tip:** What helps to bring in more traffic is having content that is relevant and important. Links are also important.

Inclusion of Keywords

Keywords are one of the first steps you need to consider when using SEO. One of the main rules in a ranking algorithm involves the location and frequency of keywords on a web page. Try to figure out what type of key words financial aid reviewers, funders, and agents are likely to use when they are searching for performing arts talent on the web. The words you imagine them typing into the search box are your target keywords. For example, say you have a page devoted to stamp collecting. Anytime someone types "stamp collecting," you want your page to be in the top ten results. Accordingly, these are your target keywords for that page. Each page in your website will have different target keywords that reflect the page's content. For example, say you have another page about the history of stamps. Then "stamp history" might be your keywords for that page.

When searching for keywords, look for words that are not single. Single words are too broad and competitive. Your target keywords should always be at least two or more words long. Usually, too many sites will be relevant for a single word, such as "stamps." This "competition" means your odds of success are lower. Don't waste your time fighting the odds. Pick phrases of two or more words, and you will have a better shot at success.

The more often you use keywords, the more relevant your site will be to the search engines, and the more likely your site will come up with those keywords in the search results. If your page contains 200 words, 2 or 3 of those words should be keywords, totaling 1 percent to 1.5 percent density. You should consider using your keywords in links and in headings of your page.

Search engines also like pages where keywords appear "high" on the page. They will check to see if the search keywords appear near the top of a web page, such as in the headline or in the first few paragraphs of text. They assume that any page relevant to the topic will mention those words right from the beginning.

Frequency is the other major factor in how search engines determine relevancy. A search engine will analyze how often keywords appear in relation to other words in a web page.

Sometimes, sites present large sections of copy via graphics. It looks pretty, but search engines can't read those graphics. That means they miss out on text that might make your site more relevant.

Position Your Keywords in Titles

Make sure your target keywords appear in the crucial locations on your web pages. The page's HTML title tag is most important. Failure to put target keywords in the title tag is the main reason why perfectly relevant web pages may be poorly ranked.

Build your titles around the top two or three phrases that you would like the page to be found for. The titles should be relatively short and attractive. Think of newspaper headlines. With a few words, they make you want to read a story. Similarly, your page titles are like headlines for your pages. They appear in search engine listings, and a short, attractive title may encourage users to click through to your site.

Use your target keywords for your page headline, if possible. Have them also appear in the first paragraphs of your web page. When it comes to the order of the text in the title element, the following works well:

Document title | Section name | Site or company name

This is probably one of the best formats for accessible title texts. Again, accessibility and SEO work together.

Whatever you do, don't use the same title text for all documents. Doing so will make it much harder for search engines, people browsing through search results, and site visitors to quickly find out what the document is about.

Build Inbound Links

Obtaining links, back links or inbound links to your site is one of the #1 rules for ranking. Every major search engine uses link analysis as part of its ranking algorithm. As a result, link analysis gives search engines a useful means of determining which pages are good for particular topics. The more links you have, the higher the ranking.

Links to your site tells search engines how important your site is. If search engines see that your website is important enough that several sites link to you, then it must be important enough for your site to rank high on the search engines.

To generate links, you need a strategy. Start by adding your site to DMOZ and Yahoo Directories. Write articles. Article marketing is a great way to obtain back links to your site and create more traffic. Submit to local and industry directories. Look for link partners and link-exchange with them. You can ask customers or suppliers to link with you. Look for relevant, high-ranking sites to link with you by e-mailing them or calling them.

Return visitors who like your content will eventually link to your site, and having lots of inbound links is great for search engine rankings, especially if those links are from highly ranked sites.

By building links, you can help improve how well your pages perform in link analysis systems. The key is understanding that link analysis is not about "popularity." In other words, it is not an issue of getting lots of links from anywhere. Instead, you want links from good web pages that are related to the topics you want to be found for. Make sure the links you use for your website are also important and high-ranking. They should have at least a "4" Google page rank.

Here is one simple means to find those good links. Go to the major search engines. Search for your target keywords. Look at the pages that appear in the top results. Now visit those pages and ask the site owners if they will link to you. Not everyone will, especially sites that are extremely competitive with yours. However, there will be noncompetitive sites that will link to you, especially if you offer to link back.

Submission to Search Engines

One of the last steps is the proper submission of your site to the search engine or directory. Submit your website to Google as soon as you register a domain name. Don't wait because you haven't built your site, haven't thought of what content to write, or don't have a business or marketing plan together yet. Submit it right away. It takes a long time to get indexed on the search engines. It takes months to get indexed, and even more months to get high rankings. So don't expect to rank high in the first couple of months after submitting your site.

Second, whenever Google notices a new website, it keeps the equitable ranking of that site for a certain amount of time, so it can analyze and determine whether your site is genuine, plausible and long-term. It does this to filter out all the Spam sites. So Google "sandboxes" your website. You are establishing site history by submitting your site early. By the time you have all your content together and developed, Google will have no reason to see you as Spam.

> **Smart tip:** URL ranking results change week-to-week due to competition, so maintaining a top ranking requires constant keywords monitoring and information rework. Search Engine Optimization never rests, much like your competition.

Provide Easy Access

Accessibility is very important. Making your site more accessible to vision impaired human users will also help search engine robots find their way around it. Remember, Google is blind, so even if you don't care about blind people using your site (which you should), you'll still want it to be accessible. This means that you should use real headings, paragraphs, and lists, and avoid using anything that may interfere with search engine spiders.

Avoid Using Frames

While it is possible to provide workarounds that allow search engine robots to crawl frame-based sites, frames will still cause problems for people who find your site through search engines. When somebody follows the link from a search result listing to a frame-based site, they will land on an orphaned document, outside of its parent frameset. This is very likely to cause confusion, since in many cases vital parts of the site, like navigational links, will be absent.

> **Beware:** If you are looking for a quick and easy way to get great results through SEO, there isn't one. Instead, expect to do some hard work, especially when it comes to the content of your site. There are no shortcuts. You will also need patience. Results do not come overnight.

Some sites use JavaScript or server side scripting to redirect anyone trying to load a document outside of its parent frameset to the site's home page. This is a very user hostile thing to do, and it definitely does not help the people visiting your site. Just lose the frames. They are bad for usability anyway.

16

Listing of Grant Directories

Nine Grant Directories That Every Performing Artist Should Know

You can save a considerable amount of time by becoming familiar with a few online grant directories. Discipline yourself to research a certain number of funders every week, rather than trying to seize the big picture all at once. This can be overwhelming. Some of the online grant directories list hundreds and even thousands of sources. The only way to become familiar with these funders is by visiting each of the sites, one at a time.

Fundsnet Services (www.fundsnetservices.com)

This is an excellent free source that lists thousands of funders. It is very easy to access and is user-friendly. Since 1996, Fundsnet Services has provided grant-writing and fundraising resource assistance to those in need of funding for their programs and initiatives. Fundsnet services allows you to search for grant opportunities in various categories, including arts, children, disability, women, health, education, computers, technology, environment, sport, and computer and technology. It also links visitors to pages on community foundations, international foundations, government funding, Canadian funders and more.

Council on Foundations (www.cof.org)

Provides links to other sites such as government grants sources and private sector foundations. It provides information on foundations awarding grants, upcoming events such as grants conferences, career programs, how to start a foundation, grant-making activities, publications, and more. The Council on Foundations details emerging issues in philanthropy and provides career information on grants, conferences, and events.

Contact: 1828 1 Street NW, Washington, D.C. 20036

Phone: (202) 466-6512

(Fax) (202) 785-3926

Foundation Center (http://fdcenter.org)

Established in 1956, the Foundation Center is dedicated to serving grant seekers, grant makers, researchers, policymakers, the media, and the general public. The Center's mission is to support and improve philanthropy by promoting public understanding of the field and helping grant seekers succeed.

The Foundation Center provides education and training for the grant-seeking process. Some of the Foundation Center tools to help grant seekers succeed are:

- Foundation Finder—allows users to search by name for basic financial and contact information for more than 70,000 private and community foundations in the U.S.
- Grant maker websites—four distinct directories with annotated links to grant-maker websites organized by grant-maker type allow users to search or browse summaries of the collected sites.
- Sector Search—a specialty search engine that indexes every page of the most useful non-profit sites on the Internet.
- 990-PF Search—a searchable database of the 990-PF tax returns filed with the Internal Revenue Service by all domestic private foundations. Users can locate and download, via .pdf (portable document files), the tax records of more than 60,000 private foundations. By looking at sections on the tax records that list giving patterns, award amounts, board members, and so forth, you can help decide if a foundation is a good match with your needs.

Associated Grant Makers (http://agmconnect.org)

Associated Grant Makers is a resource center for philanthropy. It has a reference collection of publications and other information on foundation and corporate grant making and nonprofit management including national foundations, corporate giving, IRS 990-PF forms, journals, newsletters, fundraising manuals, and proposal-writing guides. Its mission is to support the practice and expansion of effective philanthropic giving. AGM is a community of foundation staff and trustees, corporate grant makers, donors and philanthropic advisory services that builds a connection with nonprofit leaders. It is a warehouse of learning both for grant makers and grant seekers. Its events calendar offers grant-related activities offered every year.

Contact: 55 Court Street, Suite 520, Boston, MA 02108
Phone: (617) 426-2606
E-mail: agm@agmconnect.org

The Grantsmanship Center (http://www.tgci.com)

The Grantsmanship Center is primarily a training organization for grant writers. The *Center* sponsors workshops on writing grant proposals; publishes a funding newsletter, *The Grantsmanship Center Magazine*, available free to qualified agencies; and sells reprints of articles related to proposal writing and fundraising. *TGCI* magazine provides information on how to plan, manage, staff and get grants for individuals and organizations.

Contact: P.O. Box 17220, Los Angeles, CA 90017,
Phone: (213) 482-9860
Fax: (213) 482-9863
E-mail: info@tgci.com

Phyllis Edelson, ed., *Foundation Grants for Individuals*, The Foundation Center, New York, 2007

The Foundation Grants for Individuals gives a comprehensive listing available of private foundations, some of which provide financial assistance to individuals. The subjects of funding are categorized as follows: educational support, restricted to company employees; general welfare; arts and cultural support, and restricted to graduates or students of specific schools. It gives each individual listing with the application address, limitations, financial data, EIN (employer identification number), foundation type, and application information.

The Foundation Grants for Individuals should be within the reach of any serious grant writer or grant seeker. Published by *The Foundation Center*, it has over 1500 pages. The current 14th edition costs $75.

The Directory of Grants in the Humanities 2008/2009, Oryx Publishing, Phoenix, Arizona, 2008

The Directory of Grants in the Humanities contains brief descriptions of more than 4,000 funding programs that support research and performance in literature, language, linguistics, history, anthropology, philosophy, ethics, religion, and the fine and performing arts including painting, dance, photography, sculpture, music, drama, crafts, folklore, mime, and other areas. These programs fund research, travel, internships, fellowships, dissertation support, conferences, and performances. Each listing includes deadline dates, contact name and address, restrictions, and amount of money available.

The Fund for Women Artists (www.womenarts.org)

The Fund for Women Artists is founded on the belief that women artists have the power to change the way women are perceived in our society. The Fund for Women Artists is a nonprofit 501(c)(3) arts service organization dedicated to helping women artists get the resources they need to do their creative work. Created in 1994 by Martha Richards, the organization has raised over $4 million and created a website that provides free networking, fundraising and advocacy services to over 500,000 visitors a year.

Contact: P.O. Box 60637, Florence, MA 01062
Phone: (413) 585-5968
Fax: (413) 586-1303
E-mail: info@womenarts.org

17

Useful Websites Every Financial Aid Seeker Should Know

Here are some financial aid websites to explore. Some of them will suit your needs while others may not. Spend adequate time researching these places to find out which ones you are qualified for.

FastWeb

Name of Listing: FastWeb
Description: Find colleges and scholarships and apply online for the scholarship that suits your needs. The site has a lot of information on scholarships, loans, grants and how to apply for them. Requires membership before making scholarship application
Website address: http://www.fastweb.com
Contact information: 444 North Michigan Avenue, Suite 3000, Chicago, IL 60611
E mail: n/a

College Savings Plan Network

Name of Listing: College Savings Plan Network
Description: An informative website with a focus on fleshing out the 529 Plan. It offers a series of articles on the 529 Plan.
Website: http://www.collegesavings.org/
Contact information: n/a
E mail: n/a

ARTS Program, National Foundation
for Advancement in the Arts

Name of Listing: ARTS Program, National Foundation for Advancement
  in the Arts
Description: Scholarships for performing, visual and literary artists.
Website address: http://www.artsawards.org/
Contact information: National Foundation for Advancement in the Arts
  youngARTS program, 444 Brickell Avenue, P-14, Miami, FL 33131
  Phone: (305) 377-1140
E-mail: info@nfaa.org

College Board

Name of Listing: College Board
Description: A comprehensive source for all students planning to attend
  or who are already in college. It assist students in finding a college,
  applying for college, writing college essays, filling out financial aid forms,
  taking college centers, SAT centers, and more.
Website address: www.collegeboard.com
Contact information: 45 Columbus Avenue, New York, NY 10023-6917
E-mail: n/a

Student Financial Aid Resources by State

Name of Listing: Student Financial Aid Resources by State
Description: Provide information on the state's education programs, colleges and universities, financial aid assistance programs, grants, scholarships, continuing education programs, and career opportunities. This
  is run by the Department of Education.
Website address: http://wdcrobcolp01.ed.gov/Programs/EROD/org_list.
  cfm?category_ID=SHE
Contact information: n/a
E-mail: n/a

Saving for College

Name of Listing: Saving for College
Description: 529 Plans, contributions by grandparents into long-term col-
  lege funds, Coverdell accounts and others are fleshed out.
Website address: http://www.savingforcollege.com/
Contact information: n/a
E-mail: n/a

FinAid

Name of Listing: FinAid
Description: Provides information on scholarships, loans, savings, military
aid and more.
Website address: http://www.finaid.org/
Contact information: n/a
E-mail: n/a

AmeriCorps

Name of Listing: AmeriCorps
Description: National network of programs that engages more than 70,000
Americans each year in intensive service to meet critical needs in com-
munities throughout the nation. Financial aid is given to participants.
Website address: www.americorps.org
Contact information: 1201 New York Avenue, NW, Washington, D.C. 20525;
Phone: (202) 606-5000
E-mail: questions@americorps.org

American Student Assistance

Name of Listing: American Student Assistance
Description: Gives information on education loans, workshops and semi-
nars on financial aid, and how students can apply for aid.
Website address: http://www.amsa.com/
Contact information: American Student Assistance, 100 Cambridge Street,
Boston, MA 02114
Phone: (800) 999-9080
E mail: brightbeginnings@amsa.com

Scholarship Page

Name of Listing: Scholarship Page
Description: This website has been created by a student who didn't have
money to get through college, but somehow found a way to get an edu-
cation through financial aid. It provides detailed listings of where to
look for financial aid.
Website: www.scholarship-page.com/
Contact information: The Scholarship Page, 13014 New Arden Court, Oak
Hill, VA 20171
E-mail: Does not accept e mails.

College Connection Scholarships

Name of Listing: College Connection Scholarships
Description: Provides direct links to colleges, tips on the scholarship
  process, and sample college essays
Website: http://www.collegescholarships.com/
Contact information: 1508 Seton Villa Lane Wilmington, DE 19809
E-mail: staff@collegescholarships.com

College Scholarship Search

Name of Listing: College Scholarship Search
Description: The College Scholarships, Colleges, and Online Degrees page
  is designed to offer college-bound, graduate school-bound, and career
  school bound students of all ages information easy access to information about a wide variety of subjects which include: free college scholarship and financial aid searches, SAT and ACT test preparation tips,
  and more, colleges and universities throughout the United States.
Website: http://www.college-scholarships.com/
Contact information: n/a
E mail: n/a

Review

Name of Listing: Review
Description: Provides information on how to fill out the FAFSA and PRO-
  FILE; the difference between need—based aid and merit-based aid, gov-
  ernment-sponsored loans, and more.
Website address: www.review.com
Contact information: The Princeton Review, 2315 Broadway, New York
  10024
Phone: (212) 874-8282
E-mail: helpme@review.com

Eduprep

Name of Listing: Eduprep
Description: Gives listings of some leading scholarship and financial aid
  programs. If you are unsure about which search engines to look for, visit
  this website and it will lead you to the necessary sources.
Website address: www.eduprep.com/scholarship.asp
Contact information: n/a
E mail: collegeprep@lagcc.cuny.edu

GoCollege

Name of Listing: GoCollege

Description: Offers information on federal student loans, private loans, scholarships, Pell Grants and other alternatives. The Financial Aid section will guide students step by step to discover what options will best suit their needs. Financial aid investing options like College 529 Plans and baccalaureate bonds are also explained here.

Website address: www.gocollege.com

Contact information: n/a

E mail: n/a

National Association for College Admission Counseling

Name of Listing: National Association for College Admission Counseling

Description: Provides all the information college students would need to know about federal, private, and state financial aid programs. It covers types of financial aid such as scholarships, loans and grants. Federal student aid programs, institutional aid, and state aid are also covered in great detail.

Website address: http://www.nacacnet.org

Contact information: 1631 Prince Street, Alexandria, Virginia 22314

Phone: (703) 836-2222

E-mail: info@nacacnet.org

Chase Student Loans

Name of Listing: Chase Student Loans

Description: Loan consolidation, loan defaults, finding scholarship money and grant search are some of the topic covered. It discusses the differences between applying for a federal vs. private loan. Students interested in knowing the current interest rates for Federal Stafford and PLUS loans, this website provides up to date information.

Website address: http://www.chasestudentloans.com/

Contact information: n/a

E-mail: studentloans@chase.com

College Is Possible

Name of Listing: College is Possible

Description: College Is Possible (CIP) is the American Council on Education's K–16 youth development program that motivates middle and high school students from underserved communities to seek a college education. As the umbrella organization for higher education and a presidential association, the American Council on Education (ACE) is uniquely positioned to build a bridge between colleges and universities and their local K–12 community with commitment at the executive level. Learn about student financial aid programs, basic facts about college prices and student aid, recommended websites, books, and brochures, and how to choose the right college.

Website address: www.collegeispossible.org

Contact information: American Council on Education, One Dupont Circle NW, Washington, D.C. 20036-1193

Phone: (202) 939-9300

E-mail: comments@ace.nche.edu

Music Websites

Here are some music websites for musicians to explore. Some of them may suit your needs while others may not. Determine which ones are likely to fund your specific request.

American Music Therapy Association, Inc.

Name of Listing: American Music Therapy Association, Inc.

Description: Creates public awareness of the benefits of music therapy and increase access to quality music therapy services in a rapidly changing world.

Website address: www.musictherapy.org

Contact information: 8455 Colesville Road, Suite 1000, Silver Spring, Maryland 20910 Phone: (301) 589-3300

Fax: (301) 589-5175

E-mail: info@musictherapy.org

The American Musical Instrument Society

Name of Listing: The American Musical Instrument Society

Description: An international organization founded in 1971 to promote better understanding of all aspects of the history, design, construction, restoration, and usage of musical instruments in all cultures and from all periods. Under awards, musicians can access information on the Curt Sachs Award, Frances Densmore Award and more.

Website address: http://www.amis.org/awards/index.html

Contact information: The Guild Associates, Inc., 389 Main Street, Suite 202, Malden, MA 02148

E-mail: amis@guildassoc.com

American Musicological Society

Name of Listing: American Musicological Society
Description: Founded in 1934 to advance research in the various fields of music as a branch of learning and scholarship. 3,600 individuals and 1,200 institutional subscribers from over forty nations participate in the Society.
Website address: http://www.ams-net.org/awards.html
Contact information: American Musicological Society, Inc.,
6010 College Station, Brunswick ME 04011-8451
Phone: (207) 798-4243
Fax (207) 798-4254
Toll-free tel./fax: (877) 679-7648
E-mail: ams@ams-net.org

Society of Ethnomusicology

Name of Listing: Society of Ethnomusicology
Description: Multidisciplinary in concept and worldwide in scope. Members' interests range from Japanese shakuhachi performance practice to popular music in New York; from the conservation and display of Native American musical instruments to teaching world music in public schools. Members of the Society for Ethnomusicology are scholars, students, performers, publishers, museum specialists, and librarians from numerous disciplines. Some of these disciplines include anthropology, musicology, cultural studies, acoustics, popular music studies, music education, folklore, composition, archiving, and the performing arts, just to name a few.
Website address: www.ethnomusicology.org/
Contact information: n/a
E-mail: semexec@indiana.edu\

The Aaron Copland Fund

Name of Listing: The Aaron Copland Fund
Description: In general, grants range from $1,000 to $20,000.
Website address: www.coplandfund.org/
Contact information: c/o American Music Center, 30 West 26th Street, Suite 1001, New York, NY 10010-2011; Re: Aaron Copland Fund Performing Ensembles Program
Tel: (212) 366-5260 ext. 29
E-mail: n/a

Koussevitzky Music Foundation

Name of Listing: Koussevitzky Music Foundation
Description: The Foundation considers applications from performing
  organizations for the joint commissioning of composers.
Website address: www. koussevitzky.org
Contact information: Foundation Administrator, Koussevitzky Music
  Foundation, Inc., c/o Brown Raysman LLP, 900 Third Avenue, New
  York, NY 10022
Phone: 212-895-2367
E-mail: info@koussevitzky.org

Music Research

Name of Listing: Music Research
Description: Advancing active participation in music-making across
  the lifespan by supporting scientific research, philanthropic giving
  and public service programs from the international music products
  industry.
Website address: http://www.music-research.org/
Contact information: n/a
E-mail: info@nammfoundation.org

The George London Foundation for Singers Inc.

Name of Listing: The George London Foundation for Singers, Inc.
Description: Established by George London in 1971 as a grants program
  for outstanding young professional opera singers during their early
  careers, often at a financially difficult time. It is dedicated to the sup-
  port and encouragement of the next generation of great singers. Five
  career grants of $7500 and five encouragement grants of $1000 yearly
Website address: www.georgelondon.org
Contact information: P.O. Box 231276, New York, NY 10023
Phone: (212) 877-6347
Fax: (212) 877-6348
E-mail: londonFoundation@aol.com

Opera Index

Name of Listing: Opera Index
Description: New York tax-exempt corporation whose mission is to assist
  young singers at the very early stages of their careers with cash awards
  totaling $39,000, based upon a vocal competition.
Website address: www.operaindexinx.org

Contact information: 151 Central Park West, #1W, New York, NY 10023-1514

Phone: (212) 877-6778

E-mail: contact@operaindexinc.org

Jazz Musicians' Emergency Fund

Name of Listing: Jazz Musicians' Emergency Fund

Description: The JMEF is committed to helping jazz professionals, especially older musicians, overcome their hard times and to help them get back on their feet, making emergency funds available for immediate needs.

Website address: www.jazzfoundation.org/emergency_fund.php

Contact information: Jazz Foundation of America, 322 West 48th Street, 3rd Floor, New York, NY 10036

Phone: (212) 245-3999

E-mail: pledge@jazzfoundation.org

MusiCares Foundation

Name of Listing: MusicCares Foundation

Description: MusiCares provides a safety net of critical assistance for music people in times of need. MusiCares services and resources cover a wide range of financial, medical and personal emergencies, and each case is treated with integrity and confidentiality.

Website address: www.grammy.com/MusiCares

Contact information: Each region has its own toll-free help line: (800) 687-4227 (West Coast), (877) 626-2748 (Central) and (877) 303-6962 (Northeast).

E-mail: MusiCares@grammy.com

Society of Singers Financial Aid

Name of Listing: Society of Singers Financial Aid

Description: The Society helps singers meet financial needs resulting from crises or other circumstances. Charitable grants may be provided toward basic necessities of life such as food, shelter, utilities, medical/dental assistance, HIV/AIDS treatment, substance abuse rehab, psychotherapy and other basic expenses.

Website address: www.singers.org

Contact information: Society of Singers, 6500 Wilshire Blvd., Suite 640, Los Angeles, CA 90048;

Phone: (866) 767-7671

E mail: help@singers.org

The Rhythm and Blues Foundation

Name of Listing: The Rhythm and Blues Foundation
Description: Provides emergency financial assistance and career recognition
   awards to artists and practitioners of rhythm and blues music who worked
   and/or recorded rhythm and blues music in the 1940's, 50's, and 60's.
Website address: www.rhythm-n-blues.org
Contact information: Rhythm and Blues Foundation, 100 S. Broad Street,
   Suite 620 Philadelphia, PA 19110, Phone: 215-568-1080
E mail: kmvconnelly@aol.com

Music Maker Relief Foundation

Name of Listing: Music Maker Relief Foundation
Description: Helps the pioneers and forgotten heroes of Southern musical traditions gain recognition and meet their day to day needs. Criteria for recipients are that they be rooted in a Southern musical tradition,
   be 55 years or older and have an annual income less than $18,000. Life
   Maintenance—Grants for necessities such as food, medical needs, housing. Emergency Relief—Substantial one-time grants to recipients in crisis (medical, fire, theft, etc.).
Website address: www.musicmaker.org
Contact information: Music Maker Relief Foundation, Eno Valley Station P.O. Box 72222, Durham, NC 27722-2222
Phone: (919) 643-2456
E-mail: info@musicmaker.org

Sweet Relief Organization

Name of Listing: Sweet Relief Organization
Description: Provides financial assistance to all types of career musicians
   who are facing illness, disability, or age-related problems. The applicant
   must be a musician who has regular public performances, or performed
   on at least three widely released recordings (audio or audiovisual), or
   written music that has been performed on three widely released recordings, or published on three occasions.
Website address: www.sweetrelief.org
Contact information: 65 South Grand Avenue, #209, Pasadena, CA 91105
Phone: (888) 955-7880
E mail: info@sweetrelief.org

Franklin Furnace Fund for Performance Art

Name of Listing: Franklin Furnace Fund for Performance Art
Description: Awards grants of $2,000–$5,000 to performance artists, allow-

ing them to produce major works anywhere in the state of New York. Artists from all over the world are invited to apply.

Website address: www.franklinfurnace.org

Contact information: 80 Arts—The James E. Davis Arts Building, 80 Hanson Place, #301 Brooklyn, NY 11217-1506, Phone: (718) 398-7255 E-mail: mail@franklinfurnace.org

Actor Websites

Many acting websites list auditions for both union and nonunion acting work, tips and resources for becoming a better actor, and employment opportunities for day jobs within the show business industry, such as receptionists, script readers, web designers, and even film crews. Here are a few starting points. Always pay careful attention about revealing your personal information to any of the sites.

Acting Depot

Name of Listing: Acting Depot

Description: Resume writing for actors, job hotlines, extra work, and acting agents are some of the areas covered.

Website address: www.actingdepot.com

Contact information: n/a

E-mail: n/a

Actor News

Name of Listing: Actor News

Description: Free e-mail casting and online resources for performing artists. Gives listings of calls for auditions

Website address: www.actornews.com

Contact information: n/a

E-mail: GipGibson@theHiddenLoot.com

Actor Store

Name of Listing: Actor Store

Description: Gives a diverse collection of theater and acting resources. Also gives a listing of acting schools.

Website address: www.actorstore.com

Contact information: n/a

E-mail: n/a

Screen Actors' Guild

Name of Listing: Screen Actors' Guild
Description: SAG is the nation's largest labor union representing working
    actors. The Guild exists to enhance working conditions, compensation,
    and benefits, and to be a powerful, unified voice on behalf of artists' rights.
Website address: www.sag.org
Contact information: 5757 Wilshire Blvd., 7th Floors, Los Angeles, CA
    90036
Phone: 1 (800) SAG-0767
E-mail: saginfo@sag.org

Canadian Actors' Equity Association

Canadian Actors' Equity Association
Description: The professional association of performers, directors, chore-
    ographers, and stage managers in Canada, who are engaged in English-
    language live performance, including stage, opera, ballet, and dance.
Website address: www.caea.com
Contact information: 44 Victoria Street, 12th Floor, Toronto, ON M5C 3C4
E-mail: info@caea.com

ActorSource

Name of Listing: Actor Source
Description: Teaches actors how to craft a resume, acting scams, termi-
    nology that may be heard while on the set, how to write a proper cover
    letter and many other acting-related services.
Website address: www.actorsource.com
Contact information: n/a
E-mail: actorsource@gmail.com

Actor Point

Name of Listing: Actor Point
Description: A recommended website for actors interested in aid as well
    as launching a successful career. Teaches how to audition, headshot tips,
    avoiding acting scams, how to launch an acting career, and more. Also
    has a job advertisement section with casting calls. There is also a data-
    base featuring over 650 actors.
Website address: www.actorpoint.com
Contact information: n/a
E-mail: n/a

ActingBiz

Name of Listing: Actingbiz
Description: How to get great headshots, preparing for an audition, acting success tips, finding an agent, and casting calls are some of the areas covered in this website. Also lists film schools, training programs, unions, guilds, and associations.
Website address: www.actingbiz.com
Contact information: n/a
E-mail: n/a

North American Performing Arts Managers and Agents

Name of Listing: North American Performing Arts Managers and Agents
Description: NAPAMA comprises diverse group of managers, agents, self-managed artists, affiliated business vendors, and presenters—all industry colleagues in the field of the live performing arts.
Website address: www.napama.org
Contact information: NAPAMA, 459 Columbus Avenue, #133, New York City, NY 10024
E-mail: info@napama.org

Backstage

Name of Listing: Backstage
Description: Offers regular columns that list the latest film, television, and theater work available, mostly in the Los Angeles and New York areas, but occasionally in other cities as well. Some of the listed work is union work, some is non-union work that often includes some amount of pay, and a large number are student films or plays with little or no pay available.
Website address: www.backstage.com
Contact information: Back Stage West, 5055 Wilshire Boulevard, Los Angeles, CA 90036
Phone: (323) 525-2356
E-mail: n/a

Variety

Name of Listing: Variety
Description: Information on the latest happenings in Hollywood, acting, Grammy awards, and other events
Website address: www.variety.com
Contact information: n/a
E-mail: erin.maxwell@variety.com

Creative Capital

Name of Listing: Creative Capital
Description: Offers grants to individuals in the performing & visual arts, media, new fields. Grants up to $20,000 are offered.
Website: www.creative-capital.org
Contact information: 65 Bleecker Street; Seventh Floor , New York, NY 10012
Phone: (212) 598-9900
E-mail:

Princess Grace Awards for Theater Artists and Playwrights

Name of Listing: Princess Grace Awards for Theater Artists and Playwrights
Description: Dedicated to identifying and assisting emerging young artists in theater to realize their career goals through scholarships, apprenticeships, and fellowships. Awards are based primarily on the artistic quality of the artist's past work, his/her potential for future excellence, and the appropriateness of the activities to the individual's artistic growth.
Website: www.pgfusa.com
Contact information: 150 East 58th Street, 25th Floor, New York, NY 10155
Phone: (212) 317-1470
E-mail: info@pgfusa.com

Grants, Awards and Scholarships in Puppetry

Performing artists in the field of puppetry have a few sources offering aid specifically in the field. They are not as plentiful as other performing arts like music and acting, however. Here are a few of them.

The Arlyn Award

Name of Listing: The Arlyn Award
Description: A search for outstanding design in the puppet theater. It is a cash prize of $500.00. Any puppeteer, anywhere in the world is eligible to enter. Submit a portfolio of not more than ten original designs and photographs of a single production premiered. Enclose a brief outline of the designer's intent, and, if possible, a videotape (edited to 10 minutes) of scenes showing how effectively the designs work in the performance.
Contact information: Arlyn Award Society, c/o NVCAC, 335 Lonsdale Avenue, North Vancouver, BC, V7M 2G3 Canada

The UNIMA Exchange Cultural Commission

Name of Listing: The UNIMA Exchange Cultural Commission

Description: For over 25 years UNIMA-USA has offered scholarships to underwrite professional puppetry training abroad for North American UNIMA members. Study in different countries and different cultures actively encourages "building bridges of international understanding" with puppeteers from around the globe.

Puppetry training may be undertaken with either a recognized puppetry professional or a professional program outside of North America. The Exchange Cultural Commission of UNIMA, in collaboration with a number of International Puppet Festivals, now offers scholarships for UNIMA members to attend international festivals. These scholarships cover housing, meals and free entry to the performances.

Website address: http://www.unima-usa.org/scholarships/index.html#1

Contact information: Alberto Cebreiro Exchange Cultural Commission, UNIMA Ronda del Port, 5-70, 46128—Alboraya (Valency), Spain

E-mail: alberto.ce@teleline.es

Puppeteers

Name of Listing: Puppeteers

Description: The Endowment Fund makes financial grants to active puppeteers for projects that will further the growth and development of the art of puppetry. Awards range from $100 to $1000. The first priority of the Endowment Fund Committee is the allocation of funds to support the development and creation of new professional puppet productions.

Website address: www.puppeteers.org

Contact information: Michael Nelson, P.O. Box 2296, Yontville, CA 94599 (707) 257-8007

E-mail: mail@magicalmoonshine.org

Emma Louise Warfield Memorial Fund

Name of Listing: Emma Louise Warfield Memorial Fund

Description: Established to enable individuals to attend a national festival who lack the financial means to do so otherwise. Puppeteers, puppet makers, and puppetry students 22 years old and older may apply. All applicants must be members of the Puppeteers of America, Inc.

Contact information: Kamala Kruszka P. of A. Scholarship Committee Chair 9612 Twain Way Bakersfield, CA 93311

Phone: (888) 568-6235

Emergency Grants

Individuals may qualify for emergency expenses to help with day-to-day living expenses, including:

- Health insurance
- Hospital bills
- Loan and debt payments
- Disaster relief
- Expenses
- Rent/mortgage
- Addiction recovery
- Food and clothing
- Child care
- Utility bills

Sources Funding Emergency Aid

It may be worth your time and effort to know a few places that award emergency grants. You never know when disaster might strike. Here are a few sources awarding emergency aid to performing artists.

Actors Fund of America

Name of Listing: Actor's Fund of America
Description: Provides for the social welfare of all entertainment professionals—designers, writers, sound technicians, musicians, dancers, administrators, directors, film editors, stagehands—as well as actors. Professionals in film, television, radio, theatre, dance and music all turn to the Actors Fund in times of need.
The Actors Fund Human Services Department offers a wide range of social services to working professionals, persons with AIDS, seniors and the disabled and others in need of help. In addition, emergency financial grants may be provided for essentials such as food, rent and medical care.
Website address: www.actorsfund.org/
Contact information: The Actors Fund, National Headquarters, 729 Seventh Avenue, 10th floor, New York, NY 10019
Phone: (800) 798-8447
E-mail: info@actorsfund.org

Musicians Foundation

Name of Listing: Musicians Foundation
Description: Helps professional musicians by providing emergency finan-

cial assistance in meeting current living, medical and allied expenses. Financial assistance is limited to musicians working in the United States. All professional musicians, regardless of genre, are eligible to apply.

Website: www.musiciansfoundation.org

Contact information: Musicians Foundation, 875 Sixth Avenue, Room 2303, New York, NY 10001.

Phone: (212) 239-9137

E-mail: info@musiciansfoundation.org

Craft Emergency Relief Fund

Name of Listing: Craft Emergency Relief Fund

Description: Provides direct financial aid educational assistance to craft artists, including emergency relief assistance, business development support, resources, and referrals.

Website address: http://www.craftemergency.org/

Contact information: CERF, P.O. Box 838, Montpelier, VT 05601-0838

Physical Address: 28 Elm Street #2, Montpelier, VT 05602

Phone: (802) 229-2306

E-mail: info@craftemergency.org

Elizabeth Greenshields Foundation

Name of Listing: Elizabeth Greenshields Foundation

Description: Grants for representational artists in early stages of career, for study, travel, rent, materials, etc. Each grant is $10,000 (Canadian).

Website address: n/a

Contact information: Elizabeth Greenshields Foundation, 1814 Sherbrooke Street West, Suite 1, Montreal, Quebec H3H 1E4 CANADA

Phone: (514) 937-9225

E-mail: greenshields@bellnet.com; egreen@total.net

Change

Name of Listing: Change

Description: Grants for emergency expenses incurred by medical catastrophes, fire, theft, natural disaster, accident, or to avoid eviction, etc. No fee; submit detailed letter detailing emergency. Deadline: Open.

Website address: n/a

Contact information: Change, Inc., P.O. Box 54, Captiva FL 33924

Telephone: (212) 473-3742

E-mail: n/a

The Artists' Fellowship

Name of Listing: The Artists' Fellowship
Description: Private, charitable foundation that assists professional fine
   artists (painters, graphic artists, sculptors) and their families in times of
   emergency, disability, or bereavement. Assistance is given without expec-
   tation of repayment.
Contact information: Artists' Fellowship, Inc., 47 Fifth Avenue, New York,
   N.Y. 10003
Telephone: (646) 230-9833

The Pollock-Krasner Foundation

Name of Listing: The Pollock-Krasner Foundation
Description: The Foundation's dual criteria for grants are recognizable
   artistic merit and demonstrable financial need, whether professional,
   personal or both. The Foundation encourages applications from artists
   who have genuine financial needs that are not necessarily catastrophic.
   Grants are intended for a one-year period of time. The Foundation will
   consider need on the part of an applicant for all legitimate expenditures
   relating to his or her professional work and personal living, including
   medical expenses. The size and length of the grant are determined by
   the individual circumstances of the artist.
Website address: http://www.pkf.org/
Contact information: The Pollock-Krasner Foundation, Inc., 725 Park
   Ave., New York, NY 10021
Phone: (212) 517-5400
E-mail: grants@pkf.org

Writers Emergency Assistance Fund

Name of Listing: Writers Emergency Assistance Fund
Description: Exists to help established freelance nonfiction writers across
   the country who, because of advancing age, illness, disability, or extraor-
   dinary professional crisis are unable to work.
Website address: http://www.asja.org/weaf.php
Contact information: American Society of Journalists and Authors Char-
   itable Trust 1501 Broadway, Suite 302, New York, NY 10036
E-mail: n/a

Off the Beaten Path

Some financial aid is less publicized, making it more difficult for performing artists to learn about their availability. Here are a few of those off the radar:

I Have a Dream

In 1986 Eugene Lang created the "I Have a Dream" foundation to help other people start similar projects. Students can't apply for this assistance. They can only hope someone will adopt their class. $300,000 is given per class. The website is www.Ihad.org.

Dollars for Scholars

Dollars for Scholars is a national network of 800 community-based, volunteer-operated scholarship foundations affiliated with the Citizens Scholarship Foundation of America (CSFA). All funds are awarded by a local awards committee to students of the community. Ask your counselor if your community has a chapter, or check http://citizens. scholarship-foundation.org.

President's Student Service Scholarships

The Corporation for National Service provides $500 matching scholarships to students who have received at least $500 from a local community organization and who have performed at least 100 hours of service in the past 12 months. Visit www.student-service-awards.org

Prudential Spirit of Community Awards

These $1000 awards go to two students in each state who have demonstrated "exemplary, self-initiated community service." Schools may nominate one honoree for every 1500 students. Inform your counselor of your good work.

Delta Service Corps

The Delta Service Corps places workers age 17+ in existing community organizations across some of the low-income regions in states such as Arkansas, Louisiana, and Mississippi. Corps members receive a $4725 education voucher for each of two years of full-time service. Check www.ladeltacorp.org.

Public Allies

Ten-month program designed and run by young people for young people who want to help solve some of the nation's most pressing social problems. Currently more than 100 "Allies" between the ages of 18 and 30 receive a stipend ($15,000 plus health and education benefits) while working on projects in public safety, education, human needs and the environment. Public Allies is a highly competitive application process. See www.publicallies.org.

Teach for America

Recent college grads spend two years teaching in under resourced public schools nationwide. 3000 people compete for 500 opportunities. Go to www.teachforamerica.org.

Fulbright Grants and Teaching Assistantships

Fulbright grants send you to campus in 1 of 140 countries to take courses. Knowing the local language is key. It also awards approximately 1,800 student grants to non-U.S. nationals to study in the United States annually. Approximately 3,200 new and continuing student fellows are currently in the United States on Fulbright grants. The website is www.iie.org.

Rhodes Scholarship

American Rhodes Scholars are selected through a decentralized process by which regional selection committees choose 32 scholars each year from among those nominated by selection committees in each of the fifty states. Rhodes Scholars are elected for two years of study at the University of Oxford, with the possibility of renewal for a third year. All educational costs, such as matriculation, tuition, laboratory and certain other fees, are paid on the scholar's behalf by the Rhodes Trustees. Each scholar receives in addition a maintenance allowance adequate to meet necessary expenses for term-time and vacations. The Rhodes Trustees cover the necessary costs of travel to and from Oxford, and upon application, may approve additional grants for research purposes or study-related travel.

A Rhodes scholarship provides tuition, fees, and maintenance costs for two to three years of graduate work at Oxford University. Only 32 awards to American students are given each year. The website is www. rhodesscholar.org.

Rotary International Ambassadorial Scholarships

Rotary Ambassadorial Scholarships are one- and two-year fellowships for study abroad to foster international understanding among people of different countries. See the website at www.rotary.org.

Community Money Contacts

Most communities offer scholarships to help their young citizens. The grants vary in size from $100 to several thousand; they are usually circumscribed in their geographic coverage and you must learn about them yourself. There is no central registry. Read your local papers carefully, especially the page devoted to club and community affairs. Visit your Chamber of Commerce. It might keep track of local businesses and corporate scholarships. Also visit the American Legion Post. The legionnaires take a special interest in helping people with their education. And finally, ask your high school counselor.

Community service scholarships are available to students. If you have demonstrated a solid commitment to serving your community, you may be able to turn your good deeds into college scholarship money. For more information on both of these programs, contact your guidance counselor or your principal.

18

Financial Aid Myths

There are many myths out there about financial aid. Many artists never even try to apply for aid because of certain misconceptions blocking their motivation about ever winning grants and scholarships. Getting these myths out in the open may help you to muster courage and go forward with your financial aid search.

Myth 1: There Is Less Aid Available Than There Used to Be.

This is not true. There was over $129 billion in student financial aid available for the academic year 2004–2005. This is almost $10 billion more than academic year 2003–2004. These statistics were taken from the study titled "Trends in College Pricing," College Board, 2005.

Myth 2: You Have to Be a Minority to Get Aid.

This is not true. There are no criteria within the federal or institutional methodologies that factor in minority background. Both federal and institutional need analysis systems are race-neutral. The FAFSA does not even ask applicants to submit race information. Colleges will use the estimated family contribution and simply subtract it from the cost of attendance to determine financial need. Also, colleges are committed to access and affordability regardless of ethnic background.

Myth 3: Only Students with Good Grades Get Financial Aid.

It is a misconception to think that you have to be an "A"-grade student to get financial aid. Schools not only consider grades but also service to the community, participation in the arts, athletics, and academic major as criteria. More importantly, eligibility for student aid from the federal government and grants from individual colleges are based on the student's financial need, not academic record.

Myth 4: Private Schools Are Out of Reach for My Family.

In many cases, attending a private college or university may be more affordable than a public institution. Private colleges and universities have more institutional aid to award to students. Also, private colleges will award money to students based on academic merit and financial need in order to attract a diverse student body. Nationally, more than 70 percent of students attending private colleges and universities will demonstrate financial need and will receive aid packages including free money, loans, and on-campus part-time work opportunities.

Myth 5: Seeking Financial Aid Is Complicated.

Wrong. The process of seeking financial aid for performing artists is relatively simple, but there is a path to follow. Eligibility for the overwhelming bulk of financial aid comes from government and private sources. But no one gets financial aid unless she/he asks for it. Perseverance is key. You may not win financial aid right away, but you have to keep applying steadily.

Myth 6: It Is Only Available to the Poor.

False again. Some federal programs provide help only to low-income students. But others spread the wealth to anyone who shows financial need. Any student can borrow money at a below-market interest rate and not start repaying until he or she leaves school.

Myth 7: Only High School Counselors Can Secure Financial Aid.

Sure, counselors can help, but they are not going to hand you financial aid on a platter. No one is going to hand it all to you. At some level, you have to seek it. Counselors' knowledge of the process runs the gamut from extremely high to total ignorance. Some counselors work closely with college financial aid officers, attend their conventions, speak their language, and know as much about the process as the best of them. Others barely know the difference between a Pell Grant and a Perkins Grant. If you have one of the informed ones, you are lucky. If not, you will have to get personal advice from financial aid offices on the campuses you are considering. Friends who recently have gone through the process can be a big help.

Myth 8: College Is Too Expensive for Our Family.

This is not true. Both private and public colleges are awarding significant amounts of financial aid to make their colleges affordable. U.S. citizens have no excuse to say the aid available to them is limited. There is plenty of it to go around. Financial aid for international students is rather limited, especially for those without U.S. citizenship or permanent residency status. The key is that you have to apply for aid. No student should rule out a college because of its sticker price. Financial aid will reduce the price according to family circumstances.

Even with respect to "expensive" colleges, once student financial aid is taken into account, the net cost of attending a private college is substantially less than the published tuition and fees price. Private colleges over the last decade have increased student aid by more than twice as much as tuition: 197 percent increase in aid versus 86 percent increase in tuition.

> **Stat fact:** According to College Board's study "Trends in College Pricing 2005," 46 percent of undergraduate students in public and private four-year colleges are enrolled in institutions with published tuition and fees less than $6000.

Myth 9: My Parents' Income Is Too High to Qualify for Aid.

Don't believe that you are ineligible for aid due to family income. Any family concerned about meeting the cost of a college is encouraged to apply. Maybe if your parents are millionaire status, it might be a challenge to prove a need, but a very small percent of the population falls into this category.

Merit scholarships are awarded based on specific criteria—for example, high school average, SAT scores, rank in class, and service. The largest growth in institutional aid budgets is merit money. Colleges are competing locally, regionally, and nationally for talented, gifted students. Many colleges are offering merit money in order to improve their rankings in college guides. Your parents' income should not limit you from getting aid.

Myth 10: My Parents Saved for College, So We Won't Qualify.

Saving for college will provide the applicant with more opportunities. Both student and parental savings will reduce student's indebtedness. Remember that the largest component of student aid is low-interest loans. Savings will provide money to assist the family in paying both direct and indirect college costs.

19

Marketing Tips

Marketing Tips for Performing Artists

Pursuing the right marketing strategies is critical to the financial success of your career and education as a performing artist. When seeking financial aid to further your performing arts career, having some accompanying materials at hand may be useful. Sometimes you may attach these along with grant applications or scholarships. Either way, marketing and publicity are important for financial aid, especially for professional artists.

The tips below provide some ideas that you can mesh into your marketing plan. All of them might not work for you. Select the ones to suit your specific needs. They are intended to help you establish visibility, credibility, and marketability. Following these marketing tips may get you more financial aid.

Newsletters

Start a newsletter. Newsletters are one of the least expensive and most effective public relations tools that exist for drawing attention. This is especially true with e-newsletters. By sending out a quality newsletter on a regular basis you can keep current clients, potential clients, the media, and other important sources updated about your work.

Here are some points to address in your newsletter:

- What's unique about your skill?
- Who are your clients? This tells you what kind of audience you are addressing
- What services are you proudest of? Describe them briefly
- Have you won any awards?

242

- Allow room for photographs
- Encourage readers to send you e-mail
- Include a "Safe Unsubscribe" feature
- Provide a list of URLs where readers can find out more information
- Include a headline for every article, and a caption for every picture
- Double-check your spelling and grammar. If you are weak in these areas, have someone else read the newsletter with an editor's eye before e-mailing it
- Carefully cultivate a mailing list. Keep it in good shape and work on expanding it

Press Releases

You can write a press release about nearly anything newsworthy that is related to your work. Some topics include a schedule of performances, an award that you just won, or the display of new technology or technique. Some magazines, newspapers, and public radio stations promote press releases for free. Do a little bit of legwork to find out if there are any sources that promote press releases at no extra charge in your area.

> **Smart tip**
>
> - Tips for writing press releases
> - Submit the press release well before the publishing deadline
> - Keep the press release short
> - Follow the guidelines
> - Write to catch the eye and hold the reader's interest
> - Include a good photograph or two with the press release

Pro Bono and Philanthropic Work

Pro bono work is particularly effective when you want to promote your art, whether it be music, singing or dance, in a new area or when you want to re-vamp your image. Let's assume you are a musician. Offer services to homeless shelters, welfare organizations, hospice centers, and community schools. Do a benefit for your local hospital. Pro bono work does not necessarily have to be related to your performing arts work, but anything that can help to increase the visibility in your community.

Charitable work always reflects well. It shows that you venture beyond yourself. Community involvement shows to the people that you take a genuine interest in their well-being outside your business parameters. It provides your music with more exposure, which will increase client loyalty and sales. Here are some examples of pro bono work

- Performing for free on AIDS day at the local hospital
- Sponsoring a fundraiser organized by a local nonprofit
- Doing a free demonstration at the local school

Cultivate Referrals

People inevitably listen to a personal recommendation over a sales pitch. Word of mouth is a strong means of promoting your image as a performing artist. Referrals are among the most profitable fruits of marketing. A referral from a present customer is stronger than an ad in the local paper.

In order to get quality referrals it is important to have ongoing frequent contact with your clients. Simply ask your present customers for a referral.

Using Yellow Pages to Market Your Performing Arts Services

Yellow Pages are a powerful way to acquire new customers. If you play wedding music, for example, include that information on the ad.

Subscribe to Performing Arts Magazines

Subscribing to performing arts magazines helps you to keep in touch with the latest trends in the industry. There are many magazines to choose from. Sometimes magazines may publish information about awards, grants, and scholarships.

Promote Your Website Every Day

Be sure your web address is printed on your business cards, reception area, brochures, and all other business-related paraphernalia. Offline marketing is as important as online marketing.

Contact Your Local Writers to Promote Your Art in Local Magazines and Newspapers

Get writers interested in the work that you do as a performing artist. If you treat them well and they like you, their write-up can be a hundred times more effective than an ad in a glossy magazine. Magazine and newspaper editors are constantly looking for fresh ideas, both in writing and photography. You can increase business by getting a feature article published in a newspaper or trade magazine. Getting your art into a trade journal is a sure way to market your services.

Flying High with Flyers

A flyer is a standard 8.5" × 11" letter-sized sheet of paper that can be used to create awareness, present information, and promote your work. Flyers have a local reach. You can often work with a flyer-distribution company or the post office to target a very specific neighborhood or area. The cost of flyers can be very low if you focus on a particular area. If you are having a dance recital, sending out flyers within your local community is a great way to get publicity.

Print Ads

Print ads are one of the most powerful and popular methods of advertising. Consistency is one of the most important elements of successful advertising. Keep the same image and layout throughout your ad campaign. When advertising in a local magazine or newspaper, keep the logo and photo the same in each ad. Even when the text changes, your ad layout still will become familiar to consumers, thereby helping to build your image as a performing artist.

An advertisement should be easy to read, easy to-understand, and should stand out while readers flip through a publication.

Building Bridges, Not Boundaries

Building relationships with other local businesses is an excellent way to increase visibility. Join your local Chamber of Commerce, Rotary, and church council. Collaborate with your competitors instead of avoiding them. All these are ways of building bridges instead of boundaries locally, nationally, and internationally.

Business Cards

Your business card can become a powerful tool for promotion. Ideally it should include your name, address, phone, and fax. Think of your business card as a mini advertisement. Your aim is to get people who read it to call you or visit you with regards to a service. Create custom full-color designs that will creatively connect you with your target market, while visually building your image. Use quality paper, make it easy to read, and keep it simple.

Despite the availability of expensive designs and die cuts, the most recommended form is a standard size business card that fits neatly into a wallet, card case or Rolodex. What is important is that you include all of the basic information about yourself as a performing artist. Leave enough white space and don't clutter your card with too much information.

Putting a Press Kit Together

The press kit serves as your paper representative. It should say who you are and what you do in as eye-catching and concise a fashion as possible. You should distribute a press kit liberally because it will be one of your main goals for selling your act. Give or send it to everyone and anyone who asks.

Glossy Photos

You will want both black and white and color photos for your press kit. You can also submit photos via CD or e mail, or have presenters download images from your website. Whatever their format, these photos are important. They are the images that you present to the world, and they should convey instantly who you are, what you perform, what style, and which genre. The photos should include a good headshot, if necessary.

Posters

This is a very good promotional tool to hand out liberally to presenters, to sell, or when mailing out applications for aid. They are not very expensive to print, especially if you stick with black and white and maybe one color. Places to hang posters include store windows, bulletin boards, walls, and telephone poles in the town where you are performing.

Brochures and Bulk Mail

Basically, a brochure should display at least one photo, what you do, and how to contact you. The style (typeface, layout, and copy) should be in keeping with your kind of music. The look should say something about you right away, before the person ever reads it.

There are many categories of bulk mail, including nonprofit, automated, and so forth. Bulk mail also saves you the step of having to put stamps on each one. You must have a minimum of 200 pieces, and they must be identical and sorted by ZIP Code. Go to www.usps.com or type "bulk mail" into your search engine to get more information on bulk mail.

Press Clippings

Sooner or later someone is gong to write something about you or your performing art work. You can even help this along if you know someone who can write a freelance piece to send to your local paper to get published. Many papers accept articles like this. At least you know it will be a favorable chapter this way. Once an interview, article, or review gets published, reproduce it liberally.

Biographies

People want to know about you and your performing act. Include a biography with your publicity and promotional material. Discuss about what sparked the love of music in you, how you first got started, which musicians have influenced you the most, etc.

Audio/Video Demos

If you don't have a good representative demo that someone can listen to, you won't get anywhere. No one hires without hearing an act. A demo usually consists of around three songs, in the case of a musician. Few busy folks will listen to more. Put your very best song or performance first.

People prefer CDs to tapes. Sending a poor demo is worse than sending none. Again, remember this is representing you and your music, so make it your best work.

Glossary

Accelerated degree program: Intense shortened course of study; typically three years of year-round course work.

Accreditation: Process by which a school demonstrates that its programs meet a certain set of academic and educational standards as determined by a regional or national accrediting association.

Acknowledgment report: A form that summarizes the financial data from the financial aid form and shows the estimated family contribution. Parents will receive this form in order to confirm the information and make changes if necessary.

Advanced placement exam: A test offered by the College Board during a student's senior year in high school; allows you to earn credit toward college requirements.

American College Testing Program (ACT): One of two standard college entrance examinations; the other is the SAT.

AmeriCorps: A community service program introduced by the Clinton administration as a way to repay past loans or fund future study.

Assets: Anything that is owned. When determining financial need, assets include cash, real estate, personal property, investments, savings accounts, etc.

Award letter (financial award letter): A letter that is sent to the student from the financial aid office outlining the financial aid package offered to the student. The student then needs to sign and return this letter to accept the aid that is offered.

Campus-based financial aid program: A financial aid program that is sponsored by the federal or state government, but administered locally by the individual schools; typically run by the school's financial aid office.

Cancellation (forgiveness): A deduction from the original balance a student owes on a load. Cancellations are granted for work in a certain profession or under other specific conditions.

College Scholarship Service (CSS): One of the two services that the government and colleges rely on to determine the family's expected contribution.

Conditional scholarship: A type of scholarship for which specified conditions must be met, and, if they are not, the scholarship is revoked or converted into a loan.

Congressional methodology: A standard formula developed by Congress under the Higher Education Amendment of 1986. This formula is used to evaluate parents' income and assets, in conjunction with the number of children in the family who are college-aged and their anticipated college costs. This evaluation helps determine the estimated family contribution (EFC) figure and the student's eligibility for financial aid.

Consolidation: A payment option for students with multiple loan debts. Consolidation allows borrowers to combine the principals and pay in one monthly installment for up to twenty-five years.

Cooperative educational plan (co-op): A program that allows students to split time between work and study in order to earn money to finance their education. This can be done either through work and study during the same term or alternating one term for work and one for study. The job usually pertains to the student's major.

Default: The failure to repay a student loan according to the terms that were specified in the promissory note. Upon default, the school, lender, or government agency can take legal action to ensure repayment.

Deferment: A postponement of the payment of the principal and the interest on a loan to a future date. Many of the federal loan programs have some sort of deferment program.

Dependent student: A classification that says that the student is dependent on his or her parents for financial support.

Disbursement: The paying out of money from a scholarship, grant, or other source.

Education IRA: An account in which parents can deposit up to $500 a year that is slated specifically for future college expenses.

Eligibility: The degree to which a student qualifies for financial aid, usually expressed in a dollar figure; eligibility is based on a number of criteria.

Eligible noncitizen: A government term for people who are not citizens of the United States, but through special circumstances still qualify for federal student assistance programs.

Emergency loan: Temporary, low- or no-interest loan assistance given to students to help them cover costs until their financial aid is received; usually granted immediately and without question.

Estimated family contribution (EFC): The estimated amount of money a student's family can contribute to the student's total cost of college. A standard formula, called the Congressional Methodology, is used to compute the EFC and combines both the parents' and student's estimated contributions. The total EFC figure is used in calculating a student's eligibility for financial aid.

Estimated student's contribution: The calculated amount you should be able to provide to cover a portion of the expenses incurred while attending college. It is calculated from your expected income, assets, and benefits.

Federal direct student loan (FDSL): A Stafford, PLUS, or consolidated loan that is sponsored by the federal government.

Federal Family Education Loan Program (FFELP): Federally backed program through which private lenders provide PLUS or consolidated loans to students.

Federal Supplemental Education Opportunity Grants (FSEOG): Government grants administered through each school's financial aid office.

Federal work-study: Campus-based program through which students are paid a government-subsidized wage to work. Work-study jobs are usually related to the student's field of study and are typically allocated for students who have demonstrated adequate financial need.

Financial aid package: The total aid that is given to the student, including public and private funds. This will include all scholarships, grants, loans, and work-study that are included for the student. The financial aid package is shown in detail in the award letter.

Financial aid profile form: A new form and procedure, administered by the College Board/College Entrance Examination Board.

Financial aid transcript: A record of all the federal financial aid that a student has ever received. Many schools require this form from the student when transferring to another school.

Financial need: Used to describe a family's financial situation relative to anticipated college costs; typically, a low-income family will have a high degree of financial need and, therefore, qualify for any number of need-based aid programs.

Financing programs: Commercially offered services that often provide sound additions to federal- and state-funded loan programs.

Forbearance: Specified amount of time in which a loan does not need to be paid back; usually used by students who don't qualify for deferment but are unable to make loan payments.

401(k) plan: A program in which employees of participating companies automatically transfer a percentage of their pre-tax salaries into mutual funds. Companies often match a certain percentage of these funds to encourage employees to save.

Free Application for Federal Student Aid (FAFSA): Federal form widely used to apply for federal aid.

Free money: Financial aid that accrues no interest and does not need to be paid back.

Grace period: A period of time after college graduation—typically six to twelve months—in which a student does not have to begin repaying a loan.

Grant: Financial gift that does not need to be paid back. Most grant awards are based on the financial need of the student.

Guarantee agency: The state agency that administers the governmental aid programs in their state. This agency deals with insuring the loans and sets limitations within federal guidelines.

Guaranteed Student Loan: More commonly known as the Stafford Loan.

Guaranteed tuition plan: Guarantees a single, agreed-upon student tuition rate from enrollment to graduation; often used as an incentive for enrollment.

Half-time: A student must be attending school at least half-time in order to qualify for many types of federal aid. The criteria for half-time varies from college to college. General guidelines are as follows:

- For schools using semester, trimester, or quarter systems, a minimum of six semester or quarter house per term.
- For schools not using academic terms to measure progress, at least twelve semester hours or eighteen quarter hours are required.
- For schools using clock hours to measure progress, a minimum of twelve clock hours per week.

Hope Scholarship: This is not an actual scholarship granted by an organization but rather a tax credit plan that began in 1998 in which parents get a deduction for college expenses they can't otherwise cover.

Income contingent: A loan repayment schedule based on the borrower's ability to pay.

Independent student: A student who is financially independent. In order to be classified as independent, a student must meet certain federal criteria.

Interest: Charge for borrowed money; generally a percentage of the amount borrowed (see principal).

Lifetime Learning Credit: A tax credit plan in which taxpayers can get a credit of up to $10,000.

Loan: Money that is borrowed from the government, a bank, credit union, or other lender that must be paid back; usually accompanied by interest charges.

Loan consolidation: A repayment option for students with more than one outstanding loan; this lowers monthly payments and makes the repayment process simpler.

Loan default: The failure to repay a loan according to the terms agreed to in the promissory note; a lender may take legal action to get the money back.

Loan deferment: A postponement of a loan's repayment; many federal loan programs have a deferment program.

Loan delinquency: Failure to make loan payments when they are due; delinquency can result in loan default.

Loan dismissal: Also known as cancellation or forgiveness. A situation in which a loan, or portion of a loan, no longer needs to be paid back; almost always based on very specific and limited circumstances.

Need analysis: The actual process that the CSS and the ACT use when determining the amount of financial need for each student.

NMSQT: see Pre-Scholastic Aptitude Test/ National Merit Scholarship Qualifying Test.

Origination fee: A fee that a lender may charge in order to subsidize the cost of a low-interest loan. This fee is taken out as a percentage of the loan when it is originally issued.

Parental contribution: The expected amount contributed by your parents toward your college expenses.

Parental Loans for Undergraduate Students (PLUS): Loans given by the same financial institutions that give Stafford Loans.

Pell Grant: Need-based type of federal financial aid that does not need to be paid back; only available to undergraduate students.

Pell Grant Index (PGI) Number: An index number appearing on your Student Aid Report (SAR) that determines the amount of Pell Grant money to be included in your financial aid package. The number is the result of a series of calculations based on your SAR.

Perkins Loan: A low-interest, need-based loan given by schools; payback begins nine months after a student leaves school.

Pre-Scholastic Aptitude Test/ National Merit Scholarship Qualifying Test (PSAT/NMSQT): Taken during junior year of high school; a preparation for the SAT and a qualifying test for the National Merit Scholarship.

Principal: In terms of loans, this represents the amount of money borrowed, not including any interest charges (see interest).

Promissory note: A legal note that a student must sign when awarded a loan; stipulates conditions and repayment terms.

Satisfactory academic progress: A certain level of academic achievement, usually measured by grade point average, that must be achieved and maintained by the student while earning a degree. The grade point average standard is different for each school, so you must check each school to find their standard for academic progress.

Scholarship: A financial gift that does not need to be paid back; scholarships are awarded based on a variety of criteria, including academic excellence, demonstrated talent, race, religion, group affiliations, state of residence, etc.; scholarships can also be awarded on the basis of need.

Scholastic Aptitude Test (SAT): One of two standard college entrance examinations; the other is the ACT.

Specialized aid: Aid programs based on a wide range of criteria intended to encourage targeted populations of people to pursue higher education.

Stafford Loan: A loan given by banks, credit unions, loan associations, and schools; also known as the Guaranteed Student Loan, or GSL.

Statement of Education Purpose: This is sent with the Student Aid Report (SAR) and you must sign it to assure the government that the money awarded will go exclusively to education-related expenses. The school you attend or apply to may have a similar report that you must sign.

Student Aid Report (SAR): Report sent to students who have applied for federal financial aid; contains information used by financial aid officers to help them evaluate students eligibility for government aid.

Student loan interest deductions: Tax deductions provided for qualified independent students who are paying off college loans.

Student Loan Reform Act (SLRA): An act passed by Congress in 1993 that alters the way students obtain and repay educational loans; brought about the direct lending program and introduced the idea of community service as a repayment option.

Subsidized Loan: A loan that does not accrue interest until the recipient leaves school.

Supplemental Education Opportunity Grants (SEOG): A campus-based grant program that usually is a supplement to Pell Grants.

Tax Relief Act of 1997: Recent tax law changes benefiting students and their parents who are paying for college.

Total cost of attendance: An estimated total of all college costs used in determining a student's eligibility for financial aid; total costs include such expenses as tuition, books and supplies, housing, meals, personal expenses, transportation/travel, and miscellaneous expenses.

Tuition prepayment plan: Allows future tuition to be paid at current rates; some plans allow for payment years in advance.

U.S. Armed forces Reserve Officer Training Corps Program (ROTC): A program offered by the Air Force, Army, Marines, and Navy that provides scholarships and on-campus officer training. Administered by the military's college-based officer training program. Participants can receive full college tuition plus a monthly stipend, typically in return for a time commitment of active and reserve duty in the Armed Forces.

Unsubsidized loan: A loan that accrues interest while a student is still in school.

Waiver: An arrangement by the school that allows nonresidents (out-of-state students and foreign students) to attend that school at the resident tuition rate.

Bibliography

Bellia, Anthony J. *Financial Aid for the Utterly Confused*. New York: McGraw-Hill, 2007.

Braverman, David. *The Standard & Poor's Guide to Saving and Investing for College*. New York: McGraw-Hill Companies, 2004.

College Board Guide to Getting Financial Aid. New York: College Board, 2007.

Eaker, Sherry. *The Backstage Handbook for Performing Artists: The How-To and Who-to-Contact Reference for Actors, Singers, and Dancers*. New York: Back Stage Books, 1991.

Financial Aid Student Guide. Washington, D.C: U.S. Department of Education, 2000.

Finney, David F. *Financing Your College Degree: A Guide for Adult Students*. New York: College Entrance Examination Board, 1997.

Garrett, Sheryl. *On the Road: Saving/Paying for College*. Chicago: Dearborn Financial Publishing, 2006.

Garrison, Larry, and Wallace Wang. *Breaking Into Acting for Dummies*. New York: Wiley Publishing, 2002.

Jazwinski, Peter. *Act Now: A Step by Step Guide to Becoming a Working Actor*. New York: Three Rivers Press, 2006.

Kiyosaki, Robert T. *Guide to Investing: What the Rich Invest In, That the Poor and Middle Class Do Not*. New York: Warner Books, 2000.

Leider, Anna J. *Don't Miss Out*. Alexandria, VA: Octameron Associates, 1999.

_____. *Loans and Grants*. Alexandria, VA: Octameron Associates, 2000.

O'Neil, Brian. *Acting as a Business: Strategies for Success*. Portsmouth, NH: Heinemann, 1999.

Ordovensky, Pat. *Peterson's USA Today Financial Aid for College*. Lawrenceville, NJ: Peterson's Guides, 1994.

Parker, Yana. *The Damn Good Resume Guide*. Berkeley, CA: Ten Speed Press, 1996.

Paying for Graduate School without Going Broke. New York: Princeton Review Publishing, 2004.

Peterson's Study Abroad. Lawrenceville, NJ: Peterson's Guides, 2006.

Pres, Josquin des, and Mark Landsman. *Creative Careers in Music*. New York: All-worth Press, 2000.

Ragins, Marianne. *Winning Scholarships for College*. New York: Henry Holt and Company, 1994.

Ripple, G. Gary. *Do It Write: How to Prepare a College Application*. Alexandria, VA: Octameron Associates, 1999.

Saint Nicholas, Michael. *An Actor's Guide: Your First Year in Hollywood*. New York: Allworth Press, 1996.

Shih, Patricia. *Gigging: A Practical Guide for Musicians*. New York: Allworth Press, 2003.

Smith, Brenda. *Best Kept Secrets for Winning Scholarships*. www.bestkeptsecret-sofwinning.com, 2003.

Smith, Rebecca. *Electronic Resumes and Online Networking*. Franklin Lakes, NJ: Career Press, 1999.

Sponholz, Melanie and Joseph. *College Companion: The Princeton Review*. New York: Random House, 1996.

Stone, Cliffie. *You Gotta Be Bad Before You Can Be Good*. Canyon Country, CA: Showdown, Inc., 2000.

Tyson, Eric. *Personal Finance for Dummies*. Hoboken, NJ: IDG Books Worldwide, 1995.

VGM Career Books. *The Guide to Basic Resume Writing*. Chicago, IL: Public Library Association, 2004.

Waschka, Larry. *The Complete Idiot's Guide to Getting Rich*. New York: Alpha Books, 1999.